There is an old saying,
That upon some solemn shore,
Beyond the sphere of grief,
Dear friends shall meet once more

Pro Charis per carus monumentum quod diligo quod motum,
meus inspiration finis vobis
1994–2009

DENBY & DISTRICT IV

Chronicles of Clerics, Convicts, Corn Millers & Comedians

CHRIS HEATH

Wharncliffe Books

By the same author:

Denebi – Farmstead of the Danes
(Richard Netherwood 1997)

A History of the Denby Dale Pies
(J R Nichols 1998)

Denby & District – From Prehistory to the Present
(Wharncliffe Books 2001)

Denby & District II – From Landed Lords to Inspired Industrialists
(Wharncliffe Books 2004)

Denby & District III – From Medieval Manuscripts to Modern Memories
(Wharncliffe Books 2006)

'Ye Old Townships' – Denby Dale, Scissett, Ingbirchworth & District
A Denby & District Archive Photograph Album
(Wharncliffe Books 2007)

'Ye Olde Townships' – Skelmanthorpe, Clayton West, & District
A Denby & District Archive Photograph Album
(Wharncliffe Books 2007)

First Published in Great Britain in 2009 by
Pen & Sword Wharncliffe Books
an imprint of
Pen & Sword Books Ltd
47 Church Street
Barnsley
South Yorkshire
S70 2AS

ISBN: 978-1-84563-124-6

A CIP catalogue record for this book is available from the British Library.

Typeset in 9.5/12pt Palatino by Concept, Huddersfield.

Printed and bound in England by
CPI UK

Pen & Sword Books Ltd incorporates the imprints of
Pen & Sword Aviation, Pen & Sword Maritime, Pen & Sword Military, Wharncliffe Local History, Pen & Sword Select, Pen & Sword Military Classics, Leo Cooper, Remember When, Seaforth Publishing and Frontline Publishing.

For a complete list of Pen & Sword titles please contact
PEN & SWORD BOOKS LIMITED
47 Church Street
Barnsley
South Yorkshire
S70 2AS
England
E-mail: enquiries@pen-and-sword.co.uk
Website: www.pen-and-sword.co.uk

Contents

Acknowledgements

Abigail McCallum, Brian Elliott, Bryan Heath, Carol Heath, Charles Hewitt, Chris Sharp, David and Molly Green, Ellen O'Flaherty (Trinity College Library, Dublin), Jon Wilkinson, Karen Heath, Monica Price, Paul Heath, Phillip Brook, Rev. Simon Moor (Silkstone Church), Richard Littlewood, Roni Wilkinson, Stephen and Yvonne George, Sue McClarron at Launceston Archives – Tasmania, Staff at the Borthwick Institute – York, Thomas Richard Cowan, Trevor Elam, Wendy Hawkins and Gillian Nixon at Barnsley Local Studies Library.

Any errors or omissions are entirely the fault of the author. Whilst every effort has been made to trace the copyright owners of the illustrations in this book the author wishes to apologise to anyone who has not been acknowledged. If an error has occurred this will be corrected in any subsequent reprint of this work.

Introduction

Three years ago, I wrote in the introduction to Denby & District 3, *You never know, if enough material comes in, I might, one day, write volume IV!* Well, here it is and it is very much a volume about people, or perhaps the lives of people and their successes, failures, trials and tribulations.

I have returned to the thirteenth century, partly because this period of history fascinates me and also because of a number of previously unknown documents held in Scotland. These have shown further associations between the Balliol and Burdet families, Lords of Denby, but working together on behalf of the King of England. Indeed, we now know that Sir Robert Balliol, was once the Sheriff of Northumberland and dealt directly with Peter Burdet who was the Constable of Berwick Castle. It was Peter Burdet who handed over the keys to the castle when John Balliol was chosen by Edward I to become the new King of Scotland. Rather than go over old ground I have included the salient points of the new records and have endeavoured to draw up a time frame which includes the most important events from the twelfth, thirteenth and fourteenth centuries regarding Denby and its Lords. The lack of definite dates for most of these events means a certain amount of informed guess work, in order to try and get as near to the true picture as possible. The result is a model that I hope portrays a clearer understanding of this early period and is something that may be worked upon by others.

I have returned to Denby church and its clergy largely because of my involvement with an exhibition held there in October 2008. Much of the detail I had included in Volume 1 was already well known and all I did was draw the facts together. I had not questioned very much of it but on returning to the matter I discovered glaring holes and omissions and decided to go back to as much of the original source material as possible. This of course, led me to discover much more, never before published information, including a number of curates who had been long forgotten. These included a non-conformist firebrand who was imprisoned for his beliefs at York. This man was actually born at Denby and held the curacy of the chapel in the village of his birth briefly before his career led him to pastures new. I have also tried to examine the lives and families of these men, the results of which, though mixed, are fascinating. I met an ancestor of the Rev. Job Johnson in Denby churchyard, who was tracing his family history and so we swapped details. Following the Rev. A B Orr was a monumental task as he was Vicar of so many different parishes during his career and his family connections were a complete surprise and a bonus during the research.

In March 2008, a gentleman from Scotland got in touch with me, asking me if I would like some old photographs of Denby Dale and its environs. He was a member of the Green family of Denby Dale and knew some of his family's history. As the Greens were an integral part of central Denby Dale, the opportunity to remember them was too good to miss and so their story is included, along with the new photographs. The story with the George family, also once known as Kelso, developed out of the fact that my Mum grew up living next door to them in Norman Croft. The present generation, were more than happy to see their fascinating family story recorded and were more than generous with photographs and information.

Elijah Hinchcliffe was very much a chance find, though I was more than pleased to discover him. I had always wanted to research a transported convict but there were far too many normal, well-behaved individuals living in the district. Yes, as we have seen from reports in the *Barnsley Chronicle*, there were plenty of rogues, but none were forcibly sent 12,000 miles from home, never to return, for their misdemeanours. Elijah took some following and I was lucky enough to learn the details of his trial, and particularly his crime, something central to the chapter, due to the efforts of a work colleague. A man who had never been to an archives in his life (and probably never will again) included the job on a visit to Chester and came up trumps – thanks Tom – you're a diamond! Even with this, the chapter ended quite suddenly for a long time, as I had no way of following Elijah in Australia after he was released. Almost at the end of the writing of this book a lady from Launceston Archives in Tasmania got in touch after reading a letter that was published in *Ancestors* magazine. Within two weeks I had all the details I required. Thanks to the selfless research she undertook on my behalf, Elijah's story is now complete.

The final chapter includes the last of the reports I have taken from *the Barnsley Chronicle*. Due to the immense amount of time it takes to wade through the bound yearly volumes I am unlikely to do any more, so enjoy them, particularly the 'ghost' in Denby Dale. I have also used this chapter to include previously unpublished photographs, not used elsewhere in the book, some complement the text but others are simply there by their association with a particular village.

Finally, I would like to thank everybody I have worked with over the past twelve years, without whom, the story of Denby and District would not have been possible. I must also apologise to all those individuals who have made contact regarding information that I have been unable to follow up on, due to time constraints. Were I to live ten lifetimes I would not be able to record all that I should or would like.

The pursuit of ones ancestors and their lives, *genealogy*, has undergone a massive change due to the development of the Internet. The publication of many parish registers and census returns alongside on-line resources which grow and improve every year, means that more and more people are able to undertake their own personal journey into the past. We can only wonder at the stories that are waiting to be told. As this book is very much about individuals, it mirrors the pursuit of local history, it is the goodwill of the people involved that make the journey back in time so stimulating.

Chris Heath
May 2009

Chapter One

Balliol & Burdet and the Scottish Connection

We have examined the Scottish and Royal connections of the de Denby, Balliol and Burdet families in previous volumes but new documents have the uncanny knack of coming to light all the time. As they emerge they do one of two things, add to or, alter the history already written. These documents are particularly useful if they cover a period of time about which our knowledge is less full. The following documents cover the period 1279 to 1333:

1279

Robert de Balliol states that he is ready to put to view what he has said concerning Geoffrey de Neville, and asks the king hear his plea, as Geoffrey claimed to have rendered account for five years, but has concealed certain sums received from various people.

First the account is to be viewed in the Exchequer, and if he has not accounted an inquisition is to be made concerning this and other articles.

Places mentioned: York; Kyrkeby Morheved [Kirkbymoorside], *Fountains Abbey, Holmcultram* [Abbey Town], *Northumberland.*

People mentioned: Geoffrey de Neville; William de Lec; William de Croft; Peter de Romeyn; Master of St Leonard's Hospital, York, Simon de Evesham; Abbot of Whitby; Baldwin Wake; Abbot of St Mary's, York; men of Kirkbymoorside; Henry le Vavasour; Abbot of Fountains; Abbot of Holmcultram; Foresters of Northumberland.

1282

In the same year at the bridge [of boats] *which the king had caused to be prepared between Snowdonia and Anglesea, sixteen knights whose names follow were drowned:- The lord William de Audley. The lord Lucas de Taney. The lord Richard de Wells. Amaury Burdet. Peter de la Mare. Philip* [Robert ?] *Burnell. William Burnell. Henry Tyes. Howel, son of Griffin. Roger de Clifford, junior. William de Lindsey. William the Butler, son of Richard the Butler. Thomas de Halton. William de Odingsels. Peter de la Quarere. Walter le Jay. And as many esquires, and three hundred footmen, and with great difficulty the lord Otho de Grandison escaped. Also the head of prince Llewelin was sent to London.*

We do not at present know who Amaury Burdet was, but this man was almost certainly related to the family which came to Denby as his name is intrinsic to the family.

1283 August 20

Between: 1. Jordan son of Godfrey de Menthorppe and John his son of the same 2. Amaric de Eyvill and Emma his wife Jordan has quitclaimed to Amaric one toft and two bovates of land in the vill and territory of Menthorppe. Witnesses: Sir Thomas de Metham, Sir Robert de Baliol, Knights, Robert de Osegoteby, John son of Nicholas of the same, John of the castle, Thomas de Luceby of Southe Duffeld, Gamel of the same, John de Averagnes of Skipwithe, Adam de Hirland of the same, Robert de Akethorpp, Thomas Lubyas de Brakenholme and Richard de Clyf, clerk.

1291 October 18

Receipt by Peter Burdet for 25l. 12s. 6d. received from the Chamberlain of Scotland as his wages for keeping Berwick Castle. Berwick.

1291 December 16

Receipt by Peter Burdet, castellan of Berwick, for 43l. received from the Chamberlain of Scotland and his associate in part payment of his wages. Melrose.

1292 April 25

Receipt by Peter Burdet, constable of Berwick Castle, for 27l. received from Philip de Linton, constable of Berwick, in part payment of his wages. Berwick Castle.

1292 June 19

Receipt by Peter Burdet, constable of Berwick castle, for 14l. 3s. 3d. received from Philip de Linton in part payment of his wages. Berwick.

1292 June 29

Receipt by Peter Burdet, castellan of Berwick, for 13l. received from the same in part payment of his wages.

1292 September 28

Receipt by Peter Burdet, castellan of Berwick, for 42l. 14d. 4d. received from the Chamberlain of Scotland and his associate. Roxburgh.

1293/4

Release by John, son of Roger Cok, to Sir John, Earl Warenne, of all lands and tenements descended to him from Thomas Cok his uncle, and Robert Cok his brother, in Steynford, Fithlake, and Conesburgh. Witnesses:- Sir Gerard de Hedone, Sir Francon le Tilis, Sir Robert de Balliol, Sir Anselm de Gyse, Peter de Lound,' Robert le Breton, John Petipas, and others. York.

1296 November

Warrant for the allowance of expenses incurred by Robert de Balliol upon the invasion of Northumberland by the Scots.

1297/8

Receipt of Walter de Stansfield, one of the keepers of the King's horses, for fodder etc, supplied by Robert de Balliol, sheriff of Northumberland, 1mark.

1298 December 28

Receipt by Peter Burdet, the King's pantler, for wheat at Newcastle from the sheriff of Northumberland.

A 'pantler' was the officer in a great family who had charge of the bread and other provisions.

1299 August 3

Warrant for Robert de Balliol, late sheriff of Northumberland, for monies expended on Scottish prisoners delivered to him by the sheriff of York, to be taken to Newcastle and for provisions and money delivered to the keeper of Berwick for the munition of the town.

The length of Balliol's period in office as Sheriff is currently unknown but from the latter two documents it seems certain that he dealt directly with Peter Burdet and it is likely that the pair were already well acquainted. Burdet's family were already living in Denby and Balliol had been married to Margaret de Denby since at least the early 1280s.

1302/3

Receipt by William de Thorp to Richard de Bremesgrave for 2 quarters of oats from the King's stores at Berwick-on-Tweed to the use of Nicholas de Metham by bill of Sir John de Drokenesford. Northumberland.

1303 November 11

Debtor: Nicholas, son of Thomas de Metham (who held Eggborough, Osgoldcross Wapentake, West Riding of Yorkshire), knight. Creditor: Roger, son of Roger Basy (citizen and merchant) of York. Amount: 8m.

Before whom: John le Spicer, Mayor of York; Robert de Seizevaux, Clerk.

Sent by: Andrew de Bolingbroke, Mayor of York; Robert de Seizevaux, Clerk.

We have already, briefly, met Thomas de Metham above, in the document dated 1283. Thomas was the father of Nicholas de Metham who married Margaret de Balliol (formerly de Denby) after Sir Robert Balliol's death around 1309. Margaret bears him two daughters, Alice and Elizabeth. Thomas de Metham and Robert Balliol were well acquainted and young Nicholas would have grown up knowing Margaret as at least a friend.

1322

Petition: Stephen de Redenesse [Reedness, West Yorkshire] *to the King and council.*

Stephen de Redenesse states that he had 200 acres of moor with other lands and tenements in Reedness, of the gift of Robert de Balliol, of which Robert's ancestors and feoffors had been seised since the Conquest, and that he was disseised of this by Henry de Lacy, then Earl of Lincoln. Because of his fear of the Earl, he never dared to begin a suit to recover it. It is now in the king's hand, and he requests grace and a remedy.

Endorsement: The muniments which belonged to Henry de Lascy are to be searched, to see if anything can be found on behalf of the king, which might bar Stephen; and then the king will do justice.

1331

Stephen de Redenesse makes two complaints to the King and council about legal proceedings in a case between him and Peter de Saltmarrays [Saltmarsh], *and one about proceedings in a case between him and Nicholas and Margaret de Metham and John de Ousthorp, both concerning tenements in Yokefleet.*

Other people mentioned: Peter de Saltmarrays, Eluard de Saltmarrays, father of Peter de Saltmarrays, John Travers, justice; Peter de Middelton, William de Denom; Robert de Skorbourgh [Scarborough]; *Adam de Hoperton; Nicholas de Metham; Margaret de Metham, wife of Nicholas de Metham; John de Ousthorp.*

1333 September 24

Debtor: Nicholas de Metham [who held part of Laxton in Howdenshire Wapentake in the East Riding of Yorkshire], *knight. Creditor: John de Hextelsam, tailor, of York. Amount: 55s. Writ to: Sheriff of Yorkshire.*

Sent by: Nicholas de Langton, Mayor of York; William Gray, Clerk.

In order to make sense of the latter and to tie them up into a workable historical framework the following timeline will help. It is as complete as it is currently possible to get though some of the dates are approximate and are based upon the realms of probability.

The Early Lords of Denby – A Timeline

Date	Local Occurrence	Date	National Occurrence
c.1249	Probable birth of Robert Balliol, possibly to Henry Balliol (died 1246) and Lora Valoines.	**1240 May 15th**	Dafydd, younger son of Llewellyn the Great created Prince of Wales.
c.1249	Probable birth of Almaricus Burdet at Rande to Nicholas Burdet who was knighted in 1250.	**1249 Jul 8th**	King Alexander II of Scotland dies. He is succeeded by his son Alexander III.
c.1255	Probable birth of Agnes de Denby to William de Denby, the founder of the first chapel in Denby, dated to 1229/1232.	**1256**	King Henry III builds a house in the Tower of London for the first elephant seen in England.
c.1265	Probable birth of Margaret de Denby to Robert de Denby and Margaret de Hoyland (High). She was the cousin of Agnes de Denby.	**1264 May 14th**	Battle of Lewis, King Henry III and his son, the future Edward I are prisoners of Simon de Montfort.
		1265 Aug 4th	Battle of Evesham. Simon de Montfort defeated and killed by the King's forces.

Date	Local Occurrence	Date	National Occurrence
1267	23rd October. The King (Henry III) owes Robert Balliol 19/– arrears of wages.		
c.1272	Probable birth of Robert Burdet to Almaricus Burdet and Agnes de Denby.	**1272 Nov 16th**	Death of King Henry III.
		1274 Aug 19th	King Edward I is crowned at Westminster.
1275 Nov 29th	Agnes Burdet (n'ee de Denby) noted to be alive in a land grant, and also married.		
1278 May 18th	Robert Balliol was to appear before the King (Edward I) charged with Forrest Trespass.		
1279	Robert Balliol asks the King to hear his plea regarding Geoffrey de Neville as Geoffrey claimed to have rendered accounts for 5 years but has concealed certain sums from the King.		
1280	11th February. Robert Balliol was to pay his fine (for Forrest Tresspass) of 100 marks at 20 marks per annum (1 mark was worth 13 shillings and 4 pence so this was a large amount).		
c.1281	Probable marriage of Robert Balliol and Margaret de Denby.		
c.1282	Birth of Idonea Balliol to Robert and Margaret Balliol.		
1282	Amaury Burdet is drowned along with 15 other knights at 'the bridge of boats' which King Edward I has caused to be made between Snowdonia	**1283–87**	Conway castle is built. Caernarvon castle begins construction. Harlech castle built between 1283 and 1289.

Date	Local Occurrence	Date	National Occurrence
	and Anglesey, during his conquest of the Welsh. Amaury Burdet is currently unknown but the similarity of the name to the Denby generations is instructive.		
1282	2nd August. Robert Balliol served as a Knight under the Bishop of Durham against the Welsh during King Edward I conquest of the country.	**1283 Nov 25th**	Daffydd, last Prince of Wales was executed at the order of Edward I.
1283 Aug 20th	Sir Robert de Balliol, Knight, witnesses a quitclaim regarding lands at Menthorpe, it is of interest that one of the other witnesses was Thomas de Metham, father of Nicholas who would go on to marry Balliol's widow.	**1284 Feb 5th**	Margaret the 'Maid of Norway' granddaughter of King Alexander III of Scots is recognised as his heir following the death of his son, Alexander a month earlier.
1284	8th February. It was reported that Robert Balliol did good service in Wales.	**1287**	Robert the Bruce, a claimant to the Scottish throne rebels against the succession of Margaret at Strathclyde.
1291– Sep 28th 1292	Peter Burdet is paid regularly for his services as the Constable of Berwick Castle.	**1290 Dec 17th**	Death of Queen Eleanor of Castile, wife of Edward I, aged 54.
1292 Nov 18th	Peter Burdet hands over Berwick castle to John Balliol. He appears to leave here and makes for Denby, probably on the advice of Robert Balliol, though Burdet's may already have been established here.	**1292 Nov 17th**	John Balliol named King of Scots in preference to Robert Bruce after Edward I presided over 13 rival claims at Norham, near Berwick. Balliol is 42 years old and relatively unknown in his new kingdom.
c.1293	Robert Thorpe of Denby grants Peter Burdet a piece of enclosed land called 'Syndirhill' lying in a place called Thorpe in Denby the grantee paying 1d yearly.		

Date	Local Occurrence	Date	National Occurrence
1293/4	Robert Balliol was witness to a release regarding Fishlake and Conisborough.		
		1294 Jun	King John Balliol of Scots declares he will fight for Edward I against Philip IV of France.
		1295–1298	Beaumaris castle is built.
		1296 Mar	At Berwick. The Scots invade England. John Balliol refuses to pay homage to Edward I. Edward attempts to impose English rule.
1296 Nov	Warrant for the allowance of expenses incurred by Robert Balliol upon the invasion of Northumberland by the Scots.	**1296 Jul 10th**	John Balliol's rebellion has been crushed. After he failed to pay homage to Edward I in March, Edward sacked Berwick massacring 7000. Then at Dunbar, Balliol's forces were routed and Scottish castles began to be surrendered. Publicly stripped of crown, sceptre, sword, rings and even the fur from his robes, John is exiled in England with the insignia of his once independent kingdom.
1297	Robert Balliol noted to be a Knight of the Shire of Yorkshire.	**1297 Sep 11th**	The Scots rebel against the English, led by William Wallace they deliver a stunning defeat to the English at the Battle of Stirling Bridge.
1297	Robert Burdet represents his family at the Court of Arches in London regarding the right of presentment of the chaplain of Rande. Robert would have to have been 21 or over at the time.		
1297/1298	Robert Balliol is Sheriff of Northumberland. A receipt survives of Walter de Stansfield, one of the keepers of the King's horses, for fodder, supplied by Balliol to the value of 1 mark.		

Date	Local Occurrence	Date	National Occurrence
		1298 Jul 22nd	King Edward I crushes William Wallace and his rebel army at the Battle of Falkirk.
1298. Dec	Receipt by Peter Burdet, the king's pantler, for wheat at Newcastle from the Sheriff of Northumberland (ie: Robert Balliol).		
1299 Aug 3rd	Warrant for Robert Balliol, late Sheriff of Northumberland for monies expended on Scottish prisoners delivered to him by the Sheriff of York, to be taken to Newcastle and for provisions and money delivered to the keeper of Berwick for the munition of the town.		
c.1300	Marriage of Robert Burdet and Idonea Balliol, their first child, Aymer is born soon afterwards.		
1301	Robert Balliol noted to be a Knight of the Shire of Yorkshire.		
1302/3	Nicholas de Metham receives 2 quarters of oats from the Kings stores at Berwick on Tweed by a bill of Sir John Drokenesford of Northumberland.	**1302 Jan**	John Balliol, former King of Scots is freed from his imprisonment.
1304	Fine between Nicholas de Wortley and Robert Balliol and his wife, Margaret, in which Robert and Margaret recognised Nicholas to be Lord of the Manor's of Denby and High Hoyland, who had made a gift of them to Robert and Margaret for their lives and afterwards to their daughter Idonea and her husband, Robert Burdet.		

Date	Local Occurrence	Date	National Occurrence
c.1304	Robert Burdet granted the manors of Denby and High Hoyland to Robert and Margaret Balliol for their lives, in default of issue from Robert Burdet the manors were to pass to the heirs of Margaret's family (the de Denby's).		
1304	Almaricus Burdet noted to still be alive. His wife, Agnes de Denby has died by now.	**1305 Aug 23rd**	William Wallace executed in London. His head and limbs severed for public display.
1305 Jun 15th	Nicholas de Metham, son of Thomas de Metham, Knight, (who held land at Eggborough, Osgoldcross Wapentake) was in debt to Roger, son of Roger Basy, citizen and merchant of York for 8 marks. A writ was sent to the Sheriff of York by Andrew de Bolingbroke, Mayor of York.	**1306 Mar 27th**	Robert Bruce raises the Scottish flag of independence and is proclaimed King at Scone.
1308	Robert Balliol was a witness at the proving of age of one Rob. Bertram of Bothal. Robert Balliol said that on 23rd April 1287 he was attacked by robbers on his way from Corbridge and reached Morpeth on foot, his horse being killed, and that Rob. Bertram was born about that time.	**1307 Jul 7th**	King Edward I dies of dysentery en route to war in Scotland. His son, Edward II becomes King.
c.1309	Probable death of Robert Balliol aged around 60 years.		
c.1310	Margaret de Denby (aged around 45) re-marries to Nicholas de Metham and has two daughters, Alice and Elizabeth.		
1312/13	Peter Burdet is granted lands in Gosse and Seignaux in France (Gascony?) formerly in the possession of Aumanin de Budanide. (Aymer Burdet?)	**1313 Apr**	John Balliol, deposed King of Scots died in exile in France.

Date	Local Occurrence	Date	National Occurrence
		1314 Jun 24th	Robert Bruce, though outnumbered, defeats an English army of 2500 knights and 15000 infantry and wins the Battle of Bannockburn.
1322	Stephen de Reedness states that he held lands, tenements and 200 acres of moor by the gift of Robert Balliol, which had been held by the Balliol family since the conquest but that these had been seised by Henry de Lacy and he wishes to recover it.	**1327**	Death of Edward II at Berkeley castle, his son, Edward III becomes King.
		1329 Jun 7th	Death of Robert Bruce of leprosy, his son, David succeeds him.
		1330 Nov 29th	Roger Mortimer is hanged, drawn and quartered in London, for the murder of Edward II and treason against King Edward III.
1331 Jul 4th	Aymer Burdet, son of Robert and Idonia Balliol is in dispute with Nicholas de Metham regarding tenements and lands in Denby and High Hoyland. This means that Aymer is now Lord of the Manor and that his father, Robert is dead.	**1334 Jun 12th**	At Newcastle, Edward Balliol, son of John has paid homage to King Edward III, overturning the achievements of Robert Bruce who died five years ago. Two years ago, Edward returned to Scotland after eight years exile in England to claim the throne. With English help he defeated a Scottish army at Dupplin Moor in 1332 though he was driven back later that same year. In March 1333 he laid siege to Berwick in the name of Edward III and in July, together they crushed the Scots army at Halidon Hill.
1331 Oct 14th	Stephen de Redenesse complains to the King and Council regarding Nicholas and Margaret de Metham (formerly Balliol, formerly de Denby) and John		

Date	Local Occurrence	Date	National Occurrence
	de Ousthorp concerning tenements in Yokefleet. This means that Margaret was almost certainly much younger than Robert Balliol when she married him.		
1333	Nicholas de Metham is in debt to the amount of 55 shillings to John de Hextelsham, a tailor of York. Metham is noted to hold land at Laxton in Howdenshire Wapentake. A writ was issued to the Sheriff of York by Nicholas de Langton, the Mayor of York.		
1335	In front of King Edward III at York. Aymer Burdet is in dispute with Nicholas de Metham regarding lands at Denby.		
1338	Aymer Burdet ordered to supply twenty men, furnished with horses and arms for the protection of the North from the Scots.		
1344	Denby court roll notes that Simon was the servant of Isabel Langton, wife of Aymer Burdet.	**1346 Aug 26th**	Battle of Crecy.
1351 Jul 6th	Aymer Burdet was a witness at the trial of the murderers of John de Eland, this murder being the culmination of the 'Eland Feud'.	**1356 Jan 20th**	Edward Balliol hands over the crown of Scotland to Edward III at Berwick in return for a rich pension.
1359 Oct 20th	Aymer Burdet witnesses a deed granting John de Gunthwaite the water mill. He does not appear in any later records. He must have died around this time. His wife, Isabel Langton re-married to Ralph Hyde.	**1356 Sep 19th**	Battle of Poitiers.

Date	Local Occurrence	Date	National Occurrence
c.1360	Nicholas Burdet becomes Lord of Denby, mentioned in the Poll Tax of 1379, he never married and was dead by 1408, when he was succeeded by his brother, Richard.	**1362 Apr**	John of Gaunt, fourth son of Edward III inherits the title, Duke of Lancaster.
		1377 Jun 21st	Death of King Edward III.

Chapter Two

The Lives of the Clergy of Upper Denby

The roll of religion in the lives of our forebears was of far greater importance than today. In many ways, their lives were lived around it in the sure and certain knowledge that one day, each individual would meet his creator and so answer for their lives. Although I have previously examined the historical details of Denby church, within this chapter I intend to reach a little deeper and try to get to know the clerics who cared for the souls of the village's people. About some of these individuals we know very little, but further research may well add to the wealth of historical detail we have for others. We will also see the results of new research, which supplies us with never before published details of the original Chapel of Ease. Ultimately, the oldest building (and site) within most villages is that of the religious edifice. We will trace the individuals across the country and in many cases meet their families and friends. Before we do this we need to re-cap upon the history of religion in the area.

Early beginnings

Aerial photographs showing marks in the landscape indicate that there has been a settlement at High Hoyland for at least 2000 years. The remains of a Saxon cross, dating to around AD800 and other material of this period have been found, and suggest that the cross marked the site of an early Christian preaching station. A primitive road track has also been identified linking High Hoyland with Denby and Penistone.

The earliest church here that we know of, was founded about 1150 by Adam fitz Swain, grandson of the Saxon landholder, Ailric. Nothing now survives of this building, save fragments built into the later edifice. The catalogue of Rectors begins in 1250. The church has undergone a number of re-developments, over the centuries, but there is no doubt as to its antiquity and the fact that, All Hallows, High Hoyland, at one time, played host to the religious devotions of the people of Denby.

There was another option:

St John the Baptist church, Penistone, dates from at least 1200 and Denby was a part of its parish. The catalogue of Rectors here dates from 1229. All services for the people of Denby, including baptisms, marriages and burials would have taken place here.

An attempt was made to found a private chapel at Denby dated to between 1229 and 1232, by William de Denby who can be found in the following document regarding a transfer of land, dating to the thirteenth century:

Jordan de Heton to Adam, son of William de Denby, the chaplain of Cumberworth.

Penistone Church, photographed in 1928.

William was one of the most influential people living in Denby at that time, and was brother to Sir Robert de Denby, the Lord of the Manor. He gave a piece of land to Penistone church in return for which the Rector of Penistone, Godfrey de Ludham permitted William to build:

> *An oratory in my house and there to celebrate mass, ensuring only that the mother church of Penistone and Denby chapel are not disadvantaged.*

William had sworn this on the high altar at Penistone. So here we have our first evidence for an early chapel at Denby. Its location will probably always remain a mystery, though a link with the site of the present church would not be unreasonable as memories may have persisted through the centuries influencing the site of the later building. No other historical reference to it has yet been unearthed, which suggests that its life was short and that it fell out of use, possibly even with the death of William de Denby, around the end of the thirteenth century.

The de Denby family became involved in the cross border warfare, which took place between England and Scotland during the thirteenth and fourteenth centuries. So much so that they became the gaolers, at Denby, of Sir Robert Balliol, a cousin of deposed King John Balliol of Scotland. Also involved in the conflict were the Burdet family from Rande, Lincolnshire. Peter Burdet was the Constable of Berwick castle who handed over the keys to King John Balliol when Berwick was surrendered to the Scots in 1292 on the advent of him becoming King. His deposition took place in 1296, all these events being orchestrated by King Edward I of England. Sir Robert Balliol married the daughter of one of his gaolers,

Margaret de Denby and had a daughter, Idonea. She in turn married Robert Burdet, who by way of this marriage inherited the Lordship of Denby. The lordship then passed from father to son:

Lords of the Manor's of Denby and High Hoyland

Aymer Burdet 1300–1360	Richard Burdet 1470–1546
Nicholas Burdet died 1407	Aymer Burdet 1497–1574[1]
Richard Burdet (*brother of above*) died 1436	Henry Burdet 1525–1602
Robert Burdet died 1451	Richard Burdet 1550–1616
Aymer Burdet died 1485	George Burdet 1580–1636
Nicholas Burdet died 1508	Richard Burdet 1610–1666[2]

Some of the above years of birth are approximate and are designed to help the reader understand the time-scales involved.

1 *Aymer Burdet inherited only Denby after accusing his father of treason against King Henry VIII, from this point this branch of the family were not the Lords of High Hoyland.*

2 *Richard Burdet sold the Manor of Denby to William Savile in 1643.*

These early Lords owned vast areas of land in the locale. In the fifteenth century, one old charter lists lands in the following places subject to Burdet of Denby overlordship:

> *Denby, Hoyland, Nether Bretton, Barnsley, Mapplewell, Clayton, Darton, Kexborough, Langsett, Thurlstone, Ingbirchworth and Cumberworth.*

This meant that they had a choice of which church to attend and probably meant that they were itinerant. Nevertheless, High Hoyland and Penistone remained the main two.

It is unknown as to where the early burials of these Lords took place. Penistone is the leading contender, but by the time of Richard Burdet, who died in 1436, we can learn a little of his loyalties. He left 6s 8d for the adornment of the high altars in the choirs of Penistone and High Hoyland and also a personal bequest to the Rector of Penistone, Robert Pullayne of 6s 8d, (Pullayne was actually a distant relative).

Richard's son, Robert Burdet, who became Lord of Denby after his father's death, died in 1451. In his last will he requests that his body be buried *in the church of St John the Baptist at Penistone*. He left 6s 8d for the making of a cross and a further 20s for bread, ale and cheese to be supplied on the day of his funeral to the mourners.

The mould was now set as can be seen by the last will of Lord Richard Burdet (1550–1616).

> *I Richard Burdet of Denby Hall, bequeath my soul to God Almighty, my maker and redeemer and my body to be buried in the parish church of Penistone, in my choir.*

Denby Hall was in fact, much closer to High Hoyland than Penistone, but the Lords of Denby made sure that their final journeys were to the mother church.

What of the people who populated the village throughout these times? The answer is that they also attended services at Penistone. They travelled on foot, or if they were lucky, in horse-drawn farm carts, taking their infants for baptism, their lovers for weddings and their dead for burial. In the winter months, it was difficult and dangerous to cross the regularly flooded waters of Scout Dyke.

According to previously published local history a tragedy occurred, in 1626, when thirteen parishioners from Denby lost their lives on their way to church and drowned in the overflowing dyke. Such an event may well have been remembered orally for many generations but written evidence of it is difficult to find. The surviving Penistone parish burial registers only begin in 1644 and the Bishop's copies of these, held at the Borthwick Institute, York, are missing for 1626, so proving the event and naming the individuals concerned is difficult.

The situation was intolerable and the villagers resolved to petition Archbishop Tobias Mathew of York for a licence to erect a chapel. It is interesting to note that the neighbouring people of Cumberworth also petitioned the Archbishop at the same time, regarding their chapel, and received the same approvals as Denby in the June of 1627. They may have used the alleged tragedy at Scout Dyke as ammunition for their cause, though it may also be that as one parish learnt of the efforts of its neighbour the other followed suit.

The Archbishop formally agreed to the Denby request on 12 December 1627, although he was unable to consecrate it, he did allow them licence to perform religious ordinances and choir offices without prejudice to Penistone. Burials also took place, for instance Isabell Haigh was buried in December 1672, Nathaniel Haigh in April 1676 and Mary Woolsind in April 1723.

The chapel consecrated at Denby in 1627 may have been very similar to Chopwell Chapel, near Newcastle Upon Tyne, pictured here in 1908.

The money behind the new chapel came, surprisingly, not from the Burdet Lords of Denby, but the Bosville Lords of Gunthwaite.

During the thirteenth century, Gunthwaite was home to a family which took the name of the place for themselves. A charter written during the reign of King Edward III (1327–1377) mentions John Gonnildthwaite and the water mill there. The mill, rebuilt a number of times, still survives on its original site though has recently been converted into housing.

The Bosville's first arrived in England around the time of the Norman Conquest and intermarriage brought them into possession of Gunthwaite. The first member of the family to live almost entirely at Gunthwaite was Godfrey Bosville (1519–1580). He rebuilt the estate and erected a new Hall and barn. The Hall has long since gone but the Tudor barn still survives. Godfrey made a very illustrious marriage to Jane Hardwick, sister of the well known Bess of Hardwick, Countess of Shrewsbury. By this marriage he also, albeit distantly, allied himself with the Royalty of England. Amongst the children born to this union was Mary Bosville who united the two leading families of the area when she married the Lord of Denby, Richard Burdet (c.1550–1616).

Godfrey Bosville's Grandson, also called Godfrey (1596–1658), served as a Colonel for Parliament, under Oliver Cromwell during the English Civil War. During the war a regiment of Roundhead soldiers under his command were stationed at Gunthwaite but a number of these contracted typhoid fever here and died. It is believed that these men were buried under the giant oak at Gunthwaite Hall.

The money to build the new chapel of ease or district chapel at Denby was provided by Colonel Bosville. As he was the moving force behind the construction of the chapel Colonel Bosville also held the right to appoint the first minister. Following his own religious persuasion, he chose the puritan, Charles Broxholme.

At the foundation of the church at Denby religious division still abounded in England. Henry VIII's split with Rome over his desire to marry Anne Boleyn and divorce Catherine of Aragon led him to found the Church of England and Catholic belief was under threat. It returned with a vengeance under the reign of 'Bloody' Mary between 1553 and 1558. Elizabeth I was more tolerant in general although she followed the ways of the English church. Puritans evolved as a group unhappy with the limitations of the Elizabethan settlement. They tended to favour plain styles of dress and lived lives of strict morality. Common features of their attitudes towards the church were their insistence of the urgency of re-creating the clergy as a preaching body. Also, their desire to carry on the reformation of the Church of England by purifying it of ceremony on account of its retention of much of the ritual and belief of the Roman Catholics. They were later to be the fierce opponents of the Royalists during the Civil War.

Finally the villagers of Denby and Gunthwaite had a house of worship, in their own back yard. A visitation by the church authorities from York in 1627 recorded that:

In 1627 the second chapel was built at Denby, to be used only for Mattins and Evensong.

It is interesting to note that the church authorities at this time were well aware that this was the second chapel to be built here. The thirteenth century edifice may have survived for longer than has previously been thought. This also lends greater credence to the possibility that the new chapel was built on the site of the old one. There were further visitations in 1693/4, 1715 and 1720 but they have no other detail than 'all well' and so add nothing to the story.

The Clergy

Charles Broxholme 1627–1632

Charles Broxholme was probably born on 15 February 1591, at Boultham, Lincoln, the son of William Broxholme. Once ordained he was described as *a passive and patient non-conformist* and also that his *head was too big for a church door.* He supported Parliament during the Civil War as one would expect of a Bosville minister, but before this was hounded from various ministerial posts by King Charles I men for nonconformity. In October 1629, he was inhibited from preaching at Denby by the King's High Commission and was ordered to attend the Commission later in the month but he was allowed more time as he pleaded that he was unwell. He was charged with giving Holy Communion to persons who had not been kneeling and was required to give their names. In January 1630, he produced a certificate by the Penistone churchwardens that the six people who had received the sacrament not kneeling, had since received it kneeling. He continued to prevaricate and on the 8th March 1632 his suspension from office was to be posted at Denby chapel, though he managed to hold this off until August. On 2 August 1632, he told the Commission that he was still unsure of his beliefs and was suspended forthwith and ordered to pay 50s costs.

He left Denby for Derbyshire and the protection of his friend, Sir John Gell, who kept the King's men at bay. Broxholme could hardly have had a better bodyguard at the time!

Sir John Gell (1593–1671) was born to one of the wealthiest families in Derbyshire. He was the son of Thomas Gell (1532–1594) and he married Elizabeth Willoughby (1593/4–1644) the sixteen-year-old daughter of Sir Percival Willoughby of Wollaton near Nottingham in 1610.

In 1635, he was appointed Sheriff of Derbyshire and was created a Baronet in 1642. Eight months later he supported Parliament at the outbreak of the Civil War and was commissioned by the Earl of Essex to secure Derbyshire for Parliament. His enemy Lord Chesterfield seized Lichfield in 1643 and it was John Gell who sent him to London in chains after the Royalist surrender. Gell's troops became notorious for plundering and Gell himself was not averse to corruption to secure appointments for friends and relatives. His loyalty to parliament came under scrutiny when he failed to join Lord Fairfax for the Naseby campaign in 1645 which led some to suspect he had changed sides, it is certain that his influence within the parliamentarian cause began to decline at this time, soon after the death of his wife in 1644. In 1648 he attempted to secure a pardon from Charles I (whilst Charles was imprisoned at Carisbrooke Castle), by offering to lend him £900 in gold. In 1650 Gell was found guilty of plotting against the Commonwealth and sent to the Tower of London until 1652 after which he was released and lived quietly in London. At the Restoration he was pardoned by Charles II for his roll in the civil war, regained his estates and granted a position at Court until his death in 1671.

Charles Broxholme is named in a document which has survived from the civil war period which regards one of John Gell's commanders, Thomas Sanders, whose relationship to his superior was at best acrimonious.

> *Charles Broxholme, Peter Whitinge, John Crompton, Thomas Bakettell and Everard Poole to Thomas Sanders – being ministers of the gospel, we give testimony that we do concieve you are no seperatist or independent.*

Broxholme later ministered at Belper, Buxton and then South Darley in Derbyshire, to which living he was nominated by Parliament, in 1646, as Rector. He died and was buried here in 1647. The Broxholme family were related to the illustrious Greville family and Charles's brother, John Broxholme, was the MP for Lincoln in the Long Parliament which declared civil war on Charles I in 1642. Charles Broxholme also wrote *The Good Old Way or Perkins Improved* which was published posthumously in 1654.

Daniel Clarke 1632–1643

Daniel Clarke succeeded Broxholme in 1632. He was born in 1609, and was the son of Hugh Clarke (1591–1634), the Vicar of Wolston, Leicestershire. Daniel's brother was Samuel, who became a well-known Puritan biographer.

Daniel was educated at Kings College Cambridge where he took his BA in 1631 and MA in 1634. Doubtless he was nominated to the post at Denby by Godfrey Bosville and whilst at Denby, Clarke met and married Elizabeth, daughter of the Lord of Denby, George Burdet. In 1637 Clarke was cited before the Archdeacon's court for administering the sacraments in Denby chapel, it not yet being consecrated. Clarke also supported the cause of parliament during the civil war and left Denby in 1643, at the request of the House of Commons, to replace the ardent Royalist, Gamaliel Whittaker at Kirkburton. Whittaker was arrested by Parliamentary troops, deprived of his living and died *of grief and ill usage* in a Manchester prison. It was also at this time that the Burdet family sold their manor of Denby to the Savile family of Thornhill, whether this had any bearing on Clarke's departure is unknown. Daniel Clarke was described as *a painful preacher* which meant that he took the trouble to write his own sermons rather than repeat the words of others. He left Kirkburton in 1649 and went on to become the Vicar of Fenny Compton, north of Farnborough in Warwickshire, where he died in 1654 aged 45. Daniel's son by Elizabeth Burdet, Thomas, also became a member of the Clergy.

Thomas Clarke was baptised at Kirkburton in 1649. He was the third pluralist Vicar of Huddersfield, as he was also appointed the Rector of Kirkheaton, 1694–1707. Thomas Clarke married one Elizabeth Smith who died in 1707 and was buried at Kirkheaton. By her he had five children, one son and four daughters all of whom were baptised at the Huddersfield Parish Church, they were, Daniel (after his Grandfather), Frances, Elizabeth, Mary and Ann. Thomas Clarke died in 1707/8. (*For more details on Thomas Clarke please refer to Ye Olde Townships – Denby Dale etc.*)

Up until now Denby chapel had no income other than charity coming into its coffers. The diary of John Hobson recorded in 1733 that:

> *At church. Mr Parkin, minister at Denby told me that Oliver Cromwell had endowed that chapel out of a Royalists estate, which he has seized on.*

It was actually Colonel Godfrey Bosville who was instrumental in initiating that the heirs of Edward Osborne (a Royalist) should pay £25 per annum to Denby Chapel. The money was paid irregularly but eventually £1000 was forthcoming.

Rev. Miller circa mid 1640s early 1650s

Sometime after the departure of Daniel Clarke in 1643 a man we know only by the name of Miller took over as minister at Denby.

It is probable that he was the man referred to by Captain Adam Eyre in his famous diary kept between 1647–1649:

Sunday 12th December 1647 – This day I went to Denby chapel and heard an old fellow preach both forenoon and after.

It is possible that Rev. Miller has been somewhat overlooked because of the reputations of the next incumbent at Denby and his counterpart at nearby Cumberworth, during his tenure. He almost certainly shared the curacy with the following incumbent.

Ralph Ward circa 1649–1650

We now come to a previously unknown individual but a man who became something of a firebrand in the name of his faith.

Ralph Ward was born in 1629 at Denby, only two years after the second chapel was built, he is therefore, the only local boy to have been made minister at the chapel. His time at Denby was short but his life and career make for fascinating reading.

He was educated at Sidney Sussex College, Cambridge under the tuition of Mr Elias Pawson and graduated BA in 1650, and MA in 1654. He became a passionate non-conformist, a conversion largely attributed to Samuel Hammond (of York), then minister of St Giles. In Denby, Ralph would have found his beliefs encouraged by the Bosville's and other notable families in the area, as all the early ministers of the chapel were puritans. He would have grown up attending the puritan sermons of Daniel Clarke in the village.

Ralph left his post at Denby after being recommended by Samuel Hammond to become the private chaplain to Colonel Fenwick whose regiment were garrisoned at Leith in Scotland after the Battle of Dunbar (3 September 1650) in which Oliver Cromwell achieved victory over the Royalist Presbyterian Scots. Ralph was here in 1651 but during a visit to friends in Yorkshire was persuaded not to return to Scotland but to take up a post as minister at Wolsingham, Durham, he was ordained on 14 September 1653 at the church of St Johns, Newcastle. The testimonial for this reads as follows:

Forasmuch as Mr. Ralph Ward hath addressed himself to the Classical Presbytery within the town and county of Newcastle-upon-Tyne (according to the order of both Houses of Parliament of August 28th, 1648, for the ordination of ministers by the Classical Presbytery), desiring to be ordained a Preaching Presbyter, for that he is called in the work of the ministry in Wolsingham Church in the county of Durham, and hath exhibited unto the Presbytery a sufficient testimonial now remaining in their custody of compleat age, of his unblameable life and conversation, of his diligence and proficiency in his studies, and of his fair and direct call to the forementioned place: We, the ministers of the said Presbytery, have by appointment thereof examined him according to the tenor of the said ordinance, and finding him to be duly qualified and gifted for that holy office and employment (no just exception being made against his ordination or admission) have approved him; and accordingly in the Church of St. John's, in Newcastle, upon the day and year hereafter expressed, have proceeded solemnly to set him apart to the office of a Preaching Presbyter and work of the ministry with fasting and prayer and imposition of hands: And do hereby (so far as concerneth us) actually admit him into the said charge there to perform all the offices and duties of a faithful minister of Jesus Christ. As witness whereof we have hereunto subscribed our names this 14th day of September, An. Dom. 1653. John Bewick, Moderator. Rd. Prideaux, Wm. Coley, Anthony Lapthorn, John Marshe, Robt. Plaisance, Wm. Henderson, Henry Lever, Thomas Hubbart.

After this, Ralph returned to both Cambridge and Oxford universities and began MAs at both. His living at Wolsingham was worth £150 per annum where it is stated that he:

> *applied himself vigorously to his work. He laboured hard on the Lord's days and went on the week days from house to house to enquire after the fruit of his pains. The poorer sort he invited to his house once or twice a week to be catechised and instructed, promising them victuals for their bodies if they would mind the good of their souls. But to his sorrow he found they soon grew weary; and as for those of his hearers who were in better circumstances, though they carried it very respectfully to him, they generally declined his personal applications.*

Because of the latter and '*some other difficulties*' he readily accepted an offer to move to the sequestered (living held by the Parliamentarians) parish of Hartburn. The living had previously been held by a Royalist sympathiser who had been ejected by Parliament who now required a minister more suitable for their regime. Ralph's income was reduced but his future prospects greater.

At the restoration of Charles II in 1660 the former incumbent was forcibly returned to his post and Ralph was ejected from his living aged 31. He retired to Newcastle where he ran a school which had *many gentlemen's sons for his scholars.* He also preached occasionally for Samuel Hammond and a Mr Durrant.

The Act of Uniformity passed in 1662 required every member of the clergy to declare their consent to everything in the Book of Common Prayer, to renounce the Solemn League and Covenant, to be ordained according to the rites of the Church of England and to subscribe to its doctrinal articles. The act led to the ejection of 960 ministers who were described as non-conformists after they refused to consent to the latter. Many of these ejected ministers found themselves in the same situation as Ralph Ward, victims of the changes wrought by the Civil War. This effectively silenced Ralph's preaching and also caused his school to close.

After a brief retirement he became the domestic chaplain to Sir John Hewley of York and he remained at York (with one interruption) for the rest of his life. The Five Mile Act of 1665 which was introduced to try and limit the potentially permissive influence of ministers who would not conform. It prohibited them from living within five miles of any place they had served before the passing of the act, though they were allowed to travel through such places. The act was not repealed until 1812. Ralph was driven away from York because of this but by 1666 he had returned and was living with his own family and preaching privately and without disturbance from 1666 until 1672. Under the Declaration of Indulgence he managed to obtain a licence (on 10 June 1672) to act as an independent teacher at the home of Brian Dawson in Ousegate, York.

Ralph now began a more public ministry in York. He gave sermons all around York, held debates with scholars, visited the sick and often went out into the country to preach lectures on week-days but *the Devil would not suffer him, however, to live without disturbance.* Before 1672 he was put into the Spiritual Court by the churchwarden of his parish and was excommunicated for not frequenting the church and receiving the sacrament there, this was renewed from year to year.

This turned into a a writ which either confined him to his house or obliged him to be extremely cautious in his endeavours.

In 1682 Ralph was fined £20 for a conventicle (a forbidden religious meeting) and a little later a further £40 for the same. Finally, whilst holding a conventicle at the house of a Mrs

Rokeby in Micklegate at 9 am on a Sunday morning, *the place was surprised by a magistrate and constables*. The names of 32 people were recorded as being present. Some of them it was reported,

> *they found in lofts above the garretts, and Mr. Ward and Mr. Taylor in a closett locked up, and the rest in several rooms.*

Bail was given before their appearance at York Assizes when they were tried before the infamous Judge Jeffrey's (1648–89). A manuscript of the time recorded that Jeffrey's called Ward and the 12 others committed,

> *rogues, traitors, and whiggs, he tells them the King's pleasure is to root out all phanaticks through the land.*

Ward was said to have behaved himself before the judge but for the illegal meeting he was fined £50 and was sent to the prison on Ousebridge in 1684, the conditions of which were described thus:

> *the cells of which would almost have rivalled the notorious Black Hole of Calcutta; air, light, and ventilation were absent, and the waters of the river rushed in when they were above their usual level.*

A petition on his behalf failed at the next assizes though he still managed to preach from his cell to the many who went out of the city to hear him. The death of Charles II in 1685 signalled the beginning of the end for the illegality of nonconformity which ended in the Act of Toleration in 1689. Ward was kept a prisoner largely due to the charges he allegedly owed to the court. A compromise was reached and upon payment of £40 he was given his freedom on 8 March 1686 after two years in prison.

He tried to continue his preaching as before but two long years in harsh conditions had badly affected his health, particularly his asthma. He was assisted by a Noah Ward in his public services every third Sunday. Shortly before his death he told a certain *pious lady* who new and highly respected him that,

> *I hope I can say that in simplicity and godly sincerity, not with fleshly wisdom, but by the grace of God, I have had my conversation in the world.*

Ralph died on 13 March 1691 aged 62, the following epitaph has survived regarding him:

> *He was of a bold spirit and undaunted in his work, and he had prudence and meekness to govern his courage, that while it kept him true to his own conscience made him not justly offensive to others. He was eminently pious; all his sermons were preached over twice, first to himself and then to others. He was much in prayer, was not afraid of his own company, was delighted with soliloquies, and kept his heart with all diligence. He was excellent in all relations. His family was a well-ordered church, and his friendship was safe, edifying, and honourable. In a word all the worthy characters of a Gospel minister met in him He deserved quite other treatment than he met with from an unkind world, but his reward is above.*

We must now mention the other cleric who would have put Denby's Rev. Miller in the shade. His presence at Cumberworth would have been well known to the local populace but his religious views and political persuasion were poles apart from the of the Puritans of Denby.

Bishop Henry Tilson of Cumberworth 1651–1655

Henry Tilson was born at Heponstall near Halifax in 1576. He entered Balliol College, Oxford in 1593 and took a degree in arts as a member of that house four years later. He was elected soon afterwards as one of Skirlawe's Fellows of University College and took a degree as Master of that house where he can be found in 1601 aged 25. In October 1615 he became Vicar of Rochdale and whilst here he came to the attention of the ill fated, Thomas, Earl of Strafford. He became of Earl's chaplain and accompanied him to Ireland when King Charles I conferred the title of Lord Lieutenant upon him. The Earl made Tilson the Dean of the Cathedral of the Holy Trinity, commonly called Christ Church in Dublin and Vice Chancellor of the University in 1634. He later rose again and became Bishop of Elphin in 1639 but when rebellion broke out in Ireland in 1641 the Bishop's career went into decline. He was also deprived of his patron as the Earl of Strafford had returned to England at the request of the under siege, King Charles in 1641, only to be impeached by Parliament and executed.

Sir James Ware in his history of the Irish Bishops, says:

Bishop Henry Tilson on the 16th of August, 1645, delivered the Castle of Elphin in the hands of the Lord President of Connaught; his son, Capt. Henry Tilson, who was governor of Elphin, having just before joined with Sir Charles Coot in opposition to the King's interest, and about the same time his library and goods were pillaged by Boctius Egan titular Bishop of Elphin, his damages amounting to the sum of four hundred pounds.

The Bishop, made good his escape to England, where, Sir William Savile (soon to be owner of the manor of Denby) arranged for him and his family of thirteen to live at Soothill Hall, Batley. He resided here for three years always with the intention of returning to Elphin, but he never did. Henry Tilson had married Grace Chadwick, of Clegg Hall, Midgeley, on 4 June 1620. The couple had at least eleven children, including: Dorothy (born 1621), Margaret (born 1626), Henry (born 1626), John (born 1628), Nathaniel (born 1630), and Thomas (born 1636), all in Rochdale.

Stripped of his income and with a large family to support, the Bishop set up a room at Soothill Hall which became known as the Bishop's parlour in which he privately ordained and performed the offices of a clergyman for some of his neighbours and benefactors.

In 1643 Parliament passed the Root and Branch Bill by which Bishops were driven out of their diocese, Royalist clergymen were forced from their parish and the use of the prayer book made a criminal offence. Resistance did take place, the Rector of High Hoyland (Thomas Inman), being imprisoned for a time, but many clergy carried on. The resistance movement in our area centred upon Henry Tilson and the Royalist Laurence Farrington, Rector of Emley. Despite the ban, Tilson continued to ordain men at Soothill Hall, such as Timothy Wood, master at Bradford Grammar school, who was ordained in 1647, the order being signed by Henry Tilson.

Out of compassion and in order to provide the Bishop with a living, Sir William Wentworth appointed the Bishop to preach at Cumberworth by at least 1651, allowing him a sufficient salary to support his family. The antiquarian, Fred Lawton, continues the story with Henry Tilson's own words written in 1651 at a time when use of the prayer book was a criminal offence:

But you shall know that I am not altogether idle, for I pray, after the Directory of the Church of England, and preach every Sunday at a place in the mountains called Cumberworth, two

Cumberworth Church, February 1894.

Interior of Cumberworth Church around 1930.

> *miles beyond Emley, where I have, by the way Lawrence, My Gains, or host* [Rev. Lawrence Farrington, Rector of Emley – a staunch Royalist]. *It was proffered to me by a Gentleman, Mr Wentworth of Bretton, whom I never saw, saving once, before he sent unto me; and because it come – as my ecclesiastical livings and preferments have done – without my seeking and suite; and because it is lay donative and in his power to give or detain, and the engagement was passed in that parish. I took it to be pointed out for me by God, as a little zoar, to preserve my life, and did accept it; though it will not reach to 40 marks per annum; besides I trust to do God's service in the exercise of my ministry amongst that moorish and late rebelious plundering people. When I first went to Rochdale, you may remember what the old ostler at the Baytiinges willed me to do: Take with you a great box full of tar, for you shall find a great company of scabbed sheep. The first Sunday I preached in the forenoon and read service in the afternoon; and when I perceived by their murmurings that they must have two fodderings I have made good use thereof; and whereas I might have given them two sixpences, they are well pleased if I give them two groats for a shilling, which I intend to pay them, so childish are they in the right valuings of God's coin.*

Lawton continues:

> *The Bishop probably meant by this whimsical figure, that the people of Cumberworth were better pleased with two discourses of twenty minutes each, than with one of an hour.*

The letter was written at Soothill Hall, it appears that Henry Tilson travelled from here to Cumberworth every week and sometimes spent a day or two with his friend the Vicar of Emley. During his stay in Cumberworth Henry Tilson, flouted the new laws, openly consecrating Meltham church and ordaining its first vicar in Emley church in 1652 aided by Laurence Farrington and Thomas Inman. Until recently, the only chalice which Cumberworth church possessed was the one bequeathed by him.

The chalice resides today in the treasury at York Minster. It is recorded in *Yorkshire Church Plate Volume 2* by Fallow and McCall thus:

> *The silver cup is an elegant beaker, of very graceful outline. Immediately under the rim is an engraved band of interlacing ornament, not dissimilar to that commonly encircling the bowls of the older Communion cups. Below this belt, and spreading half-way down the cup, are diagonal bands of engraved ornament forming lozenge-shaped spaces about an inch in size. These bands terminate in a sort of bell-shaped flower, pointing downwards, and are very similar to the ornament often occurring at the interlacing points of the leaf pattern on York-made Communion cups of the latter part of the seventeenth century, and which is not found on any cups made elsewhere. There is no inscription, nor is the history of the vessel known. It was doubtless a piece of secular plate originally. Height 5¼ dia. At top 3½ at the base 3 in. hallmarks grouped on the bottom: (1) leop. And lys (2) sm. Italic Y (3) illegible (York, 1655).*

Henry Tilson died on 31 March 1655 and was buried in Dewsbury church.

As we have noted, Henry Tilson the younger became a Captain during the fighting in Ireland. The Bishop's younger son, Nathaniel became the father of an eminent portrait painter. Henry Tilson was born to Nathaniel in 1659. The Yorkshireman showed early promise as an artist and became well known for his skill in copying the masters. In 1685 he embarked upon an artistic exploration of Europe with Michael Dahl, returning to London in 1689. He was a pupil and later assistant to Sir Peter Lely (1618–1680) principal portrait

The seventeenth century chalice donated by Bishop Henry Tilson to Cumberworth. (Courtesy of York Minster Archives)

painter to King Charles II) and later he worked with Sir Godfrey Kneller (1646–1723, also patronised by the King). By 1690 Tilson had established a successful practice and was known *as a painter of great charm*. Tragically, he committed suicide at the age of 36 in November 1695, when he shot himself in the heart after a love affair was ended by an enigmatic patroness known only as *Mrs Green*.

John Crooke 1657–1665

John Crooke, a native of Sheffield, took over at Denby in 1657, when he settled in the village.

He was born in 1629 in Sheffield, where his father, John Crooke, was a very successful and prosperous cutler. John (senior), was also noted to be generous with his money, reputedly giving a tenth of his income to pious uses.

John Crooke (junior) was educated at St John's College, Cambridge, where he was admitted, under Mr Howe on 27 June 1648 aged 19. After gaining his MA, his first post was that of curate at the chapel in Eccleshall, Sheffield in 1656 though he arrived in Denby only a year or so later. He had married the widow of John Bridges, the assistant minister at Sheffield in 1646. John was a puritan and non-conformist which, as we have already had reason to note, became a problem when the restoration of King Charles II took place in 1660. As with Ralph Ward, John was expected to conform to the licensed services. He was another man of principal and refused to comply and was removed from his post at Denby by the Act of Uniformity in 1665.

After his ejection John only preached occasionally or privately, he was no Ralph Ward. He was also more fortunate than many of his colleagues as he had been left a good estate by his father and he used the income from this to live on when he left Denby for Wakefield. He can be found here in 1684 when he was visited by the celebrated nonconformist preacher, Oliver Heywood. The following details have survived regarding John Crooke's character:

> *He was a sober and stout (staunch) man, very sound and orthodox, of good natural parts, active and vigorous, and very able to defend the truth with argument. It was said that he was of a somewhat penurious disposition. He was, however, a small benefactor of his native parish, the curate of Eccleshall, enjoying 30s per annum of his gift. Though he was but a spare and temperate man, he was long afflicted with the gout, which at last rose upward from his foot to his throat and choked him.*

John Crooke lived in retirement at Wakefield for 22 years before he was described as having died *'of the gout in his throat'* on 9 January 1687 aged 58.

Christopher Wallbank and the forged nomination – circa 1665

At around this time the Vicar of Cawthorne, Christopher Wallbank attempted to gain the Curacy of Denby by forging a nomination which, if nothing else proves that the post was desirable.

Christopher Wallbank was appointed as Vicar of Cawthorne in 1662. Like so many clergy appointed to fill the vacant livings that arose as a result of the Act of Uniformity 1662, Wallbank was a man of his time. He was a heavy drinker and on one occasion made a mockery of the sacrament of baptism.

In 1662 he was sitting drinking with one of his parishioners, Thomas Faley. Wallbank stood up, took his pint of ale and sprinkled Hopwood on the forehead and face with it, saying:

> *I baptise thee in the name of Much Worth in the Name of the Father, the Son and the Holy Ghost.*

Hopwood, surprised by this action by the vicar, stood up with his pint and sprinkled his ale on the vicar saying:

> *I baptise thee in the name of Little Worth in the name of the Father.*

This deed was reported by the churchwardens to the Archdeacon of York who had the case heard by the Archbishops Consistory Court on the charge that Wallbank had made holy baptism a profane act and made the office of parish priest a disgrace.

The court uncovered other irregularities.

Wallbank had presented to the Archbishop of York, Letters Testimonial together with a nomination for the curacy of Denby chapel. These testimonials were signed by John Mosley, Thomas Smith, Godfrey Custon and John Roebuck, none of whom were in orders and whose characters were suspect. The whole set of documents had been forged in order to obtain the living at Denby to be held jointly with Cawthorne.

Wallbank did not perform his duties to the letter, on 25 September 1664 Elizabeth Hewitt was to perform a penance for adultery with Robert Woofinden during Divine Service. This was not performed at that time but at a private house, though the certificate was returned as though the penance had been performed according to instructions. Wallbank was also accused of being a common swearer and cursor, a brawler, a sower of discord with his neighbours and a quarrelsome person who delighted with strife within the parish. He was also accused of solemnising marriage outside the permitted hours, without any licence or banns asked and between many parties in private houses and in church.

The Archbishop heard all this and suspended Wallbank from the living of Cawthorne, he promptly left to be schoolmaster and curate at Batley where he was in charge of the Grammar School until 1688. The advent of William and Mary in 1688 and the departure of James II saw further trouble for Wallbank. He refused to take the oath of allegiance to the new monarchs and was eventually dismissed from his post.

From letters that passed from Joshua Briggs, vicar of Kirkburton, Wallbank, it would appear, then earned a living by solemnising cut price marriages at Snowgate Head in Kirkburton without banns or license and was doing a good trade. This annoyed the vicar of Kirkburton as he was losing fees that should have been his. Nothing seems to have been done to curb this and Wallbank continued to minister in the area around New Mill until his death on 16 March 1708. He was buried in his family vault at Cawthorne with his daughter, Elizabeth, who had died in 1674 and his wife, Ann who died in 1695, aged 64. The memorial tablet survives, Christopher Wallbank described *as preacher of the gospel and minister of this church.*

Timothy Kent 1665–1691

Timothy Kent took over at Denby in 1665 and continued up until his death in 1691. His wonderful stone epitaph survives in the present day church, written in Latin, it reads:

Here Timothy Kent awaits Christ's future coming;
Master of Arts and of this Church a recent minister.
A pastor, honourable and steadfast; most watchful lest any should wander.
A popular orator, constant, beneficial, and eloquent
His arguments weighty, yet cunning; how alluring of speech, yet mightier in actions.
A good man, yet greater in writing. Though stone cannot express
his peculiar excellences,
The longings of his friends will yet constantly speak.
Died, 28th August 1691

This old stone has been here for 317 years, it is only 64 years younger than the chapel itself.

Timothy Kent was also involved in one of the most notorious events to occur in Denby – accusations of witchcraft.

In 1674, Ann Shillitoe (married to Thomas) and Susan Hinchcliffe (married to Joseph) were accused by a spinster, Mary Moor who was 16 years old. A long statement alleged that the pair practised as witches and gave examples of their sorcery. Matters were complicated when Timothy Haigh accused Mary Moor of similar activities. Moor also implicated Susan Hinchcliffe's husband, Joseph. Ann and Susan were taken to Barnsley gaol and were committed for trial at York.

The villagers of Denby were unhappy and came out in support of the accused women, producing a petition as to their good and wholesome conduct and to the contrary regarding Mary Moor. It was signed by the great and the good of the area and includes some very important names from the history of Denby. Timothy Kent signed it, giving his

The bell donated to Denby Church by Lady Mary Beaumont n'ee Burdet dated 1678.

support to the so-called witches, lending even more weight to the argument for the case to be a total fabrication.

The record of the trial, now lost, but when last seen, was torn in two, which indicates that the charges were thrown out. But it had all become too much for the Hinchcliffe family. Joseph Hinchcliffe, indicted with his wife, committed suicide on the morning of Thursday 4 February 1675, his body was not discovered until Sunday. Meanwhile, his wife Susan had died praying on her deathbed for her accusers.

It was during Timothy Kent's time at Denby that the bell was donated to the chapel. Dating to 1678 it is inscribed:

> *The gift of Dame Mary Beaumont, eldest daughter of George Burdet, Esq. of Denby Hall 1678.*

Detail of the bell and hammer.

Detail of the inscription on the bell.

Dame Mary Beaumont was the daughter of George Burdet (born 1580), Lord of Denby. She was the sister of the last Burdet Lord of the Manor, Richard Burdet (1610–1666). Mary made two advantageous marriages, firstly to Richard Pilkington and then to Sir Thomas Beaumont, hence her title of Dame. Thomas Beaumont was a member of the family recorded in 1666 by Sir William Dugdale in his survey of the gentry of Yorkshire, also known as a 'visitation'. He began the Beaumont family of Whitley with William Beaumont who was alive during the reign of Henry III (1216–1272). Thomas Beaumont (1605–1668) was the son of Richard Beaumont and

Memorial tablet inside Wooley Church of Dame Mary Beaumont who died in 1682. (Courtesy of T R Cowan)

Inscription on Dame Mary Beaumont's memorial tablet. (Courtesy of T R Cowan)

Ann Kay of Lascelles Hall. He was initially married to Elizabeth, the daughter of George Armitage of Netherton, in 1626, the union producing at least five children and so when he married Mary Burdet in August 1656 (when he was 51 years old), both parties were on their second marriages. Mary was a wealthy widower by virtue of her father and her first husband and would have been quite a catch for Beaumont. During the civil wars, Beaumont had been a Royalist and had been appointed Deputy Governor of Sheffield Castle by Sir William Savile until its surrender and fall in July 1644. He later fought for the King at the battle of Pontefract where he was wounded. His reward came upon the restoration of Charles II when he became a Justice of the Peace and Deputy Lieutenant of the West Riding. He died in 1668 and left only £100 jointure (property settled by a husband on his wife at the time of their marriage for her use after his death) which left her bitter and disappointed. Mary took the matter to court before settling privately; she died in 1682 and was buried at Wooley. It is interesting to note that Mary also made a gift of a silver chalice to Penistone church dated 1673.

Gamaliel Battie 1691–1698

Timothy Kent was succeeded by Gamaliel Battie in 1691. Battie (or Batty) was born in 1669 at Scholes, Hepworth and baptised on 18 April 1669 at Kirkburton, so he was a local boy. He was the son of John Battie and Elizabeth Wood (1645–1678) and was only nine years old when his mother died. He was ordained a Deacon at Magdalen College Chapel, Oxford in

1692. His stay at Denby lasted for seven years until 1698 when he left to become Curate and Schoolmaster at Flockton. He married a woman we know only as Barbara who died in 1742.

During the incumbency of Gamaliel Batty, John Sharp, the Archbishop of York, (1691–1714 as Archbishop) wrote a manuscript regarding the various parish churches and chapels under his jurisdiction. The page regarding Penistone and Denby is headed with the date 1716 but as Sharp died in office in 1714 the manuscript was obviously written earlier, probably around the mid 1690s.

Circa. 1690's
£32 7s 6d (Value of living)
The Chapel of Denby

> *Is within the parish (of Penistone) which yet is not consecrated. It is endowed with £30 7s 6d well paid, issuing out of an estate (blank) forfeited by the late heirs for malignancy, and given to Mr Bosville in trust for finding a curate to serve here. Since the reformation the owner came to a composition with the persons concerned so that it still remains to the chapel. The curate is Mr Batty who was admitted to it at the nomination of the three trustees with the minister, Mr Hough on nomination given under his hand.*
>
> *1706 – Certified by William Norris, the present curate and his churchwarden that the value of this curacy is £31 7s 6d paid by Godfrey Bosville Esq. The rest arises from some monies that was saved in several vacancies with the consent of the immediate successors.*

William Norris 1698–(?)

The vacancy at Denby was taken up by William Norris in 1698. Norris, born in 1659 died in 1733 aged 74 and was buried at Penistone, but had left Denby some time before.

Bryan Allot c.1727

Bryan Allot was the next man to hold the curacy. He was ordained as a Deacon in 1727 and became the Curate at Penistone in the same year under the guidance of the Rev. Thomas Cockshutt who was the vicar there. He became a priest in 1730 and by 1735 had left Penistone to become the Vicar of Stretton where he remained until 1746. In 1748 he became Rector of Burnby, though this was short-lived as he became Vicar of Londesborough in the same year and stayed until 1757. His final appointment was that of Rector of Kirkheaton where he died in 1773. This may well have been the first instance of a Curate at Penistone taking charge at Denby, it is very likely that it was only ever intended as a temporary arrangement. After less than two years, he was succeeded by Jonathan Perkins in 1729.

Jonathan Perkins 1729–1753

Jonathan Perkins, was the first of a number of curates at Denby who also held the post of Master at Penistone Grammar School. He endowed Denby chapel with £200 in 1738 to pay for its expenses and to provide a salary for its incumbent. This was followed in 1739 by a further £200 allocated from the fund known as 'Queen Anne's Bounty'. This was provided by the Church of England to provide relief for poorer members of the clergy by making grants to livings worth less than £10 per annum, (raised in 1788 to £35). From 1809 it was paid by Parliamentary grants, after which, in 1816, Denby received a further £1200. A house and lands were purchased by the chapel from the grant given in 1739, the rent for which, brought in an extra £13 per annum to the living of the curate.

It would appear that the appropriation of Queen Anne's Bounty (hereafter referred to as QAB) and the gift of the curate Jonathan Perkins (which would have been part of the QAB) caused certain authorities to consider the chapel at Denby to be a separate parish. We know that burials had been taking place from at least the 1660s and probably baptisms too. The fact that three years of Bishops Transcripts survive for Denby alone (1747–1750) does not mean that Denby chapel operated independently from Penistone. Indeed we know that it did not from Archbishop Herrings visitation in 1743. The provision of Bishops Transcripts was hit and miss anyway and we know that records of happenings at Denby were kept in the Penistone registers from at least the 1620s–1852. It is unlikely that any marriages were performed at Denby before 1854. There do not seem to be any more records regarding the 1738 'parish' other than the QAB and it is from this alone that the idea of Denby being a separate parish was established when in fact it was not, it was still under the jurisdiction of Penistone until 1853. With respect to the church authorities, there is little evidence of any split, Jonathan Perkins was still subject to Thomas Cockshutt, the Vicar of Penistone and, augmentation aside, life seems to have continued much as before within the parish.

In 1743 Thomas Cockshutt, reported to his Archbishop about matters relating to his parish. It was Jonathan Perkins who supplied the following information:

(1) *We have 130 families in chapelry of Denby of which 9 are Quakers. No papists or other kind of Dissenters.*

(2) *We have one licensed meeting house for Quakers who assemble every Lords Day to the number of 80. One Elihu Dickinson teaches.*

(3) *We have one Charity School endowed with f.5 a year for teaching poor children. Sufficient care is taken to teach then in the principles of Christian religion, according to the doctrine of the Church of England, and to bring them duly to Church.*

(4) *Denby being in the Parish of Penistone, I being Grammar School master there reside in the schoolhouse, having no house or lands belonging to the chapelry of Denby.*

(5) *I do all the duty of the Chapelry myself.*

(6) *I know of none that come to Denby Chapel that are not baptised but I believe that a 100 of competent age come who are not confirmed.*

(7) *Every Sunday and Holy Day and twice on every Lords, Day, Divine Service is performed.*

(8) *The first Sunday in every month I catechise in the Chapel and every Saturday in the Grammar School by which means most children and servants in these parts are sufficiently instructed in their catechism.*

(9) *I never administer the Sacrament in the Chapel of Denby, though I believe that there are 200 communicants in our Chapelry most of which receive at different times in the Parish Church.*

(10) *I give open and timely warning of Sacrament being administered at the Parish Church the Sunday before I and the inhabitants take it at Penistone.*

Jonathan Perkins became a deacon on 26 October 1729 at Chester and a Priest on 18 July 1731 at Christ's College, Cambridge. He is mentioned twice in the diary of John Hobson:

1727 May 11th – At Penistone. Mr Perkins' son is elected schoolmaster.
1734 October 8th – Mrs Jenkins married to Mr Perkins, schoolmaster at Penistone.

As schoolmaster at Penistone he would have taken services at Denby from 1729 onwards but after his ordination as a Priest he took up the position of curate under the guidance of, Thomas Cockshutt. He married Susannah Jenkins at Penistone on 8 October 1734.

The churchwarden's presentment for the Denby Chapelry has the following to say, dated 15th June 1750:

All is well. Our schoolmaster is efficient but we have no ministers house. John Horsfall, Joseph Gaunt, Joseph Rhodes and Wm. Earnshaw, Churchwardens. 1721, July 29th – I Phillip Mitchell, Churchwarden of Penistone, do certify that John Goldthorpe presented at the last visitation for profaning the Sabbath and for not repairing to his Parish Church hath since the visitation duly frequented the said Church as witness my hand Phillip Mitchell.

Jonathan Perkins can be found acting as a witness under his superior, Thomas Cockshutt, (the Vicar of Penistone since 1722) in the two following leases.

Thomas Cockshutt, clerk and vicar of Penistone, William Fenton of Underbank and George Walker of Hunshelfe, both of Penistone, gentlemen, the only surviving trustees of the Grammar School, to Thomas Marsden of the same, tailor, and Ann, his wife, Richard Senyor of the same, clothier, and Ann, his wife, son in law and daughter of Thomas, with Jonathan Perkins, clerk and schoolmaster, also being a party. The messuage in Penistone in which Thomas Marsden dwells. For 21 years at an annual rent of £2. In consideration that Thomas Marsden has recently spent money on repairs and additional building. (4 May 1738).

Thomas Cockshutt, clerk and vicar of Penistone, William Fenton of Underbank and George Walker of Hunshelfe, both of Penistone, gentlemen, to Jonathan Rhodes of the same, husbandman, with Jonathan Perkins, clerk and master, also a party. A messuage cottage in Penistone now divided into two dwellings with adjoining croft. For 21 years at an annual rent of 30s. (10 May 1739).

He also appears alongside a possible family member in the following lease:

Mary Mitchell of Penestone, widow and administratix of Ephraim Mitchell deceased, to John Perkins the younger of the same, grocer, with Jonathan Perkins of the same, clerk, also being a party. The residue of the lease of 1 May 1720. For 10s paid by Jonathan and 5s paid by John. (10 May 1736).

Jonathan Perkins died in 1753

Samuel Phipps 1753–1778

Samuel Phipps was born on 2 October 1714, the son of John Phipps of Pule Hill Hall.

John Phipps was born in 1683 and can be found in the following deeds:

Final Concord – 1714
Plaintiff: John Phipps, gent. Deforciants: Henry Carrington, gent., William Ellison and Rebecca his wife, John Beighton and Elizabeth his wife, John Smith and Mary his wife. In 5 messuages, 3 cottages, 120 acres land, 60 acres pasture, 60 acres meadow, 15 acres wood, in Thurgoland, Barnsley, Bradfield and Cawthorne. Consideration of £300.

Deed to declare the uses of a fine – 1 Jan 1715
William Ellison of Barnsley, Yorks., yeoman and Rebecca, his wife, of the first part; Henry Carrington of Glewhouse, Worsbroughdale, Yorks., gent., of the second part; John Spencer of

> *Cannon Hall, Yorks., gent., of the third part, and John Phipps of Pulehill, Yorks., gent., of the fourth part. Reciting a final concord of Trinity term, 1711, levied in the following lands; capital messuage called Pulehill, in Thurgoland, par. Silkstone, Yorks., in the occupation of Roger Hall: several closes, as follows; Two High Fields, North Croft, Chamber Croft, Crabb Tree Acres, Birkfield, Colepitt Close, Long Lands, Well Close, New Ing, Sower Butts, Hall Ing, Two Little Fields, Chappell Flatt, Broad Close, Two Rough Fields, all containing together, 133 acres; other messuages and buildings belonging, with closes called Croft, the Urchin Hill, the New Close, the Farrfield, all in Cawthorne, and in the occupation of William Lookes. To be to the use of John Phipps for life and thereafter to the use of John Spencer.*

John was also appointed to the position of Steward of Wortley in 1707. He came to Pule Hill Hall, Thurgoland in around 1704/5.

Pule Hill Hall was once the home of the Bamford family, around 1600. One of these, John Bamford became Lord of the Manor of Thurgoland and a Justice of the Peace. He was a Royalist though his support for his King left him in a terrible financial state. Pule Hill was sold, because of this, to Thomas Keresforth (1597–1674), a member of one of the oldest families in Barnsley. At his death, his wife Anne, inherited the *capital messuage and cottage* at Pule Hill where she stayed for nearly thirty years until her last will was written in 1704/5. Ownership of the Hall passed on to the Bower family, cousins of Thomas Keresforth around the period 1680/90 but by the time of Anne Keresforth's death John Phipps had taken up residence at the Hall.

From the Silkstone parish registers we find that John had at least four children, Frances (born 1705), John (1712), Samuel (1714) and Ruth (1716), all the births occurring at Pule Hill Hall. Only two years after the birth of Ruth, John Phipps died on 4 August 1718 aged 35, he was buried at Silkstone on the 17th. We have at present very few details about his wife, though the following quote, from the diary of John Hobson is intriguing:

> *1728/9 March 15.*
> *Mrs Hilary, mother to Mrs Phipps of Puel Hill buried at Silkstone.*

This young family were now in need of help and it was provided by George Phipps of High Green near Ecclesfield. We know that at least Samuel Phipps went to live with this man for the remainder of his childhood, but who was George Phipps?

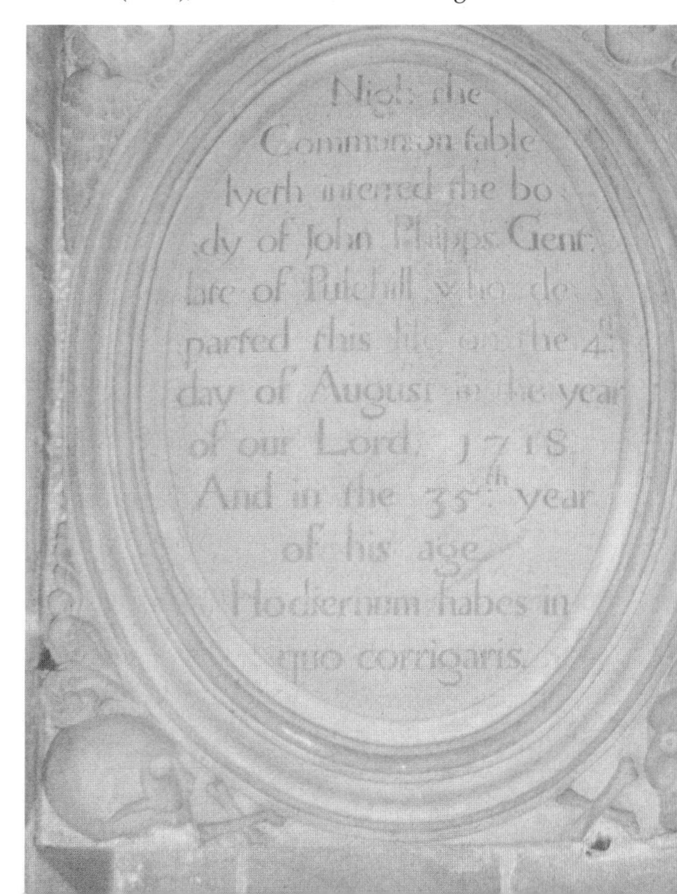

Memorial tablet inside Silkstone Church of John Phipps who died in 1718.

George Phipps was born in 1686 in High Green, the son of an elder George Phipps (1645–1726) also of High Green. He in turn was the son of Francis Phipps, born 1610 in Reading who was the son of Colonel William Phipps who fought in the English Civil Wars. George Phipps the elder was one of a family of nine all born in or around the Reading area. He was the first member of the family to reside at High Green, though his reasons for doing so are unclear. His younger brother was Constantine Phipps, who adopted the profession of law. He steadily rose in stature until he was recognised for his achievements and was knighted by Queen Anne in 1710 and became Lord Chancellor of Ireland, remaining in the post until 1714 when he returned to England and resumed his practice at the bar. He married Katherine Sawyer and had a son, William (born 1698). Sir Constantine died in 1723 and was buried in White Waltham, Berkshire.

William married Catherine Annesley, the only daughter and heiress of James, 3rd Earl of Anglesey and their son, Constantine was raised to the peerage as Baron Mulgrave of New Ross, County Wexford. His son, Sir Henry Phipps was raised further, becoming Viscount Normanby and Earl of Mulgrave and his son, Constantine Henry became the first Marquiss of Normanby.

George Phipps (born 1645) was not destined to be quite so successful as his younger brother, though he did outlive him! His death is mentioned in the diary of John Hobson:

1725/6 March 16
Old Mr Phipps of High Green buried at Ecclesfield.

He married Susanna Knutton at Ecclesfield in 1683 and as we have seen had at least one child, George, in 1686 who fostered the young Samuel Phipps. It is highly likely that Samuel's father, John, was George Phipps elder brother.

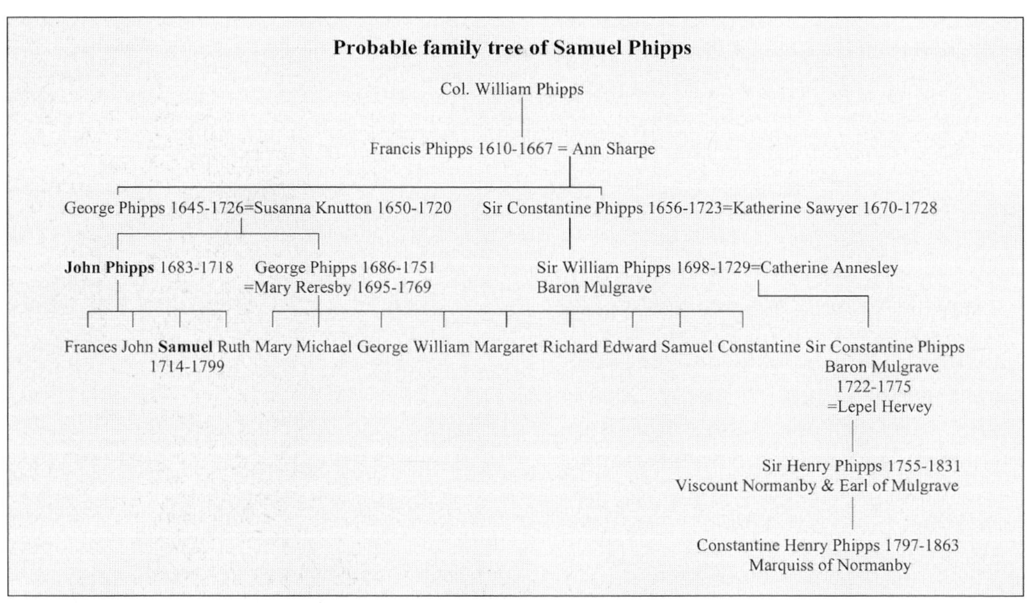

Samuel left his childhood home for Cambridge University where he gained his BA and then took up his first clerical post, that of curate of Treswell in Nottinghamshire. He was mentioned in a visitation held at Retford on 11 May 1739 (when he was 25 years old) where it was noted that he was licensed to serve here as a curate on 17 April 1739 by Richard Osbaldeston, Dean of York. His salary was £28 per annum.

In 1748 Samuel left Treswell and returned home to take up the position of curate at Penistone. He became curate of Denby on 21 June 1753. Phipps, who became a deacon in 1738/9 and was ordained a priest in 1740, went on to become Vicar of Penistone in 1761 (he was presented by Godfrey Bosville), whilst still holding his post as perpetual curate of Denby, he was also curate of Cawthorne church from 1776 until his death. He resigned from Penistone in 1798. He also served as Vicar of Silkstone from 1757 until April 1799 when he died aged 85. Phipps must have been a very busy man though he was assisted by a number of different curates in his duties, some of which were Masters at Penistone Grammar School. Samuel Phipps resigned his post at Denby in 1778.

Denby – Perpetual Curate	1753–1778
Silkstone – Vicar	1757–1799
Penistone – Vicar	1761–1798
Cawthorne – Curate	1776–1799

Samuel was a respected friend of John Spencer of Cannon Hall and was made an executor of his will. John Spencer was born in 1719 and was therefore, only five years younger than Samuel. The two boys may well have known each other from childhood, their respective

Silkstone Church circa 1900. (Courtesy of Old Barnsley)

families were certainly acquainted as the following document involves both the boys grandfathers:

Release – John Spencer of Canon Hall, parish of Cawthorne, Gent, of the first part and George Phipps of Wortley, Gent of the second part. Regarding Potters Farm at Pottershill, parish of Ecclesfield and lands adjoining for £277. 19 July 1709.

Cannon Hall had been in the possession of the Bosville family during the fifteenth century and was settled upon Richard Bosville the founder of the Gunthwaite branch. By the mid seventeenth century, their hold over it had been passed on to William Hewitt who sold it on to Robert Hartley in 1650. Hartley died in 1656 and his widow remarried to John Spencer (1629–1681), thus began the families stay at Cannon Hall.

The Spencer family had made their fortune in the local iron industry. John Spencer, the great grandson of the original John inherited Cannon Hall in 1756 upon the death of his father, William Spencer. He was to be the last of his family line as he never married. He did have two younger brothers, twins, William and Benjamin. William drank himself to death in 1759. Benjamin found himself in financial trouble around the mid-1750s and turned to the slave trade in order to secure his financial future. Although abhorrent to later generations, Benjamin was a man of his time and was, as far as he was concerned, engaged upon a legitimate venture. He bought a ship, a sloop, and called it the *Cannon Hall*. Benjamin was not to take part in the journey but would keep any of the expected profit. He paid for a crew of six sailors, their food, and the goods which were to be taken to Africa. These goods included textiles, guns and knives and steel which would be exchanged for slaves on the West African coast. The slaves were then transported to the Caribbean and sold, the profits of which were then invested in goods such as rice, indigo, rum and sugar for onward sale in Britain. Benjamin's venture set out in May 1755 but it was not a success. His slaves arrived in the Caribbean at the same time as a glut of French ships carrying cheaper slaves and consequently his slaves could not be sold. Instead they were taken to Charlestown, South Carolina and sold there. Benjamin died in 1759, two months after his brother, heavily in debt from the venture.

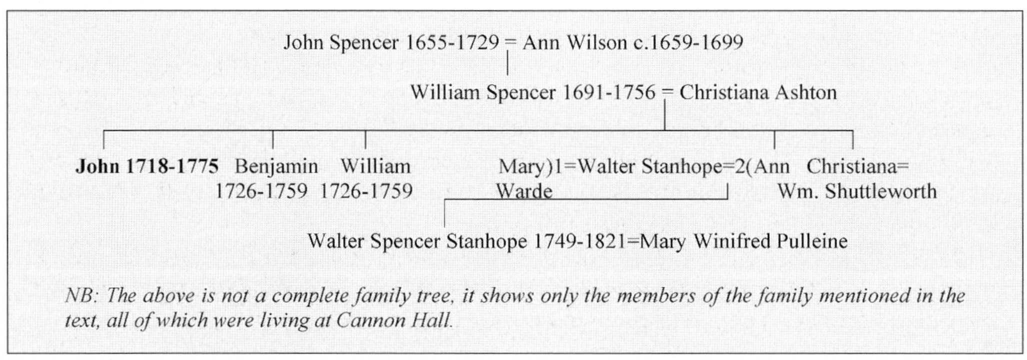

NB: The above is not a complete family tree, it shows only the members of the family mentioned in the text, all of which were living at Cannon Hall.

John Spencer died in 1775 and his nephew, Walter Spencer Stanhope inherited. Walter was the son of Walter Stanhope and Mary Spencer (sister of John). Born in 1749, he was 26 when he inherited his Uncle's estates. He became a Tory MP and was friendly with the slave abolitionist William Wilberforce who visited Cannon Hall on several occasions.

Walter used his position in parliament to argue for the abolition of the slave trade alongside Wilberforce and they achieved success in 1807 when the practise was outlawed throughout the British Empire. How times had changed, 48 years after Benjamin's death his nephew now stood against everything he had believed in, in order to make his fortune.

Samuel Phipps attitude to slavery, the tearing of men, women and children from their families in Africa, the terrible conditions on board slave ships and their treatment by their eventual owners is unknown. As a man of the cloth one would like to think he cared for the souls of these unfortunates but the practice was common and accepted, subsequently Phipps could hardly be to blame for perhaps being somewhat ambivalent.

John Spencer lived the life of a country squire, but he was also a man of his time. On Sunday afternoons he would often organise a cock fight in his park, which was, by and large an open secret. The privileged amongst his tenantry were allowed to attend and the parson, Samuel Phipps, occasionally put in an appearance himself, as if by chance! Phipps was certainly no puritan.

The following recollection of George Swift (1903–1990) of Cawthorne appeared in the book *Cawthorne 1790–1990* and gives us more insight into the characters of Samuel Phipps and John Spencer.

> *John Spencer was driving home one evening with the parson after a carousal in the neighbourhood, at which both had indulged freely in the pleasures of the table. As the old coach rumbled heavily along the lonely Yorkshire roads, to the Squire's confused brain there came the alarming sound of a horse's hoofs accompanying the vehicle. At last he turned to his companion. 'Parson' quoth he, 'do you hear that fellow pursuing us?' 'I do!' responded the parson, with bated breath. 'Tis a highwayman,' pronounced John Spencer with conviction. 'But I fear no man. Stop the coach, parson, and I will give the fellow a lesson he shall carry with his to his dying day!'*
>
> *Port, taken freely, disposes a man to be valiant, and John Spencer, despite the remonstrances of his servants, clambered out of the door, and stumbled round to the back of the coach. There, sure enough, in the dark he encountered a man, a stout fellow, who set upon him furiously. The two fought and pummelled each other, striking out manfully in spite of the fact that neither could see his antagonist, until finally the postilions, who had come to the rescue, succeeded in dragging off John Spencer, with the assurance that his enemy had fled.*
>
> *Bleeding, but triumphant, the Squire clambered back into his coach, and there met the parson, equally dishevelled, crawling in by the opposite door. 'How now parson?' panted the exhausted Squire. 'Were you, too, in it with that terrible scoundrel?'*
>
> *'I could not leave you to be killed!' panted the parson bravely; and the two heroes, grasping hands, compared notes of their bold exploits till they arrived at Cannon Hall, where they celebrated their victory in yet another bottle of port.*
>
> *It was not till the next day that John Spencer learnt from his postilions that he and the parson, having left the coach by opposite doors, had met in the dark behind it, and fought each other in mistake for the highwayman, who existed only in the imagination of each!*

John Spencer's first will was written in 1759 and named Rev. Phipps (described as of Pulehill, Silkstone) as one of his executors. This could imply that Samuel had returned to live at his place of birth and that Pule Hill Hall had remained a property of the Phipps family since the death of John Phipps back in 1718. John Spencer made his second will in 1773, again naming Rev. Phipps as executor, though now described him as of Banks-in,

Cawthorne. We know that Phipps had lived here since at least February 1768 as a mortgage has survived which states that he held a:

Capital messuage called Banks, and all buildings and lands, in Cawthorne, in the tenure of Rev. Samuel Phipps, clerk.

Described in the book *Cawthorne 1790–1990*:

Banks was a fine old house, with a spacious hall and magnificent staircase of inlaid oak, whence he (Phipps) gladly rode two miles to Cannon Hall for his frequent glass and rubber with the Squire of an evening.

The house was formerly called Micklethwaite or the Bank and had been the home of the Greene family since at least the mid-seventeenth century. It was eventually acquired by the Cannon Hall estate in 1826.

John Spencer's lands were so scattered that four years after his death, the five executors decided to make life easier by selling and exchanging the lands they held in trust. A document dating to 1796 again names Samuel Phipps as a surviving executor and states that,

All debts and legacies have now been paid by Walter Spencer Stanhope, amounting to £2250 and he has applied to Samuel Phipps (and the other executors) to be admitted in consideration, absolute purchaser of the premises, and they have agreed.

The premises refer to the estates of John Spencer.

A year prior to this and Walter Spencer Stanhope recorded in his diary,

14 November 1795 – Did business with Hardy. Heard my mother (Ann Stanhope) was ill. Went and found her very ill in bed and her face and throat much swelled. Called on Phipps.

Banks Hall, circa 1900, between Cawthorne and Silkstone and main residence of Rev Samuel Phipps. (Courtesy of Old Barnsley)

A visit to Denby chapel, during the curacy of Samuel Phipps, by Archbishop Drummond of York, undertaken in 1764, recorded the following:

> *Denby: There are 120 families and 11 Quakers taught by Henry Dickinson at the Quaker Meeting place. There is a school with a salary of £4 paid to Theophilus Swann the master. There is no vicarage house but Divine Service is performed twice each Sunday at 11am and 3pm. There are 250 communicants who walk to Penistone, for the communion is not celebrated here.*

Details of some of Samuel's other activities have survived. The following bargain and sale raised money for the poor of Silkstone and includes the names of many of the great and good of the time:

> *20 Jun 1789*
> *Henry Cutler of Collyton Rayleigh, Devon, esq., son and heir of Henry Cutler, of the first part; Rt. Hon. William Wentworth, Earl of Strafford, of Wentworth Castle, Yorks., Sir Thomas Blackett of Bretton Hall, Yorks., bart., William Bosville of Gunthwaite Hall, Yorks., esq., John Beckett of Leeds, Yorks., esq., Samuel Phipps of Silkstone, Yorks., clerk, vicar of Silkstone, John Cockshutt of Huthwaite, Yorks., esq., and John Beckett of Barnsley, Yorks., esq., all of the second part; Rev. John Mence of Barnsley, clerk, William Lawton of Barnsley, shoemaker, and Joseph Walker of Barnsley, grocer, minister and churchwardens of Barnsley, and Samuel Phipps and Edward Armytage of Silkston, minister and churchwardens of Silkstone all of the third part.*
>
> *Closes called Upper Amyas and Nearer Amyas Close, containing, by estimation 2½ acres, and being in Barnsley, and lately occupied by John Alderson at £18 p.a. rent; other close containing 1 acre 1 rood 36 poles, in Barnsley, now occupied by John Nicholson, at a rent of £1 1/– p.a.*
>
> *In trust for charitable puposes, i.e. for the use of Silkstone poor.*
>
> *The parties further agree that they will levy a fine during Michaelmas term next.*
>
> *Reciting the will of Thomas Cutler 7 Jan 1622; the will of Ellen Cutler on 27 Nov 1633; Decree of Chancery of 7 Jul 1788.*

Samuel was also in demand as a trustee on a number of last wills made during the late eighteenth century:

Will of Elizabeth Brooke of the Pond, Dodworth, Silkston Yorkshire, widow, 3 May 1766:

> *To Hannah widow of Daniel Clarke of Knaresborough Yorks., shoemaker, £100.*
>
> *Nephews Rev. Thomas Beevor of Long Elmsall Yorks., and Francis Beevor of Leeds, dyer, to have term of 500 years in ½, Dodsworth premises to provide £100 for relation Christiana (nee Oldham) wife of Philip Cotes of Knaresborough Yorks., yeoman, if she survives her husband; and term of 600 yrs. likewise for £100 for relation Elizabeth (nee Oldham) wife of Jeffry Linton of York, plumber and glazier, if survives him. ½ Dodsworth premises to relation Rebecca (late Tirwhit), widow of Robert Appleyard of Otley Yorks., ironmonger, for life, and ½ to relation Christiana Asquith of Doncaster Yorks., widow of John Asquith of Ripon Yorks., grocer, for life. Then all to Ann Christiana, d. of Edward Benson of Halton nr. Skipton in Craven Yorks., by late wife Ann daughter of Rebecca Appleyard for life and male heirs, in default to John Charles Brooke, younger son of William Brooke of Field Head, Dodworth, doctor in physic. Trustees for this to be Samuel Phipps of Cawthorne Yorks., clerk, and Richard Perkins of Dodworth Green, tanner.*

Will of Margaret Walker of Middlewood Hall, par. Darfield, Yorkshire, spinster 31 Mar 1786:

(1) to Walter Spencer Stanhope, esq., Francis Edmunds, esq., Alan Johnson esq., the Rev. Samuel Phipps, one undivided moiety of manor and lands at West Burton, Notts., in trust to sell them and discharge debts and pay legacies with the money. If these estates do not raise enough, then those in Dalton and Aughton alias Aighton, par. Rotherham, and Aston, Yorks., are also to be sold.

(2) if the Dalton and Aughton estates do not have to be sold, then they are to go to her mother-in-law Mary Walker, of Middlewood Hall, widow, for life, then to William Smith of Cowley, par. Ecclesfield.

(3) to mother-in-law, Mary Walker, a capital messuage or mansion house called Middlewood Hall, with all lands and other appurtenances, in the parish of Darfield; all lands in North Milford, Yorks; all goods and chattels, plate jewels, and personal estate.

(4) various small legacies.

Samuel Phipps died on 19 April 1799 aged 85 and was buried at Silkstone three days later. His memorial still survives inside the church as does that of his father.

We have already examined the Phipps lineage and its prominence and success, but Samuel's last will suggests even more interesting connections.

This is the last will and testament of me Samuel Phipps of Silkstone in the county of York, Clerk made this twenty second day of January in the year of our Lord one thousand seven hundred and ninety four in manor and form following that is to say first that I will and direct that my just debts, the expenses of my funeral and the charges of and attending the probate of this my will and the registering thereof at Wakefield shall be duly paid and discharged by my executors and trustees herein after appointed in manor herinafter mentioned in this my will.

He named Walter Spencer Stanhope of Cannon Hall and Joseph Beckett of Barnsley as his executors. Joseph Beckett (1751–1840) was a Barnsley businessman who became so successful that he became regarded as the 'father of the Barnsley linen trade'. He also helped develop a banking service which eventually became known as Beckett, Birks & Co, the family were also associated with the town hospital.

Samuel Phipps divided his estate into eight parts which he left to the following:

one eighth part thereof to the wife of . . . Stone of Lombard Street in the city of London, Banker. One other eighth part thereof to Lady Baring, wife of Sir Francis Baring, Baronet, of (word) Lane in the said City of London (word word) which said . . . Stone and Lady Baring are the two daughters of William Herring of Croydon in the County of Surrey, Esquire by Montague Dorothy his late wife, deceased and other eighth part thereof to Mr Francis Dawson who at present resides in the neighbourhood of Newmarket in the County of Suffolk or Cambridge. One other eighth part thereof to Thomas Dawson of Liverpool in the County of Lancaster, merchant. One other eighth part thereof to Sarah, the wife of . . . Ryan of Liverpool aforesaid, merchant. One other eighth part thereof to Lydia the wife of . . . (Moore?) (word) who resides in Liverpool aforesaid or in that neighbourhood which said Francis Dawson, Thomas Dawson, Sarah the wife of the said Ryan and Lydia the wife of the said (Moore?) and the sons and daughters of the late Francis Dawson of Liverpool aforesaid, merchant aforesaid and formerly of the town of Kingston Upon Hull. One other eighth part thereof to Sarah the wife of

> *John Foster of Brampton in the parish of Whiston in the said County of York and in case any of the said legates shall (word) to die before his her or their respective legacies shall become payable then I will and direct that the legacies of him her or theirs in so dying as aforesaid shall go and be paid to his her or their legal personal representative or representatives and as to the remaining eighth part herein I will and direct the same to be paid to the children of Joseph Walker late of Dodworth Bottom in the Parish of Silkstone in the said County, farmer, deceased, by Sarah, his late wife, also deceased which said Sarah, the wife of the aforesaid late Joseph Walker was one of the daughters of John Fleming, late of Dodworth, aforesaid, tanner, deceased, equally to be divided amongst them, share and share alike and in case of the death of any such child or children of the said Joseph and Sarah Walker before his or her or their respective legacies shall become due and payable without leaving lawful issue then this part or share of (word) or (word) so dying as aforesaid shall go and be paid to the surviving children of the said Joseph and Sarah Walker then living equally.*

He also left £50 each to his executors and dated the will 22 January 1794.

It was witnessed by John Boatson, John Rhodes and Thomas West.

On 21 November 1798 Samuel added a codicil to his will and made further bequests:

> *First it is my will and request that £300 may at, (all souls end?) after my death be paid to my servant William Kidson (Kitson??) which besides what may be due to him for the remainder of his wages I give and bequeath to him as a reward for his good long and faithful services. Item, I give and bequeath to my housekeeper, Mary Lowick £100 also to Elizabeth Haigh, my chamber maid £40.*

He also left a further £50 each for his two executors, making £100 a piece in total.

The codicil is followed by the following statement:

> *John Hardy of the parish of Bradford in the county of York, Gentleman and John Lawton, brother to Walter Spencer Stanhope esquire of Canon Hall in the county of York and made oath that they know and were well acquainted with the Reverend Samuel Phipps late of Silkstone in the county of York, Clerk, deceased, for several years before and to the time of his death and having now carefully the paper writing hereto annotated, purporting to be and contain a codicil to the last will and testament of the said deceased beginning thus. I Samuel Phipps, Vicar of Silkstone being sound in mind and body think it proper and requisite to write this codicil as an additional disposition to that made in my will reading thus –*
>
> *We verily and in (word) believe that the whole of the said codicil and new subscription there to be of the proper handwriting of the said deceased.*
>
> *Signed: Jno. Hardy, John Lawton. 21 May 1799.*

A declaration attached to the end of the will by Walter Spencer Stanhope and Joseph Beckett states that:

> *To the best of their knowledge and belief the deceased personal effects at the time of his death would not amount to the sum of £7000.*

Note that there are no bequests to any people bearing the name of Phipps.

Of the names mentioned in the main will, those of Baring and Dawson stand out from the rest.

Exactly why Samuel left money to these people is unknown, he did have two sisters and a brother but no trace of them has yet been found.

Lady Baring, the wife of Francis Baring, Baronet, was originally Harriet Herring and the wife of (?) Stone of Lombard Street was her sister, Mary Herring who in fact had married Richard Stone. The two sisters were the daughters of William Herring (1715–1801) and Montague Dorothy Dawson (1724–1789). William Herring was the first cousin of the Archbishop of York, Thomas Edward Herring (1693–1757). Thomas Herring was Archbishop at York from 1743 to 1747 and then Archbishop of Canterbury from 1747 to 1757. From this we can see that the Baring, Dawson and Stone families were all connected but their relationship with Samuel Phipps is unknown.

Francis Baring, the 1st Baronet (1740–1810) was an English merchant banker. Despite being partially deaf from an early age in 1762 he established the London merchant house of Barings, in co-operation with his brothers John and Charles. He married Harriet Herring, (who was born at Lambeth Palace in 1750), in 1767 and she contributed £20,000 to the business over the years, received from her merchant father, William Herring. Harriet also gave birth to twelve children and later emerged as a glittering social hostess. Her sister, Mary married one of London's leading private bankers, Richard Stone of Martin & Company, with whom Francis Baring's firm had opened an account. Francis Baring became director of the East India Company in 1779 and throughout various wars and disasters the family firm grew and became very wealthy. At his death in 1810 aged 70, Francis Baring's personal wealth was valued at £606,000. The company was by now being run by three of his sons. Soon after 1890, Baring Brothers & Co. established ties with King George V as his personal bank as it would with every monarch after him. As an aside, Diana, late Princess of Wales was the great grand-daughter of one member of the Baring's family. The company existed for over two hundred years and was the oldest merchant bank in London until 1995 when it collapsed after one of its employees, Nick Leeson lost £827 million speculating, primarily on futures contracts in Singapore.

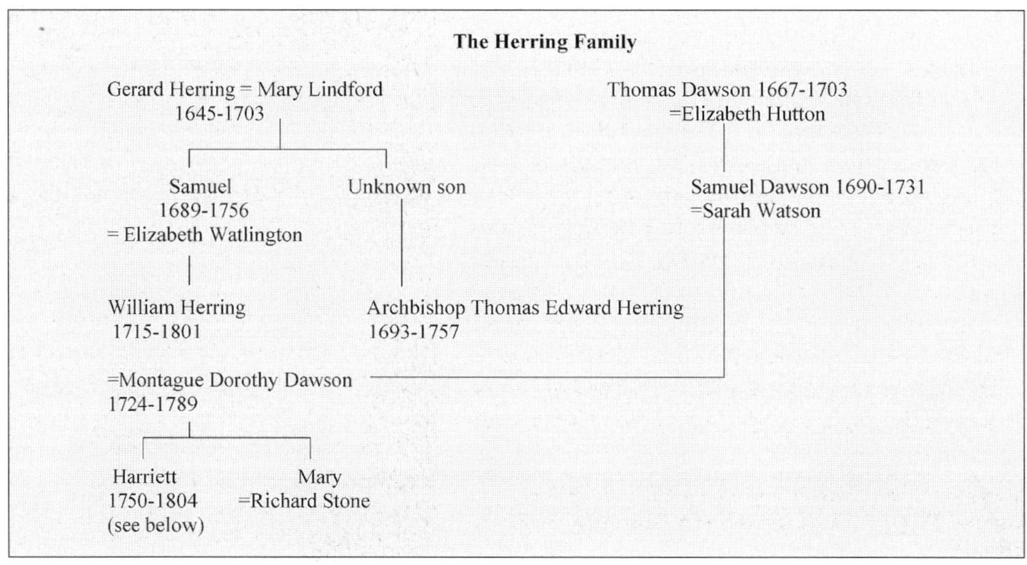

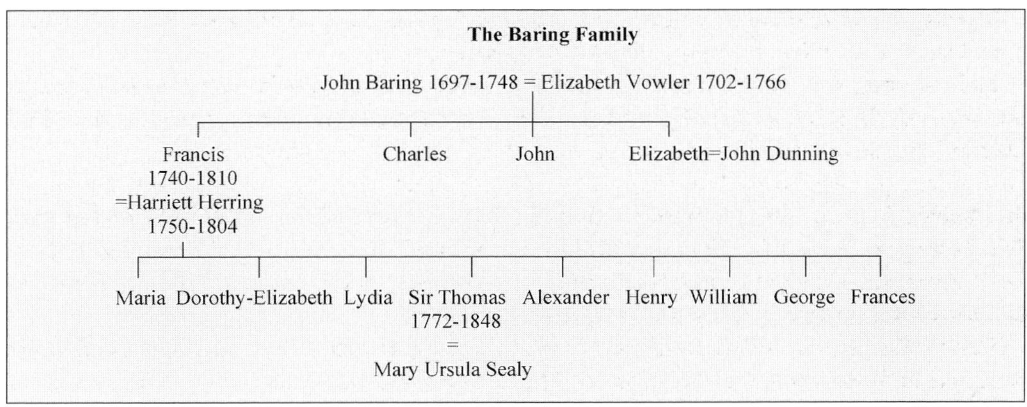

There was far more to Rev. Samuel Phipps than just 'an old parochial parson'. Bereft of his father at an age too young to remember him, he was brought up in his Uncle's home against a background where he would have met and heard all about other branches of his families success. He consorted with the great and the good of his day and at his death he left bequests to some of the biggest movers and shakers in the country in the late eighteenth century. Not all the details of his family connections are clear but this study will hopefully induce further research by others into this fascinating man.

Whilst writing his history of Cawthorne in 1882, Rev. Charles Tiplady Pratt came across the following which seems to be an appropriate epitaph:

Among sundry Parish Papers at the Vicarage, there is one dated December, 1838, in which William Stayton, George Ashton, George Greenwood, Thomas Stayton, and John Cooke sign their names to an agreement with the Minister and Congregation that they 'will faithfully observe the following Rules.' After Rules about their constant and regular attendance, and their never all absenting themselves at once without permission, it is stated that 'the singers are to endeavour as much as possible to select the easiest and most simple tunes, in order that the Congregation may join in the singing.' These singers here mentioned would be official successors of the well-known 'Cawthorne Musicians' at the end of the last century, of whom a man called Jacob Scarf sang, 'and how they go on.' Billey Clegg played the fiddle, George Schofield the Bass, Jonty Hinchliffe the hautboy while John Allott, Ned Greenwood, Dave Roberts Joe Jubb, Dickey Taylor, Wil Hutchinson,

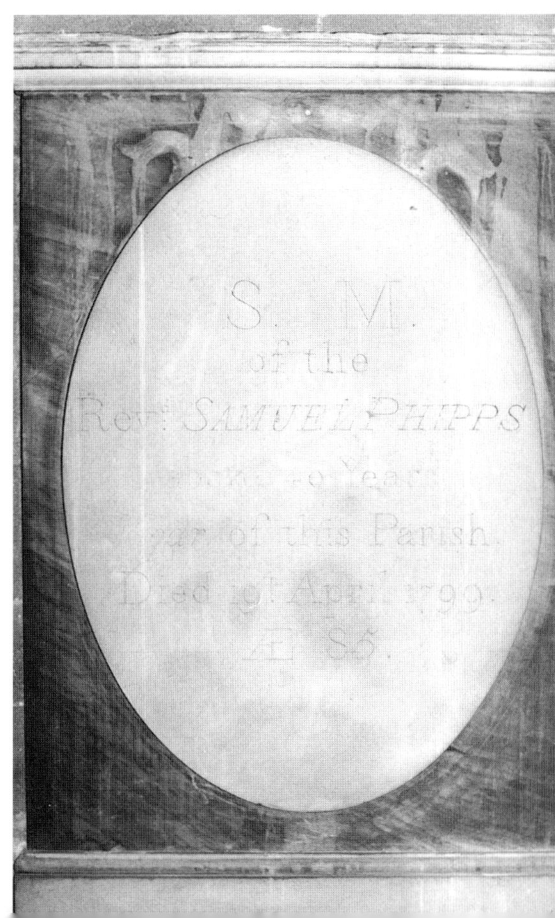

Memorial tablet inside Silkstone Church of Rev. Samuel Phipps who died in 1799. (Courtesy of Brian Elliott)

Jim Wigglesworth, John Harrison, Joe Bates, Joe Ibbetson, George Chapple, Billy English, Tommy Rhodes, Tommy Holling, Judah Hinchliffe, seem to have formed the Choir, till, as the old song says, 'Mr. Phipps would let them sing no more.'

Francis Haigh circa 1760s

Franciscus (Francis) Haigh was born in 1696/7, and was baptised at Thurlstone on 16 January 1696 the son of Johannis (John) Haigh. He gained his BA at Christ's College, Cambridge on 5 March 1720/1 when he was ordained a deacon. He became a priest on 23 September 1722. He disappears for a short while until we find him working as a preacher at Cumberworth chapel in 1723 until at least 1728, he did not remain here for long as in 1729 he was appointed as curate at Bolsterstone chapel. He also acquired the curacy of Midhope at this time where he also worked as a tutor.

Francis was mentioned in the diary of John Hobson in the year 1729/30:

> *1729/30 6 March*
>
> *Godfather to Abraham, the son of Abr*[raham] *Haigh, of Hill top: the other parties were his brother, Mr.* (Francis) *Haigh, minister of Bolsterstone, represented by Mr. Hough, and Mrs. Arabella Smith, represented by Mrs. Hannah Clarkson.*

Francis Haigh became master of Penistone Grammar School in 1751 although he appears to have remained perpetual curate at Bolsterstone.

As we have noted before, this appointment was associated with the curacy of Denby chapel and it is known that Francis did take sermons here, though Jonathan Perkins was still in the roll until his death in 1753. It is likely that he became assistant curate to Samuel Phipps at Denby after Phipps had taken on the responsibilities of Silkstone (in 1757) and Penistone by 1761.

Although these curacies supplemented his income, they also caused him to neglect his school duties. In addition to this he became blind during the last 10 years of his life, until he died in 1777.

Joseph Purslove 1778–1779

Joseph Purslove became the new perpetual curate at Denby in 1778 after Samuel Phipps resigned. He was ordained a Deacon on 25 September 1748 after attaining his BA at University College, Oxford. He was ordained a Priest on 24 September 1749. He became a curate at Silkstone church under its Vicar, John Clarkson (died 1756) in 1748 at a stipend of £30 per annum.

His stay at Denby was short, and until very recently totally forgotten, he died in 1779. He was probably sent here by the former curate of Denby and now Purslove's superior at Silkstone, Samuel Phipps. Phipps took over from John Clarkson at Silkstone in 1757. He resigned his position at Denby in 1778 and had probably lined Purslove up to take over for some time, in order to reduce his workload.

Purslove made his will on 20 April 1778 in which he described himself as of Silkstone. He bequeathed an annuity to his sister, Mary Purslove of £5 to be raised out of his lands and messuages in Bentley, Yorkshire. He also left £5 to a friend, Elizabeth Glover, widow of Thomas Glover of Fallhead, tanner. The bulk of his estate he left to his only child and heir, his daughter, Mary Mirfin Wasteneys, who was the wife of William Wasteneys of Edlington, Yorkshire, Gent.

Joseph Horsfall 1779–at least 1819

Joseph Horsfall was baptised on 14 March 1746/7, the son of Jonas Horsfall of Haworth, he became a deacon on 22 October 1769 when he took up the assistant curacy of Penistone under the watchful eyes of Samuel Phipps. He became a priest on 20 October 1771, aged 25. He had followed his elder brother, John Horsfall (born 1732), into the church, John had become the curate of Bingley in 1758.

The Horsfall family were prominent in and around the Haworth area. Westcroft Head at Oxenhope was one of the families homes. Jonas was a favoured family name and there are a number of them throughout the seventeenth and eighteenth centuries. There is a record of a Jonas Horsfall born in Haworth in 1698 and that he married Mary Smith in 1723, he is currently the only candidate for Joseph Horsfall's father.

It was also a member of this family that came to national prominence when he was murdered in 1812, when Joseph would have been 66 years old.

William Horsfall was the owner of Ottiwell's Mill at Marsden, at a time when mechanisation was driving the hand loom weavers into conditions of extreme poverty. In response to the new technology the Luddites came into existence. The name came from the threatening letters they sent to owners of the new machines which were signed 'Ned Lud' or 'General Lud'. A series of attacks on the premises of small clothiers took place during the first three months of 1812 in which the Luddites endeavoured to break these new machines. A major attack on Rawfolds Mill in the Spen Valley was defended by the militia as a result of which two Luddites lost their lives. William Horsfall developed a hatred of the machine breakers and he actively encouraged more mill owners to install the new technology. Popular legend states that he said that he *'would ride up to his saddle girths in Luddite blood'*, a sentiment well known in the locale. After attending the market in Huddersfield on Tuesday 28 April, Horsfall was attacked as he rode home, he was wounded four times, three of which were slight but the fourth was a musket ball which was to prove fatal. His brother, Rev. Abraham Horsfall, was sent for who helped carry him back to Warren House where he finally died on the Thursday.

Horsfall was not an unknown name in the Denby district. A different Joseph Horsfall, this one the son of a John Horsfall, who had died by 1782 can be found in the Carlcoates area in this year sorting out his fathers estate with his family.

An agreement was made between Joseph and his sisters, Elizabeth (wife of William Hall of Midhope), Lydia (wife of John Green of Denby) and Mary Goddard (widow), to levy a fine for the better dividing of their fathers estate between them. At some point during the latter eighteenth century Joseph's brother in law, John Green sold him the farm at Thurlstone known as Abbot Birks. Back in the seventeenth century this had been the property of Daniel Rich, son of Aymer Rich of Bullhouse (who married Alice Burdet in 1587). It descended to his son, Daniel after his death in 1679. By 1741 the property had passed to John Green of Smallshaw and then to his son, John Green who as we have noted above, married Lydia Horsfall. Joseph Horsfall sold the property in 1801 to Robert Middleton of Totties. Whether this branch of the Horsfalls were connected with the Haworth clan is uncertain.

Joseph Horsfall not only became curate at Penistone in 1769 he also became Master of the Grammar School. After the death of Joseph Purslove in 1779, an agreement must have been made between Samuel Phipps and Joseph Horsfall which saw him take up ministerial duties at Denby. Phipps had resigned in 1778 and could have taken up the responsibility again, but by now he was 64 years old and had resigned at Denby in order to concentrate on his three other churches. Jonathan Perkins had quite happily combined the roll of schoolmaster and curate between 1729 and 1753 and a precedent had been set.

The book, *A Further History of Penistone* states that:

After his death (Francis Haigh master of Penistone Grammar School), the surviving feoffees allowed the usher, Joseph Horsfall, to intrude himself into the master-ship.

If his entry into the master-ship of the school was made under dubious circumstances his leaving of it was just as peculiar!

During 1784/5 the methods and means used by Horsfall as schoolmaster came under scrutiny:

it being claimed that the master was an improper person, illegally appointed who neglected his duties.

Horsfall was supported in his case, by a petition signed by 233 inhabitants of Penistone, which approved *of the present conduct and ability of the headmaster and his assistant (Rev. Bourn),* dated 28 December 1784. Eventually, in 1785 he was made to resign from the post by Walter Spencer Stanhope of Cannon Hall, one of the Trustees of the school. Horsfall's position at Denby was unaffected and he continued to be Minister here until at least 1819.

As we have noted above, Horsfall, was assisted at the grammar school by Rev. Bourn, who was also assistant curate at Denby. He was the first employed by Horsfall for this post. Assistant curates were not shadowy figures in the background, but would have been regarded by the people of Denby as their minister, as with previous occupants in the roll. During Horsfall's tenure this may have been even more so the case.

Jeremiah Bourn – Assistant Curate 1780–1789

Jeremiah Born was baptised 26 September 1757, the son of William Bourn of Heponstall. He was made a Deacon on 8 October 1780 and now became the assistant curate of Denby. He was made a Priest on 12 October 1783. Bourn was paid £30 per annum for his services as assistant curate and schoolmaster. By 1789 he had moved on to become the curate of Emley.

John Butterfield Schorey – Assistant Curate 1794–1795

John Schorey was born 21 February 1770, and baptised on the 15 April 1770, the son of Thomas Schorey of Sandal Magna. He was educated at Queens College, Oxford where gained his BA. He became a Deacon on 5 October 1794 when he became assistant curate of Denby. He became a Priest on 4 October 1795 when he left to become curate of Scrayingham, six miles to the East of York. He earned the same £30 per annum at Denby as his predecessor.

John Mattinson – Assistant Curate 1801–(?)

John Mattinson was baptised 3 May 1774, the son of Thomas (a husbandman) and Margaret Mattinson of Newbiggin near Dacre, just to the North of Ullswater in the Lake District. He was licensed as a Deacon on 5 July 1801 and was given the position of assistant curate of Denby on the same day. At this time he was working as a schoolmaster in Barton, Cumbria, a post he had held since taking over from Thomas Myers in June 1798. He resigned this post on 24 August 1801 in order to come to Denby, for a now reduced income of £20 per annum. He was ordained a Priest on 18 July 1802.

Brice Bronwin – Assistant Curate 1816–1830 (then Curate)
To be considered below.

Samuel John Hillyard – Assistant Curate 1819-(?)
Samuel Hillyard was baptised 14 March 1784, the son of Nicholas and Mary Hillyard of St. Mary's, Rotherhithe, Surrey. He was created a Deacon by the Bishop of Exeter following letters diminutive 23 March 1819. He became assistant curate of Denby on 26 March 1819 and ordained a Priest 3 August 1823.

An anomaly occurs in 1805 when Richard Bainbridge is listed as a candidate for the curacy of Denby. He held papers as a Deacon dated after 13 June 1805 and had letters testimonial from the Diocese of Chester but appears to have been unsuccessful in his bid to become curate of Denby chapel. The record does not state why.

Whether there were other assistant curates to cover the gaps in the time periods above is not known though the York Clergy Ordinations make no reference to anyone.

Joseph Horsfall's tenure as curate at Denby lasted for some considerable time. He can still be found here in 1819, overseeing changes to the two hundred year old chapel.

Denby Chapel Alterations 1819
Until recently, documents lay dormant and unknown at the University of York regarding improvements to the chapel. Although (and unfortunately) there is no plan of the building and the proposed extensions we can begin to gain some idea of the make up and fabric of the building from them.

Granville Venables Vernon, Master of Arts, Vicar General and Official Principal of the most Reverend Father in God, Edward – by Divine Providence, Lord Archbishop of York, Primate of England and Metropolitan, lawfully authorised.

To all and singular Clerks and literate persons whomsoever and wheresoever in the Diocese of York. Greeting: We do hereby order and charge you jointly and severally, that you, or one of you do peremptorily cite all and singular the inhabitants of and within the Chapelry of Denby in the Parish of Penistone in the Diocese of York and all others in general who have or intend to have any right of titles or interest in, or unto the Chapel and Chapel Yard of Denby aforesaid personally if they can be so cited but if not personally then by publishing this, our citation in the Chapel of Denby aforesaid during the time of the Divine Service and by all other lawful ways and means so that the same may most probably come to the knowledge of the persons to be cited.

To appear before us our lawful representative in the Consistory Place within the Cathedral and Metropolitan Church of Saint Peter of York, on Thursday, being the first day of the month of April next ensuing between the hours of Eight and Twelve in the Forenoon of the same day.

To show reasonable and lawful cause if they have or know any why a License or Faculty to take down and remove or cause to be taken down and removed about seven yards in length of the North Wall of the Chapel of Denby aforesaid, opposite to the pulpit and reading desk and to erect and build or cause to be erected and built an addition to the said chapel to extend from the opening to be made in the said wall into the chapel yard of Denby aforesaid Northwards, ten yards or thereabouts and in breadth seven yards or thereabouts, such addition to be in height from the floor to the underdrawing or ceiling, ten feet at the least, the walls to be built of Delph stone similar to the walls of the chapel, the roof to be covered in slate stones and the ground or floor to be covered with flag stones in the same manor as the roof and floor of the chapel are now covered, an arch to be turned over the opening into the said Chapel and a road or passage to be made (missing word) the said intended erection to be made under the said arch into the said chapel. Also to place two windows with proper casements thereunto in each of the side walls of the said intended new erection to be in height six feet or thereabouts and in width, four feet or thereabouts and to place a door near the North end of the East side wall to open into the same from the chapel yard also to underdraw the said new erection and to erect and build or cause to be erected and built therein benches to be appropriated for the use of the children attending the Sunday School in the said chapelry and of any other persons resorting to the said chapel who are destitute of sittings there.

The whole expenses of such intended new erection and of the Faculty to be obtained for authorising the same to be defrayed by the voluntary donations of well disposed persons should be granted to the Reverend Joseph Horsfall, Clerk the Incumbent Curate and George Woolhouse the chapel warden of the said chapelry and to Benjamin Haigh, James Hargreave, John ???, Emmanuel Nicholls, Daniel Dyson and Christopher Haywood, principal inhabitants of the said chapelry and further, at their promotion to do and receive what the law shall require in this behalf.

And what you or any of you shall do in the premises, you shall duly certify us, our loyal representative at the time and place aforesaid, together with these presents. Given at York, under the Seal of our Office, this tenth day of the month of March in the Year of our Lord, One Thousand Eight Hundred Nineteen.

Extracted by Mills and Son, Proctors.

*Approved: Robert Mar***haw?*

Joseph Buckle Jones, Deputy Register

Permission to begin work was granted to the chapel trustees on 6 April 1819. The document is dated 192 years after foundation of chapel and 189 years before 2008, ie: almost exactly halfway through the history of the site. The new building work began only 26 years before a completely new church was erected, which obliterated all trace of these improvements.

Joseph Wood of Nantwich succeeded Joseph Horsfall as master at Penistone in 1786 until his death in 1836, but if he was active at Denby the records have not survived to prove it. By at least 1822, according to the trade directory, a man named John Brownhill is stated to have become the curate of the Chapel at Denby although this is a debatable subject.

A further visitation by church authorities in 1829 records a very sparsely furnished chapel:

In 1829 the furnishings of the chapel were returned as being a pulpit, a reading desk with a cushion of green shag, two prayer books, two surplices, a pewter basin for Baptisms, the Royal Arms, the Creed and Lord's Prayer on boards and a bell given by Lady Beaumont. The minister received one shilling for a funeral during the week but only sixpence for one on Sunday". The parish clerk received a salary of 20/– a year, 6/– for ringing the bell and 8d for digging a grave.

Brice Bronwin 1830–1851

We know that Joseph Horsfall was still the curate at Denby in 1819 and that Brice Bronwin had been here with him since 1816. Samuel Hillyard had also arrived in 1819. It is possible that Hillyard was brought in on the occasion of the death of Horsfall, perhaps to assist Bronwin, who was suitably qualified. Not only this but we have just one reference to another minister, John Brownhill, from Baines' directory dated 1822 which states that he was the curate in charge that year, when the evidence suggests that it ought to have been Bronwin. Evidently there is some confusion over who was in charge at Denby at this time although it goes without saying that the Vicars of Penistone, Martin Naylor, and Samuel Sunderland (from 1829), were still de facto overseers. The records state that Bronwin did not take over as perpetual curate until 1830, but with the absence of any other records for John Brownhill (who may have acted purely as an Assistant curate) I believe that Bronwin's reign began significantly earlier.

Brice Bronwin was the son of Brice and Elizabeth Bronwin of St Mary the Virgin, Pulham, Norfolk, privately baptised on 3 September 1786 and received into the church on 17 June 1787. He became a Deacon on 11 August 1816 and on the same day became Assistant Curate under Joseph Horsfall at Denby Chapel. He became a Priest on 3 August 1817, whilst assisting Horsfall.

Bronwin was an eminent mathematician and was associated with Arthur Crayley (1821–1895), one of the most famous academics in the field. Bronwin is described in a biography of Crayley:

> *The Rev. Brice Bronwin had been writing papers on mathematics since 1828 and was seasoned in the art. He had a range of mathematical interests, but elliptical functions was a speciality. Approaching his late 50s, Bronwin's scientific interests spanned the wide terrain from elliptical functions to the theory of tides and astronomy. Within the previous 5 years he had overseen the building of a new church in Denby, Yorkshire. Yet in his pastoral role he was unfulfilled 'not having care of souls' he was a curate – without a church living of his own.*

Bronwin was the incumbent at Denby, at the time of Bishop Longley's visitation in 1837.

Bishop Longley's visit in 1837 recorded the following:

> *Denby: There was no house for the curate who lived near the chapel in a private house. When I visited the chapel in autumn 1837 I found it in so miserable, filthy and ruinous a condition that I strongly recommended an attempt be made to raise money for its rebuilding. Here the population was 2000 with church seating for 200. There were two services each Sunday but there were never any celebrations of Holy Communion. For this the parishioners had to walk to Penistone. The Methodists and Ranters had built a chapel each in the parish.*

Denby's chapel of ease was in a mess. The Agricultural Revolution and later the Industrial Revolution had in some cases weakened the power of the older land-owning class. New self-made men had risen to become the new pillars of society. They were no less respectful of the need for worship but they now had the option of choosing which branch to follow. This coincided with the rise of the Wesleyan Methodists and other independent chapel organisations. These were largely built where the populations were more numerous in order to serve the needs of more people. As Denby Dykeside (later Denby Dale) grew, Denby did not and the patronage of its chapel grew smaller and its income was reduced. The remaining members of the Burdet family now lived and worked amongst the people who had once served them and the Bosville's now resided at Thorpe Hall near Bridlington. The old hall at Gunthwaite was demolished in 1830 and although the family still owned the Gunthwaite manor their influence in the parish was minimal. The Savile Lords had their fingers in too many other pies to help out an ailing chapel of ease. Not withstanding this, the people of Denby were not beaten yet.

Plan drawn by John Ellis in 1842 showing the ground floor and gallery of the rebuilt Denby Church. (Courtesy of Lambeth Palace Library)

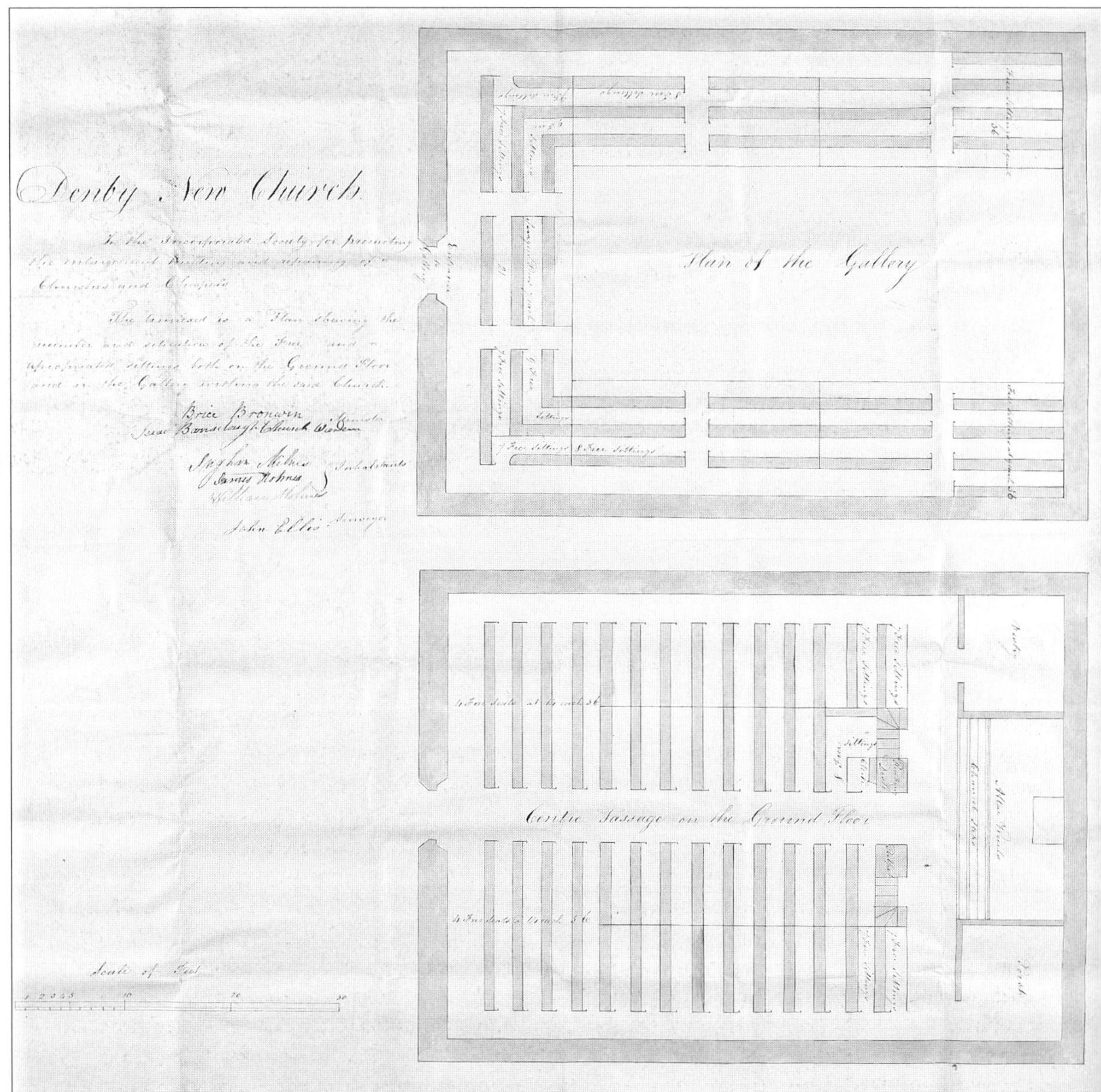

Fundraising began under the guidance of Rev. Bronwin and seven years after Bishop Longley voiced his concerns, in 1844, under Bronwin, a building committee was formed. John Ellis, a builder from High Flatts was paid £1170 to construct a new and bigger Church, which was completed in 1845. It is possible that Bronwin's mathematical background helped in the design of the new church. The plan created by John Ellis still exists, at Lambeth Palace Library. It was signed by Bronwin as Minister, Isaac Barraclough as church warden, Ingham Milnes and William Holmes – inhabitants and John Ellis.

Detail of the entrance doorway to the tower at Denby Church.

This building forms the major portion of the present Church, but consisted of a tower and nave only. The altar was at the east wall of the nave and a gallery surrounded the other three walls; box pews filled the nave, after only a short time the porch was added. In deference to the churches past, the old inscribed tombstone of former curate, Timothy Kent, was retained and placed inside the new building.

Rev. Bronwin had led the villagers to success, though by 1851 he had left the parish and relinquished his position to Job Johnson. He left Denby for pastures currently unknown, a desire probably fed by his lack of fulfilment at the chapel in Denby. His legacy to the village was the basis of the church, which survives to the present day. Brice Bronwin died in 1869.

Job Johnson 1851–1887

Job Johnson was baptised on 27 October 1816 at Greasbrough. He was the eldest son of Job Johnson senior (1787–1847) and Mary Jessop (born 1793). Job senior had travelled from Peterborough to work on the Earl Fitzwilliam estate at Wentworth Woodhouse as a labourer. He was the son of yet another Job Johnson and his wife was also called Mary. Job Johnson senior married Mary Jessop on 29 June 1813 at Wath Upon Dearne church and they went to live at Greasbrough, probably at a tenant cottage owned by the Fitzwilliam estate, where they began their family. The family moved to Nether Haugh, before 1818 where John Thomas (1818) and John Jessop (1822–1842) were born. Another change of address, before 1825, saw the family move to The Old Hall, Tankersley Park. In recent times the park has been used as a location for the 1970 film *Kes* and is now a golf course. A further five children were born here, Sarah Sophia (1825), Francis Charles (1829–1890), Elizabeth Ann (1831), Henry Edwin (1833) and Emma Elizabeth who died in her infancy. Job Johnson senior had by now been appointed 'Park Keeper' and was highly regarded by the Fitzwilliam estate. The Johnson's third son, John Jessop Johnson was involved in an accident at Sheffield and died of his injuries in 1842 aged 20. Job senior died on 21 September 1847 and was buried with his infant daughter and his third son at Wentworth old churchyard. Sarah Johnson, now widowed returned to Nether Haugh to live with her son, John Thomas and his family until she died in 1856.

In the census returns of 1851 for Cumberworth we find Job Johnson, aged 35, acting as Curate at Cumberworth church, he was by this time, married to Mary Ann Fell, thirteen years his junior, who was born in 1830 in Huddersfield. His stay at Cumberworth must have been fairly short as he was installed at Denby later in the same year and can be found earning £98 per annum in 1852.

We can find the family in the 1861 census returns:

Name	Age	Born	Occupation	Place of Birth
Job Johnson	44	1816	Incumbent of Denby	Greasbrough
Mary Ann Johnson	31	1830		Huddersfield
Mercy Elizabeth Johnson	7	1853		Denby
Sarah Catherine Johnson	5	1855		Denby
James William Johnson	3	1857		Denby

We gain more detail about the family from the next census, ten years later.

Residing at the Vicarage, Upper Denby 1871.

Name	Age	Born	Occupation	Place of Birth
Job Johnson	54	1816	Vicar of Denby	Greasbrough
Mary A Johnson	41	1830		Huddersfield
Samuel F Johnson	9	1862		Denby
Hannah M Johnson	7	1864		Denby
John A Johnson	5	1866		Denby
Sarah Fell	67	1804		Huddersfield
Hannah Fell	39	1832		Huddersfield
Robert Fell	34	1837		Huddersfield

Job and Mary had at least seven children, the eldest being Mercy Elizabeth born in 1853 followed by, Sarah Catherine 1855, James William 1857, Mary Louisa 1858, Samuel Fell 1861, Hannah Maria in 1864, John Aldous 1866.

The family are recorded in the 1881 census returns for Denby, living at the Vicarage, which for census purposes was a part of the Gunthwaite survey:

Residing at the Vicarage, Upper Denby 1881.

Name	Relationship	Age	Place of Birth	Occupation
Job Johnson	Head	64	Greasbrough	Vicar of Denby
Mary Ann Johnson	Wife	51	Huddersfield	
Samuel F Johnson	Son	19	Denby	Solicitors General Law Clerk
Hannah M Johnson	Dau.	17	Denby	Scholar
Sarah Fell	Mother in law	77	Huddersfield	Annuitant
Hannah M Fell	Sister in law	49	Huddersfield	Annuitant
Sarah Tingay	Servant	26	Brampton, Huntingdon	General Domestic

It would appear likely that John Aldous Johnson, who would have been 15 years old had died young, he is unlikely to have been with any Fell relations as the surviving members of that family seem to be living at Denby. The four elder children were old enough to have left home by now.

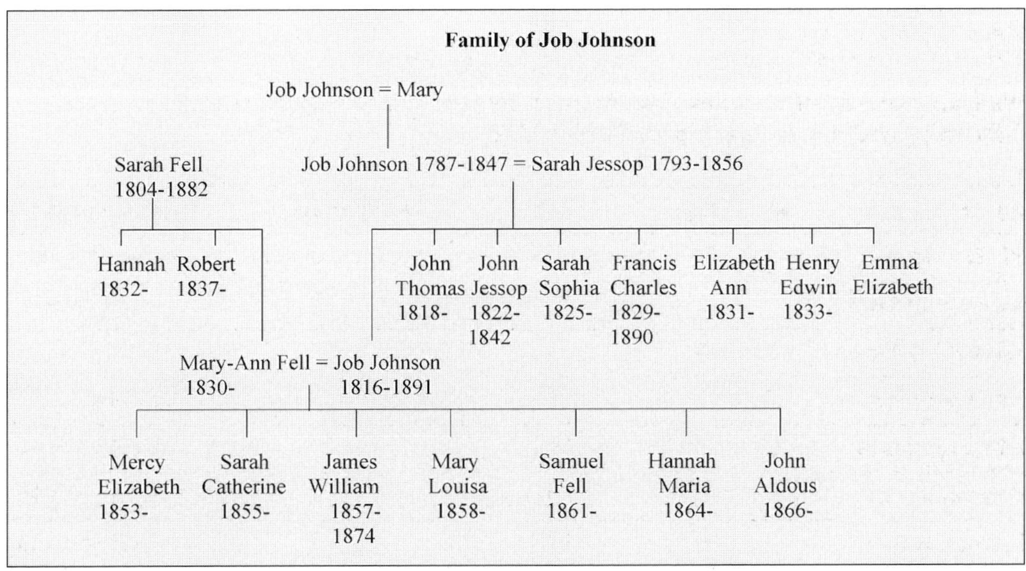

Job was active in local council and political affairs and was a highly regarded member of the local and wider community. In 1873 he was asked to write a letter of reference for a member of the highly influential local mill owners, the Kenyon's:

June 23rd 1873
It gives me very great pleasure to be able to speak very highly of Walter Kenyon and I have known him since a child. He has some very special qualities which will, in my estimation lead to

his being a good and clever man. He is very active, very industrious and takes great pains in all his engagements. He has been a pupil of mine for a long time, and I have every reason to expect great things of him. I shall be glad to know that he succeeds in the post he is now applying for.

Faithfully yours.

J Johnson

Vicar of Denby

Only a year after the latter was written, James William Johnson, Job and Mary's eldest son died. His grave at Denby reads: who fell asleep April 20 1874, aged 17 years. *Looking Unto Jesus.*

Just prior to the 1881 census survey, Rev. Johnson felt duty bound to vent his feelings on current events through the medium of the Yorkshire Post:

The Yorkshire Post – December 30th 1880.

Sir,

I am obliged at length to confess that my indignation has become master of my patience, which has long thriven to bear with the feebleness and imbecilic indifference of our gracious Queen's present advisers (unfortunately for this country) called the Government in the matter of the management, both at home and abroad (but especially in Ireland) of our public affairs.

The gravestone of James William Johnson in Denby churchyard.

Had Lord Beaconsfield been in office, the proper and only right step would long ago have been taken and murder, misrule and defiance of law in open day would not have been allowed to take place – fright and fear would not have been for weeks upon the loyal and peaceable inhabitants of the land.

Messrs. Parnell & Co. would long ago have been called to account for the treason they have been allowed so long to utter and the scandal of such a sight in view of the whole world would not have been heaped upon our beloved Sovereign and her empire to gratify the weakness and ignorance of her so called ministers.

I may be permitted, I hope, to say that I am more than astonished that the inhabitants (especially the common-sense working men) of our large towns have not ere this, risen en-masse and at once expressed their due sense of shame and righteous anger at such child play and said that these things should be so, no longer; and further, that Messrs. Bright and Chamberlain are not either the sound or true exponents of public opinion in this great country in matters so all-important to the welfare of the empire of Queen Victoria.

Dec. 28/80 J Johnson-Vicar of Denby

It was Rev. Johnson who oversaw the next fundamental change in the churches history.

On 12th December 1853 an order in council was signed by Queen Victoria finally making Denby into a separate Parish, which was now to include the townships of Gunthwaite, Ingbirchworth, High Flatts, Birdsedge and Denby Dykeside (now Denby Dale) all of which were previously under Penistone authority. Denby church had begun recording baptisms and burials in its own parish registers in 1851, as we have seen, prior to this all these were copied into the Penistone registers. After the order of December 1853 the first entry in the marriage register at Denby, was recorded by Job Johnson on 22 February 1854. The chapel of ease was now but a memory and the new church was a fully independent arm of the Church of England.

Soon after this, only the second memorial tablet of three (the others being Timothy Kent grave stone and the War Memorial) was erected inside the church. It was in memory of Charles Kilner, a professor of music. He was christened at Denby on 25 October 1795, the son of William Kilner, he died on 10 June 1858. The tablet was erected from the proceeds of an oratorio held in the church on 11 August 1858. The memorial is crowned by a violin and bow crossed under a cloth.

Job Johnson was also active in the foundation of a church day school at Denby. It was built on a site next door to the church on land donated by Thomas Kaye of Bradford in 1864 and cost £750. One of the earliest Masters of the school was Charles Hargreaves who originated from Kearsley in Lancashire. His wife, Achsah was from Kirkburton though their children were born in Slaidburn, before he took up his post at Denby, sometime before 1870.

A further visitation by the church authorities took place in 1870 which recorded the following:

Denby was a parish of 1700 people – it included a large part of Denby Dale. The new church could hold 300 but the average congregation was 40 and there were no communicants. The pews in church were rented out and the services were depressingly dull. Dissent was rising and at a meeting to elect new trustees for the management of the church school all those elected were in favour of secularising education.

Not exactly a great advertisement for Rev. Johnson's services, one can only hope that they improved over the next few years.

Rev. Johnson was also responsible for the construction of a purpose built vicarage for himself and his successors in the village. He made an agreement between the trustees of the Bosville estate and himself for the sale and purchase of 4,840 square yards of land in Denby, opposite the church, for £60 on the 12th November 1872. The vicarage was built on this land during 1873 at a cost of £1,800.

Prior to this the Denby curates had lived in one of the cottages nearest to the chapel, which formed part of the site of Highfield Farm almost adjacent to the church grounds.

Job Johnson became involved in many aspects of community life and became a highly respected member of the community both in Denby and the surrounding area. The following report is from the *Barnsley Chronicle*:

> *11 April 1885 – St. John's, Denby – Vestry Meeting*
> *The Vicar, the Rev. J Johnson, took the chair at the annual vestry meeting, held on Tuesday. The churchwardens presented the offertory accounts. Votes of thanks were passed to the wardens and sides-men for their services during the past year. The Vicar re-nominated Mr Henry Lockwood as his warden and Mr Frank Newsome was unanimously elected people's warden. Messrs. J A Johnson and J Wood were appointed sides-men for the current year.*

By 1887, aged 71, Rev. Johnson took the decision to retire and to move to Huddersfield. That he was highly regarded by the great and good of his district is illustrated by the list of people who chipped in to his retirement presentation. The total amount raised was £140 12s 6d. He remained in touch with some members of his old flock, indeed he made a gift of a Bible on the occasion of the marriage of Harry Heath and Elizabeth Barraclough in 1888, inscribed:

> *To Mr and Mrs Harry Heath on their wedding day, with the best wishes for their happiness from the Rev. Job Johnson and his family.*

He left Denby after 36 years, a burial entry is recorded in the Huddersfield area for December 1891 for Job Johnson, aged 75.

Alexander Barrington Orr 1887–1894

The early life of Alexander Barrington Orr is at present largely unknown. He was born in 1847 in Ireland, to Alexander and Mary Orr (who was born in 1818, also in Ireland). That the Orr family

Rev. Job Johnson with his wife Mary Ann, circa 1880.

were of good stock is undoubted, his career indicates this. His later marriage into the Pollexfen family is also highly suggestive of his background. The Orr family are known to have made their fortune manufacturing soda water and seem to have been well established in and around the Sligo and Donegal areas of the country.

At has also been noted, in some sources, that one member of the Orr family, name currently unknown, left the Emerald Isle for America and who ended up fighting in San Antonio, Texas, at the battle of the Alamo on 6 March 1836. The fort was defended by 187 men, against the Mexican army of General Santa Anna which numbered 5000 troops. Reports at the time suggested that around 1000 Mexicans were killed before the fort was overrun and Colonel's William B Travis and Jim Bowie were dead, Bowie bayoneted to death. The body of Colonel Davy Crockett, who had arrived in Texas only two weeks earlier was found badly mutilated, it would appear that he survived the actual battle but was then brutally executed on the orders of the Mexican General. There were no male survivors. On 21 April, Texan troops led by General Sam Houston crushed Santa Anna's army at San Jacinto and took Santa Anna prisoner. If there was a member of the Orr family here, then he died along with all the others. It must be said at this point, that there are numerous lists of the defenders of the Alamo and most differ wildly. There seems to be little certainty as to exactly who did fight here and without further corroboration the story must remain little more than an historical possibility.

What of Alexander?

The first details that we have of him come from his college entrance records. He entered Trinity College, Dublin University in 1865 at the age of 19. The son of Alexander Orr who was a barrister. Alexander junior was listed as being a pensioner (i.e., he paid a fixed annual fee for his education) and as a member of the Church of England. His place of birth was given as Dublin and his schooling was listed as private. His tutor in college was Mr Stubbs.

He gained his BA at Trinity College in 1870 when he was 23 years old. Later in the same year he was ordained a Deacon at Ripon. A Deacon was a clerk in Holy Orders who assisted a Priest. By the time of the census taken in 1871 Alexander was noted to be the head of his household the address of which was, Orchard Lodge, Great Malvern. He was living with his mother, Mary, by now aged 53, and his younger sister, Catherine S Orr, who was 16 years old at the time and therefore born in 1855.

Alexander took on his first curacy at Elland in West Yorkshire between 1870 and 1871 though he was not here for long as by the end of 1871 he had become the curate at Irton in Cumberland. By 1874 he had returned to Worcestershire and was the curate at Newland. These three curacies in quick succession would have been highly instructive in preparing Alexander for the rest of his career. Whilst at Newland he took the next step in his clerical career and was ordained as a priest.

During the early part of 1875 Alexander returned to the land of his birth to take up the post of Vicar Choral (a cleric appointed to sing in a Cathedral choir) at Limerick Cathedral. It is unlikely that this was his first return to Ireland since leaving in 1870 but it is the first visit that we know about. The wandering spirit in him saw another move later in the year to take up the position of curate at Shipton Under Wychwood, Oxfordshire where he remained from 1875 until 1877. Yet another move followed later in 1877 when he can found acting as curate at Northam, Hampshire and this was followed with a similar position in 1878 at Ford, Northumberland.

Now aged 31 years old, Alexander had not been idle on the personal front, as the following quote illustrates:

Elizabeth, now 30, humorous, gentle, always good tempered, had been courted and won by the Rev A B Orr. J B Yeats watched the premarital sparring with amusement. Orr, a good man, extraordinarily kind and generous. He believed himself of a higher social standing than his fiancée and felt that her dowry should be large, as she belonged to a family that were not gentlefolk. His own family having made a fortune manufacturing soda water.

The Elizabeth concerned was Elizabeth Anne Pollexfen, born in Ireland in 1843 (and therefore 4 years older than Alexander) and known to all as 'Lolla'. Lolla was one of 12 children born to William Pollexfen (1811–1892) and Elizabeth Middleton (1819–1892) in Ireland between 1838 and 1857.

The Pollexfen family were of wealthy status but only recently. They made a fortune from their milling and shipping companies. The shipping business was known as the Sligo Steam Navigation Co. Elizabeth's father, William was a director of the Sligo Gas, Light and Coke Co. and a prominent member of the Butter Market. The family were also wealthy enough to own and race horses at the major meets. William Pollexfen also passionately believed that Ireland should remain under the British crown. Elizabeth's elder brother, George (1839–1910) later inherited the majority of his fathers wealth. Elizabeth was educated at the convent in Sligo and retained friends amongst the nuns there for many years.

Alexander Orr married Elizabeth (Lolla) Pollexfen in 1878 in Ireland though this date could be spurious. A daughter, Geraldine E W Orr is recorded in the 1881 census returns as being 5 years old which means she was born in 1876, two years before the marriage of her parents.

By this marriage, Alexander also related himself to another prominent Irish family, one member of which, became one of the most famous writers and poets of the twentieth century.

Lolla Pollexfen's elder sister, Susan Mary (born 1841) met John Butler Yeats (born 1839) through his acquaintance with her two elder brothers at school. As we have seen in the quote above, it was J B Yeats who commented on Alexander Orr's courtship of Lolla Pollexfen. John Butler Yeats was the son of Rev. William Butler Yeats (1806–1862) and Jane Grace Corbet (1811–1876) and one of 11 children. J B Yeats initially trained as a barrister but abandoned this career and became a portrait painter but was frequently in financial difficulties. John and Susan Mary had six children between 1865 and 1875, the first of which was christened William Butler Yeats. Mary Yeats was frequently embarrassed about her husbands need to borrow money and was disappointed that when she had married him she had thought that he would become a successful barrister, not a painter! For his part, John Butler Yeats knew that there was a history of mental illness in the Pollexfen family and feared that it may occur in his own children and attributed their less favourable qualities to this notion. The Yeats family lived in Ireland and London and moved homes a number of times.

William Butler Yeats is a name that will be familiar to many as a playwright, poet and author. Born in Dublin in 1865 he was one of a talented brood of children. His sisters became successful graphic artists and his brother, Jon Butler (Jack) Yeats is widely acknowledged as the greatest Irish painter of the twentieth century. W B Yeats became an ardent Irish nationalist, encouraged by his love for the political activist Maude Gonne. He founded the Irish Literary Society and the prototype of an Irish National Theatre during the 1890s. He became disillusioned with politics until he was stirred by the Easter Rising of 1916. He was also awarded the Nobel Prize for literature in 1923. He finally married in 1917 to Georgie Hyde Lees who was 27 years his junior and who gave him two children. Yeats and James Joyce became the most important Irish literary voices of the twentieth century.

In 1887, W B Yeats mother, Susan Mary, suffered a stroke, though she made a reasonable recovery. Later in the same year she travelled to Yorkshire to see her sister, Elizabeth 'Lolla' Orr, taking with her, her youngest daughter, Susan Mary, to stay at the vicarage of a little village where Alexander Barrington Orr had recently become the Vicar.

We last left him and his family at Ford in Northumberland where he can be found in the 1881 census returns living at the Parsonage:

Name	Age	Born	Occupation	Place of Birth
Alexander B Orr	34	1847	Curate of Ford & Etal – BA, Clergyman	Ireland
Elizabeth A Orr	38	1843	Priests Wife	Ireland
Geraldine E W Orr	5	1876	Scholar	Ireland
Susan W A Orr	4	1877		Southampton
Edith A W Orr	2	1879		Ireland
Robert S P Orr	1	1880		Ford
Elizabeth Allan	16	1865	Nurse & Domestic Servant	Ford

He left Ford in 1881 to became the Curate at Norham in Bedfordshire until 1884. Whilst he was the Curate here he wrote his first published work in 1882 entitled*: A Chart of Eucharistic Doctrine.* In 1885 he took the position of Curate of Sedbergh, North Yorkshire and remained here until 1887. Never a man to linger in any one position, he uprooted his family again, which by now consisted of six children, to the village of Upper Denby. The following entries have survived in the Yeats family archives:

1887 – December. Susan Yeats and Susan Mary Yeats go to stay with Elizabeth Pollexfen Orr at Denby near Huddersfield; Susan Yeats suffers another stroke and falls down a back stair.

1888 – 12th April. Susan Yeats and Susan Mary Yeats arrive at Bedford Park from Denby.

Susan Yeats was 46 when she suffered her first stroke and 47 when the had the second one at Denby vicarage, this one leaving her completely dependant on the help of others, though she lived a good while longer. The stroke probably accounts for the length of her stay with her sister and brother in law, Alexander. One assumes that they had initially only intended to spend Christmas here. Already a deeply unhappy woman regarding her husband she had been very distressed when he had enrolled their children into an art school, seemingly to follow in his footsteps. Twelve years after her second stroke she died, aged only 59. Susan Mary Yeats would have remembered her visit to Denby well as she was 21 years old when she visited, she died in 1949 aged 83.

We can find the Orr family at Denby in the census returns of 1891:

Name	Age	Born	Occupation	Place of Birth
Alexander B Orr	44	1847	Clerk in Holy Orders – Vicar of Denby	Ireland
Elizabeth A Orr	48	1843		Ireland
Susan M G P Orr	14	1877		Southampton
Robert A P Orr	11	1880		Ford
Marian G K Orr	9	1882		Ford
Gertrude E W Orr	8	1883		Norhill
Monica T P Orr	3	1888		Sedbergh
Alice Long	39	1852	Housekeeper	Bishopstoke
Charlotte Brook	21	1870	General Servant Domestic	Penistone

One of Rev. Orr's first acts as the new Rector of Denby was to form a Church Council:

Memorandum from Rev. A B Orr, Denby Vicarage, Huddersfield to Mr H Heath, November 10th 1887.

Dear Sir,

In order to promote the harmonious co-operation of Priest and people I have decided on forming a 'Church Council'. The office of this body will be to consult with and advise me in matters concerning the performance of Divine Service, and otherwise touching the interests of the Church in Denby. May I ask you to make one of the Council, and (if possible) attend a meeting to be held at the Vicarage on Saturday evening, Dec. 3rd 1887, at eight o'clock, for the purpose of constituting the same.

Your faithful servant in Christ.

A B Orr

Your speedy answer will oblige.

Harry Heath did respond to his Vicar's call and became a member of the council, he had been very involved with the former Vicar, Job Johnson's time at the helm and would have been a natural choice. Five months later, Rev. Orr married Harry Heath to Elizabeth Barraclough on 24 April 1888 in the church. The meeting held to convene the council took place just before the arrival of Susan Yeats and her daughter.

Just prior to the latter Rev. Orr had sent a postcard to the teachers of Denby Sunday school:

A meeting of the teachers of Denby Sunday school will be held in the Vicarage on Wednesday evening, November 9th, at eight o'clock. Any teacher not attending (unless unavoidably hindered) will be held to have resigned.

A B Orr, Denby Vicarage, Oct.29th, 1887.

Evidently Alexander had developed his own ideas about how a parish church should be run and was making his presence felt in no uncertain terms. It was also in Rev. Orr's time that a large part of Denby Dykeside was ceded from Denby to Cumberworth parish, this occurred in 1892.

The wandering instinct returned to Rev. Orr in 1894 when he uprooted the family again in order to become the Rector of Drumtochty, South West of Aberdeen in Scotland. In a slightly odd exchange, the Vicar of Drumtochty, Romeo Edwin Taglis, came the other way and became the Vicar of Denby. There must have been some management in these swap over appointments but the reasons are currently unknown. Whilst at Drumtochty Alexander wrote his second and final published work – *King Longbeard* in 1898. He and his family remained at Drumtochty until 1900. He left here to become the Curate at Bourton on the Hill, Gloucestershire in 1901 aged 54.

Here our knowledge of Alexander Barrington Orr ends, the name is unusual and it is very likely that he died in 1910 aged 63 at Godstone in either Staffordshire or Surrey. His wife, Lolla, lived on until 1933 when she passed away aged 90. Details of the lives of their seven children are currently unknown. Alexander presided as Vicar, Rector or Curate at, at least 13 different parish churches distributed all over the British Isles and Ireland. He was linked by marriage to the Yeats and Pollexfen families of Ireland and was the Uncle of the celebrated W B Yeats. His personal life and family connections and associations with well known public figures would make interesting reading had it ever been written down. For just seven years this man was the Vicar of Denby and events such as the coming of the Yeats family may just have excited interest in some of the villagers who were aware of their Reverend's interesting family history.

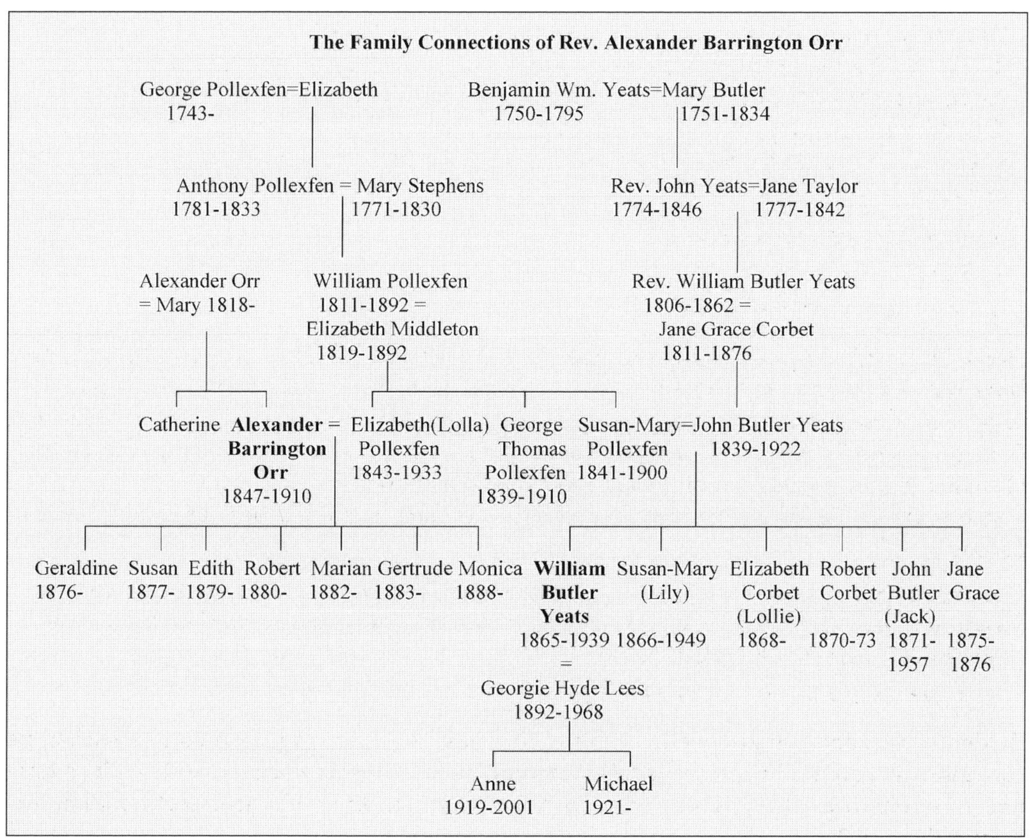

Romeo Edwin Taglis 1894–1926

Romeo Edwin Taglis was born in London in 1860. His father died whilst he was a teenager and his mother, Clara, re-married to Henry Goodered, a piano forte tuner. Both Henry and Clara were born in London, but they moved the whole family up to the north of England before 1881, when they can be found living at 18 Budle Street, Elswick, Northumberland. Romeo was at this time working as a solicitor's clerk. By 1891 he had left the family home, where Henry Goodered was now described as a Professor of Music. Romeo's sister, Adelina N Taglis (born 1863) was at this time living with her stepfather and her 13 year old stepbrother, Herbert W Goodered. Clara is not mentioned on the census return and it is likely that she was dead by now. Sometime before 1890, Romeo had decided that his vocation in life was bound up with religion and so he took up holy orders. He was duly ordained and took up his first position as the Rector of Drumtochty, south west of Aberdeen. He remained here until 1894 until he was replaced, as we have seen, by the outgoing Vicar of Denby, Alexander Barrington Orr. Romeo headed in the opposite direction and arrived in Denby in 1894, initially an outsider, but he soon made his presence felt.

He was responsible for the large scale renovation and rebuilding operation undertaken at Church during 1900/1901. The interior of the nave was almost entirely rebuilt. The gallery was taken down, stone pillars and arches were raised, dividing the centre aisle from the north and south portions of the nave. A barrel roof was placed over the centre aisle and a new chancel was built with a crossed rafter roof. The interior of the Church was now a copy of one, which the Vicar had seen in Italy. A vestry was added to the south side of the chancel and new pews replaced the old-fashioned box pews in the nave. The organ, which had been in the gallery was now put in the chancel against the vestry. Thus rebuilt, the building was re-opened and consecrated on Wednesday 19 June 1901.

A sale of work booklet, produced in 1928 included a piece written by the former headmaster of Denby school, Arnold Jackson about the late Rev. Taglis:

> *Denby was very fortunate in having Mr. Taglis for its Vicar. He possessed high genius as well as a charming personality. His great ability and special talents for administrative work were recognised by the clergy. He was one of the four proctors, selected from the clergy in the Wakefield diocese, to sit in convocation, and as such he represented the country parson. This was a great honour for a Vicar whose Parish was in a remote country district. He also was a member of the following bodies:*
>
> *The Church Assembly, The Committee for the Appointing of Bishop's, Diocesan Dilapidation's Board, Diocesan Board of Patronage. He was also the rural Dean of Silkstone.*
>
> *Although occupied so much in national and diocesan affairs Mr. Taglis found much to be done in Denby. During his vicariate extensive alterations were made to the church and school.*
>
> *He is however, best known to us as a loving tender hearted man. Possessing much charm, a joyful spirit, a pleasing way of meeting anyone with a smile and a warm handshake, he made many friends. At the Sunday school festival he was always happiest amongst the children. He was interested in the young men and was President of the cricket and football teams. He will be remembered for his work in connection with the local branch of the British Legion. His courtesy will not be easily forgotten. At all times he was so approachable that we always felt we had a friend sharing in our joys.*

The grave of Rev. Taglis in Denby churchyard. As is traditional, his plot faces those of his flock in order that he can lead them into Heaven.

Rev. Taglis ended his days at Denby, his grave is inscribed:

> *Romeo Edwin Taglis, Priest, for 32 years Vicar of Denby, died 24 September 1926 aged 67. Also, Margaret his wife, died 11 April 1940 aged 78.*

Gervase Orton Tibbits 1926–1938

Gervase Tibbits was born in 1881 and gained his Licentiate in Theology at Hatfield Hall, Durham in 1904 aged 23. He was ordained a deacon in 1905 and a priest in 1907 at Wakefield. He became the curate of Birkenshaw and Hunsworth, half way between Brighouse and Bradford between 1905–1908. He moved on to St John the Baptist church at Barnsley between 1908–1913, leaving here for Saint Saviours, Fairweather Green, Bradford between 1913 and 1918. He was enticed back to Saint John's at Barnsley at the end of the First World War in 1918 where he remained until 1926 when he left to take up the position of Vicar of Denby. A highly respected member of the community, he died here in 1938 aged 58 and was buried in the churchyard on 7 January. His income in 1937 was £371 per annum plus the vicarage. As a memorial to their former Vicar, the parishioners of Denby subscribed and installed electric lighting in 1939.

Rev. G O Tibbits, with the local scout troop in front of the main door of Denby Church, circa 1930's.

Other additions to the church during Rev. Tibbits time include:

13 March 1930 – The erection of a carved reredos (a screen or panel behind an altar or seat or a choir screen) in memory of Lady Hinchliffe.

18 March 1931 – The removal of the organ to the north aisle and erection of a screen between the vestry and the chancel and the nave and oak panelling to the east wall of the chancel.

9 May 1934 – Arrival of a new brass lectern and oak communion table.

Reginald Jackson Sheard 1939–1944

Reginald attended St. Augustine's College, Canterbury before being ordained in Knutsford, Cheshire in 1920. He became a Priest at Wakefield in 1923. His first appointment was to the curacy of Brighouse between 1924 and 1926. During 1926 he decided upon a slightly different career direction and left England to become a missionary in Pawa in the Dominican Republic from 1926 to 1928. Keeping his missionary zeal alight he moved on to Guadalcanar in the Solomon Islands between 1928 and 1931. Reginald spent five years abroad before deciding that he was ready to return to England and swapped these exotic locations to become the curate of Liversedge from 1931 to 1933. His next move was to Brownhill, near Peterhead in Scotland where he remained from 1933 until 1939. Upon the death of Rev. Tibbits at Denby, Reginald took up the chance to succeed him and to lead the villagers of Denby through the horrors of World War Two until 1944. His salary at

Rev. R J Sheard, circa 1940.

Denby was slightly lower than his predecessor at £352 per annum, plus the vicarage. Plans were made during Rev. Sheard's tenure to build a new vestry. W Wrigley, architect and surveyor of Wakefield was asked to quote for this on 11 April 1940, but no further action was taken.

Norman Aubrey Moore 1944–1981

Norman Moore was born on 3 June 1909 and was ordained a Deacon in 1935 and a Priest in 1936 at Wakefield. His first post was that of the curate at Mount Pellon, near Halifax between 1935 and 1938. He moved on to Thornhill Lees (inclusive of St. Mary's church, Savile Town), near Dewsbury between 1938 and 1944. He left here to become the Vicar of Denby, succeeding Rev. Sheard.

It was during his first year that he organised the men of the Parish to entirely re-decorate the interior of the chancel and nave. The following year saw the centenary of the construction of the Church and a booklet, written by Rev. Moore was produced. Rev. Moore also oversaw the addition of a clock to the church tower on 17 August 1950. The cost of £270 was raised by the efforts of two sisters, Annie Haigh and Lucy Kaye who went collecting from door to door from 1948 until 1950. The dedication was attended by the Bishop of Pontefract.

Norman Moore married Norah Cicely (1907–1978) and had a daughter, Robyn. He died on 17 December 1982. His gravestone at Denby notes that he was an Associate of Kings College, London and bears the Latin inscription *Laus Deo* – Praise Be to God. Rev. Moore

Left to right: J Turton (churchwarden), Clr. Kaye, Mr White, the Bishop of Pontefract, Mr Colin Crossland (churchwarden), Rev. N A Moore and Mr Waldie on the occasion of the addition of a clock to the tower of Denby Church in August 1950.

held the curacy of Denby for 37 years, only Joseph Horsfall accrued more years during his time in the post with 40 years.

The lives of the men who became the curates of Denby encompass a wealth of history and connections. They lived through turbulent times and witnessed fundamental changes in the worshipping habits of their flocks. Currently without a Vicar (since the retirement of Terry Robins in 2008), the future is uncertain. But how many people, who do not regularly attend services here, would miss the opportunity to baptise, marry or be buried here should the worst happen and the building and its past be shut up forever?

Gravestone of Rev. Moore and his wife, laid flat just to the right of the church doorway.

The Clergy of Denby

Charles Broxholme (Perpetual Curate)	1627–1632
Daniel Clarke (Perpetual Curate)	1632–1643
? Miller (Perpetual Curate)	Circa mid 1640's to mid 1650's
Ralph Ward	1649–1650
John Crooke (Perpetual Curate)	1657–1665
Timothy Kent (Perpetual Curate)	1665–1691
Gamaliel Battie (Perpetual Curate)	1691–1698
William Norris (Perpetual Curate)	1698–
Bryan Allot	c.1727
Jonathan Perkins (Perpetual Curate)	1729–1753
Samuel Phipps (Perpetual Curate)	1753–1778
Francis Haigh (Assistant Curate)	Circa. 1760's
Joseph Purslove (Perpetual Curate)	1778–1779
Joseph Horsfall (Perpetual Curate)	1779–1819*
Jeremiah Bourn (Assistant Curate)	1780–1789
John Butterfield Schorey (Assistant Curate)	1794–
John Mattinson (Assistant Curate)	1801–
Samuel John Hillyard (Assistant Curate)	1819
John Brownhill	1822
Brice Bronwin (Ass.Cur. 1816) (Perpetual Curate from 1830)	1830–1851
Job Johnson (Vicar)	1851–1887
Alexander Barrington Orr (Vicar)	1887–1894
Romeo Edwin Taglis (Vicar)	1894–1926
Gervase Orton Tibbits (Vicar)	1926–1938
Reginald Jackson Sheard (Vicar)	1939–1944
Norman Aubrey Moore (Vicar)	1944–1981
Norman Stanley Fox (Vicar)	1982–1984
Robert Christopher Shaw (Vicar)	1985–1990
David James Clarkson (Vicar)	1991–2003
Terry Robins (Vicar)	2003–2008

*Till at least 1819.

Before we complete this chapter it would be remiss of me to ignore the possibility of examining the clergy of Denby's near neighbour at Cumberworth. I investigated the churches history in *Denby & District III* and have only a limited amount of new information to add to the catalogue of Ministers, which I will list below for the first time.

Aerial view of Denby Church and school.

The Clergy of Cumberworth

c.1250	**William de Denby**
1299	**Sir John de York**
1328	**Simon de Tickhill**
1323	**Henry de Metheley**
1365	**John Burdet**
1372	**Ferrour de Shirburn**
1412	**John Walker**
1603	**Adam Meller**
1649–1651	**Timothy Broadley**
1651–1655	**Bishop Henry Tilson**
1655–1676	**Robert Allenson**
1677	**William Bray BA**
1685	**Samuel Charlesworth**
1686	**Henry Audesley**
1716	**Obadiah Porritt**
1723–28	**Francis Haigh**
1734	**William Hoggart**
1822 until at least 1837	**William Roulton (who lived in Penrith, and never came to Cumberworth so all his duties were carried out by: Christopher Blencow Dunn (Curate)**
1851	**Job Johnson**
1852	**William Shields**
c.1855	**George Bird**
1874	**W Collinson-Adamson**
1875	**W Hirst**
1899–1912 (at least)	**Adam Currie FRGS L Th**
1932–1936 (at least)	**John James Cowan BA**
1941	**Arthur E Snow assisted by T V Briggs**
1944	**T V Briggs**
1954	**Geoffrey Warwick**
1966	**A Hesselgreaves**
1991–2003	**David James Clarkson**
2003–2008	**Terry Robins**

Adam Meller became the Priest of Bishopthorpe, just to the South of York, on 24 July 1601, prior to his time at Cumberworth.

Robert Allenson was ejected from the living at Mirfield in 1655, of which he had been Vicar from 1639. He was almost immediately installed at Cumberworth and did not resume his duties at Mirfield after the Restoration. He was evidently welcomed at Cumberworth as he remained here until his death in 1676. He was buried in the churchyard on 8 December. Allenson was married and had five children.

Henry Audsley was ordained a Priest on 21 December 1689. He gained his BA at St. John's College, Cambridge. As a Deacon he would have been no more than a curate at Cumberworth.

Obadiah Porrit was born in 1668, the son of Robert Porrit of Birstall. He attended Lincoln College, Oxford, where he gained his BA in 1691. He was ordained a Priest on 19 June 1698. It was during Porrit's time that Archbishop Sharp wrote his manuscript regarding the churches in his diocese, he has the following to say about Cumberworth:

Cumberworth £18 15s

This also an ancient parochial chapel, endowed (but by whom or when I know not) with (word) to the value of £25 per annum. My Lady Eglinton presents it as a free donative at her disposal, exempt from all Episcopal jurisdiction, but yet Porrit, her chaplain (who writes himself Rector thereof) and the church warden do appear at or (word). The chapel consists of seven farms and three cottages.

(A note added to the bottom of the entry notes Francis Haigh as curate in 1723).

William Hoggart was born 22 January 1707/8 in Bampton, Westmoreland, the son of Lancelot and Mary Hoggart of Butterwick Crag. He became curate of Cumberworth on 22 June 1734 and was ordained a Priest in the same year. He became curate at Silkstone in 1735.

Christopher Blencow Dunn became the curate of Witnash on 10 April 1825 at a stipend of £60, his patron was Charles Woolsey Johnson, the Rector of Witnash, near Royal Leamington Spa, Warwickshire. Christopher was married to a woman we know only as Eliza and had at least three children at Cumberworth, namely: Lavinia Ada in 1834, Christopher B N, in 1836 and Clarissa Isabel in 1838.

Adam Currie attended Durham University before his ministry began.

The following detail concerns the Rev. George Bird who was rector of Cumberworth around 1855:

Husbands authorised to beat their wives.

Wife beating advocated by a clergyman, &c. A very large number of wife beating cases have recently been brought before the magistrates at Whitehaven, where there exists a sect of professing Christians who propagate the opinion that the practice is in accordance with the word of God. The Rev. Geo. Bird, formerly rector of Cumberworth near Huddersfield has established himself there, and drawn together a congregation; and within the last few weeks it has transpired that he holds the doctrine that it is perfectly scriptural for a man to beat his wife. About six weeks ago, James Scott, a member of Mr Birds congregation, was summoned by his wife for brutally beating her because she refused to attend the same place of worship that he did. When before the Magistrates Mrs Scott said she had no wish her husband should be punished if he would promise not to ill use her again. When asked by the magistrates whether he would make the requisite promise, he refused, saying "m I to obey the laws of God or the laws of man?' as he would not give the promise, the magistrates committed him to prison for a month with hard labour. The Rev. Mr Bird has since delivered a course of lectures on the subject of Scott's conviction. He contends that it is a mans duty to rule his own household; and if his wife refuses to obey his orders he is justified, according to the law of God, in beating her in order to enforce obedience.

The Examiner October 11th 1856

The road leading to Cumberworth Rectory, circa 1930s.

Cumberworth Rectory, February 1894. The Vicar stroking the dog may have been Adam Currie or W Hirst.

Inside Cumberworth Rectory, February 1894.

As Cumberworth church came under the authority of the Vicars of Silkstone it may be useful at this point to include a catalogue of the incumbents of that church. The long gaps between the various ministries at Cumberworth may have been filled by curates from Silkstone, though it is just as feasible that the chapel was closed at these times.

John Apley	1284
Richard de Huntingdon	1307
Thomas de Mideley or Middleton	1344
John de Cornubia	1347
Henry de Graynaby	
Thomas Marrick	1362
Richard Bate	1375
Ralph Ellys	
Richard de Ulleston	1402
Roger Gleston	1412
Richard Thurnescoe	1420
Robert Thornton	
Robert Law	1457
William Wilcock	
Clement Wymer	1515
John Nichols	1521
Thomas Wilson	1545
William Inkerfield	1553
James Wylde	1570's
Robert Usher	1580–1609
John Brooke	1609–1615
William Saxton (Curate)	1610
William Bardon	1615
Francis or Isaac Sanford	
George Burdett (Curate)	1626
Edward Hudson	
John Spofford	1642–1662
Loy Kett	1662–1666
John Richardson (Curate)	1662
Thomas Sherman	1666–1677
Thomas Peigham	1677
John Beever (Curate)	1683
Nathaniel Wainhouse	1699–1708

John Clarkson	1708–1756
Joseph Wood (Curate)	1734
William Hoggart (Ass. Curate)	1735
Joseph Purslove (Curate)	1748
Francis Dodsworth	1756–1757
Samuel Phipps	1757–1799
John Goodair (Curate)	1780
John Smith	1799–1804
George Desmeth Kelly	1804
Richard Paver (Curate)	1817
Sir Robert Affleck	1834

All of the above were Vicars unless otherwise stated.

It is also interesting to note that two men baptised in Cumberworth became priests, though not in the village of their christening.

Chadwick Hepworth was baptised at Cumberworth on 25 July 1738, the son of Joseph. He gained his BA at Trinity College, Cambridge and became a Priest 21 May 1769 taking up the position as curate of Fylingdales.

William Hodgson was baptised at Cumberworth on 25 July 1746, the son of William, Vicar of Wadworth. He was educated at Queen's College, Cambridge where he gained his BA. He became a Deacon 5 March 1770 and became a priest and the curate of Campsall on 28 October 1770.

Glossary

Curate — Assistant to a Rector or Vicar.

Deacon — Clergyman without the full status of Priest.

Incumbent — A Rector, Parson, Vicar or minister of a Parish.

Parson — In its strictest sense, a rector rather than a Vicar, but now used to denote either.

Perpetual Curate — Incumbent of a Parish Church where the Great Tithes have been annexed by an ecclesiastical body or lay person. In Denby's case the original lay person was Godfrey Bosville.

Priest — In a pre-Reformation sense, the head of a province, usually an Archbishop. After this it had a more general use for all members of the clergy.

Rector — Originally the incumbent of a parish who received all the tithes, offerings and dues. When an ecclesiastical body (i.e. a monastery) annexed a benefice it became, nominally, the rector and appointed a deputy to administer the parish, this deputy was known as a Vicar. After the reformation many monastic estates fell into lay hands and subsequently lay Rectors became common. This was how the Burdet and Bosville's acquired the right to nominate Vicars for churches like Denby and Penistone.

Chapter Three

The Green Family – Corn Millers of Denby Dale

Advertisement for Mad Dog Marketing 2008

With over 20 years experience in the pet food and animal feeds industry; from product development to nutrition, and sales and marketing; Mad Dog Marketing Ltd is an expanding family business that provides a full range of quality extruded animal feeds and pet food to customers throughout the UK and Europe.

Set-Up in 2003, Head office is based at the family mill which is situated in Denby Dale (Huddersfield), where the family have milled feeds for around 400 years. The company provides a range of top quality dry, and complete animal feeds which are manufactured onsite to high standards. The range of feeds and mixed colours and cereal proteins are made by the process of extrusion and can be tailored and marketed to the customer's individual requirements. A full range of complete working dog food is available with a diet to suit all requirements from Wheat Gluten Free, to Weight Control, and Puppy Care to Senior Diets. Each product is highly palatable, nutritionally balanced and is fortified with vitamin and minerals.

Mad Dog Marketing Ltd is a family business owned by the Green family. The Company Directors are brothers Matthew Green, Company Director and David Green, Company Secretary and Technical Manager. The day to day running of the business is taken care of by Donna Williamson, General Manager and Accounts; educated to degree level with extensive experience in Sales and Marketing. The company is based at Victoria Corn Mills, Denby Dale, with manufacture in Norfolk, UK.

But who were the people that created the platform for this business and how did they come to be in Denby Dale at all?

The Green family are one of the longest established tribes in and around the Denby Dale area. The earliest individual to occur in records was a George Green who took on a lease from the distant Lords of Skelmanthorpe, Hamnet and Robert Hyde in 1597/8. It is interesting to note that George Green was a millwright and that the land he leased was at Cuttlehirst, Highbridge in Scissett. Evidence for the existence and antiquity of Highbridge Mill dates back to at least 1246. Highbridge may be a corruption of Eilrickelbrig, shortened to Eibrigg in the fourteenth century. It was named after the former eleventh century Saxon landholder Ailric who owned much of the Upper Dearne Valley before the Norman Conquest and retained a good proportion of it afterwards. George Green leased the land here in partnership with Peter Hawksworth,

with a water corn mill and kiln being erected at Skelmanthorpe on the East part of the way, and also lands adjoining the West or South West part of the way.

The lease was for 61 years from 1597 and by a later agreement they were to have a moiety of the mill, kiln and watercourses and half of the profits. In 1657 the mill was released to Thomas Walker and of George Green we here no more.

A Christopher Green paid £25 rent for the mill and Downings farm at Gunthwaite in October 1657, he was still there in 1676 when the rent was noted to be £10 per annum. A later George Green paid a half yearly rent of £4 for the Lower corn mill in Denby Dale (below Miller Hill bridge) in 1701/4. This may be the same George Green who was recorded in the Wakefield Manor Book of 1709 as paying 8d in Skelmanthorpe and Cumberworth. A William Green was also recorded, living in the same area.

From the latter we can clearly see a common theme running through the various occupations of members of the family, that of corn milling.

The surname Green is one of the most common and widespread throughout England. In its old English form it was written 'Grene' and it derives from two main sources.

(A) As a topographical name from someone who lived near a village green.
(B) From someone who was fond of dressing in this colour, (or perhaps of someone who had the job of dressing up as the 'Green Man' for May Day celebrations).

The particular Green family that we will follow began recorded life in Emley in 1599 with John Green who married Ann. The family continued at Emley as follows:

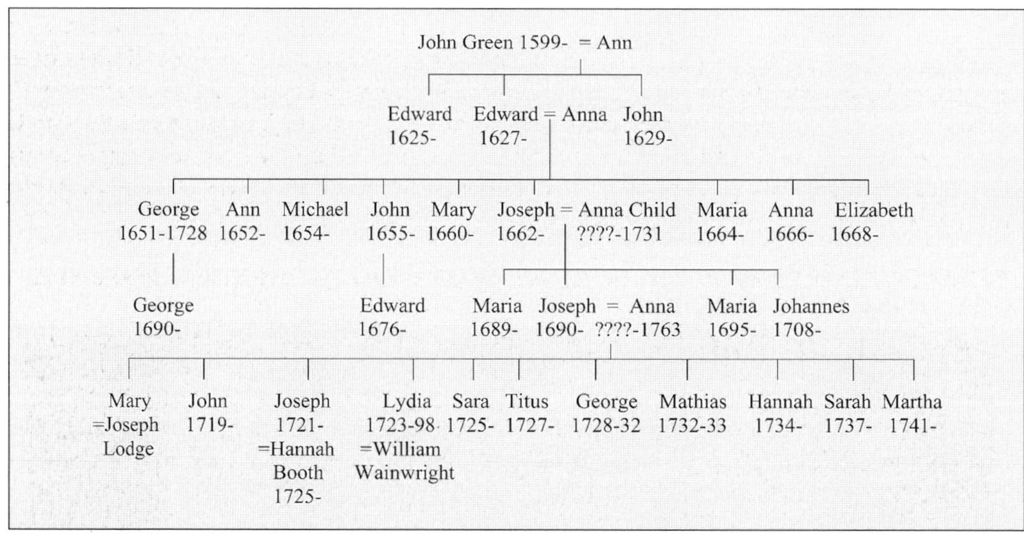

It may be that the George Green we have noted above to be a miller at Denby Dale in 1701/4 may be the George Green recorded in the tree as being born in 1651. This man was certainly the correct age to be in such a position, old enough to have served an apprenticeship and to be in business himself. It is possible, nay even probable, considering the families association with milling that he was taught by his own father, but without further evidence we cannot say for certain and we do not know Edward Green's occupation.

The descent from John to Joseph (born 1721) is somewhat bereft of details and their occupations are at present unknown. The family lived in and around Emley and

Skelmanthorpe but it was the children of Joseph Green and Hannah Booth who began to move around the district.

They had at least eight children including Francis in 1753 from whom the Denby Dale branch descend.

The eldest son, Stephen, born in 1746 became a farmer at High Hoyland. He married Jane Knight (1745–1826), and had at least three children. Stephen was also noted to be an innkeeper at High Hoyland in 1793. The pub he ran was undoubtedly the *Cherry Tree,* named after the orchard which once existed behind the present day inn and which appears in historical records back until 1281 when the Archdeacon of York visited the area and remarked upon it. At the time Stephen Green was the landlord, the pub was known as *The Globe.* On top of these jobs, Stephen was also a *'breeches maker'* according to the High Hoyland baptismal records. Stephen died in 1814.

Francis Green (1753–1836) married Hannah Bottoms (1763–1853) and settled down at Skelmanthorpe. Francis styles himself a clothier in the christening records of his children at High Hoyland church where their first child David, was baptised in 1787, being followed by at least four more, including Francis in 1809.

David Green appears to have been the first member of the family to settle in Denby Dale. He married Hannah Dyson and had five children, the first of which, Noah, was born in Skelmanthorpe in 1815 when David was noted to be a weaver. The other children were all born here, the last of which was Jane, born in 1819, when David was recorded as a spinner. Jane's baptism took place in 1820, at Emley, as with all the others, but sometime between now and 1822 the family moved in to the neighbouring village of Denby Dale. David Green was listed in a trade directory of 1822 as a shopkeeper and carrier and again in Pigot's directory of 1834, similarly as a shopkeeper and carrier, from Denby Dale to Huddersfield every Tuesday. It may just have been that David was offered a business opportunity though the nature and circumstances of the foundation of the business are currently unknown. He is next recorded in the 1841 census returns for Denby Dale.

David Greens Bible, dating to 15 March 1809, family information was still being entered long after his death in 1844.

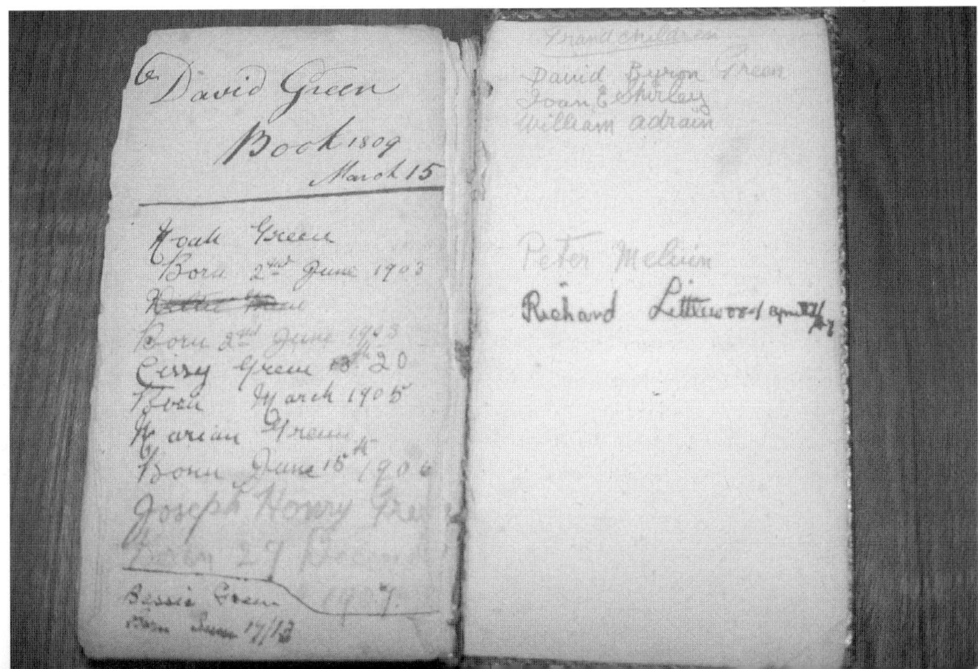

Name	Age	Occupation
David Green	50	Shopkeeper
Hannah Green	55	
Noah Green	25	Grocer
David Green	15	Agricultural Labourer
George Fitton	25	Cloth Maker
Jane Fitton (n'ee Green)	20	
Alfred Fitton	1 month	

NB: The enumerators in the 1841 census rounded ages up or down, thus they are only a guide.

Jane Green had married George Fitton and was evidently living with her parents at the time of the census with her new born son.

There is no mention of corn dealer or miller in this census return though it is obvious that Noah had joined his father in the family business, which would certainly have sold corn. At the top of the original census page in the 'place' column is written 'Hartcliffe', which indicates that the family shop and home have been located in the same place ever since.

In the same 1841 census returns we can also find that David's brother, Francis had also come to Denby Dale and was working as a fancy weaver.

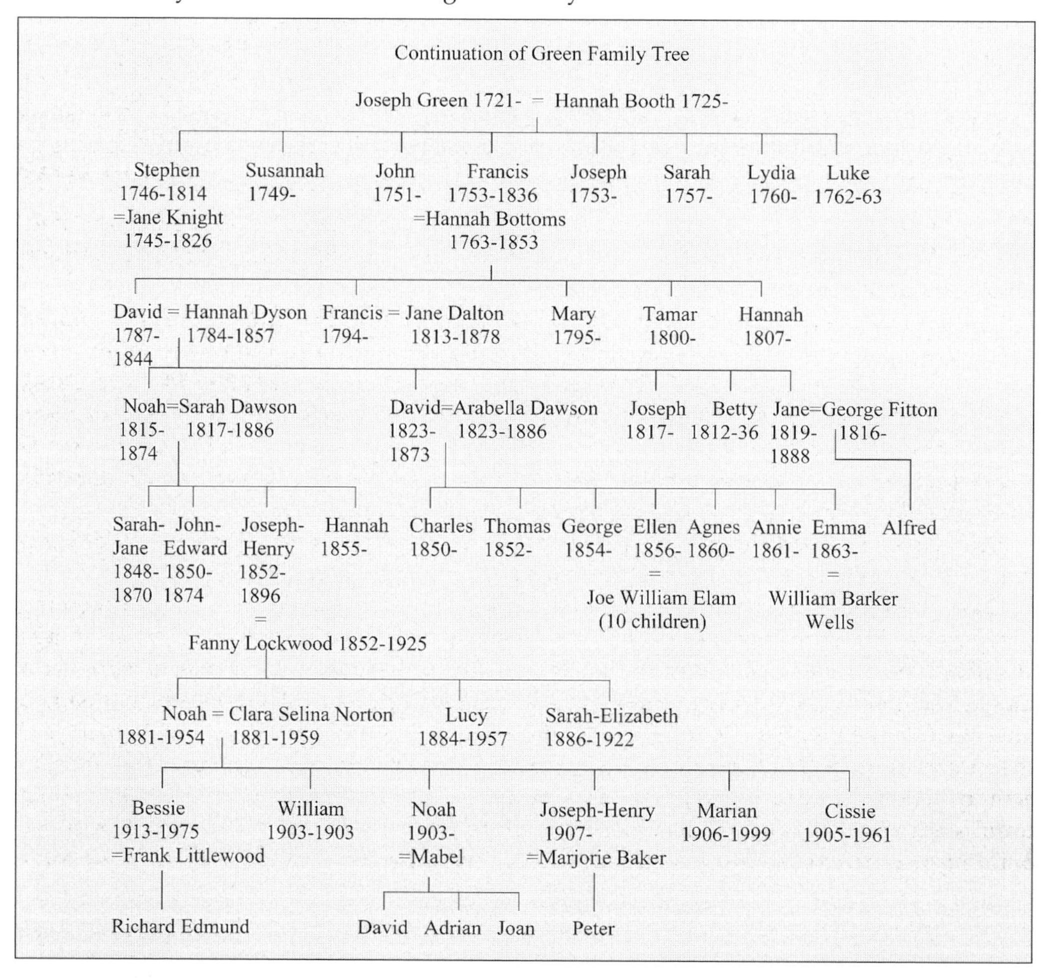

David Green died in 1844 aged 57 but he left the business in the capable hands of his eldest son, Noah (1815–1874). His second son, David, who we have already noted to be an agricultural labourer, took the next logical step up in his chosen field as he can be found listed in the 1851 census returns for Denby Dale working as an independent small farmer.

1851 Census Returns – Denby Dale

Name	Age	Occupation	Place of Birth
David Green	28	Farmer 8 acres	Cumberworth
Arabella Green	28	Farmer's wife	Bretton
Charles R	1		Cumberworth

The farm in question was Wood Nook Farm behind the Victoria Corn Mill. It is likely that David ran the farm with his brother, Noah, as he is also listed as a farmer in 1851:

1851 Census Returns – Denby Dale

Name	Relationship	Age	Occupation	Place of Birth
Noah Green	Head	36	Grocer & Farmer	Denby
Sarah Green	Wife	35		Bretton
Sarah Jane Green	Dau.	3		Denby
John Edward Green	Son	7 m		Denby
Hannah Green	Mother	67		Skelmanthorpe

As can be seen, Noah and David were now married and had begun families of their own. The brothers married two sisters from Bretton, respectively, Sarah and Arabella Dawson who were born into a farming family.

Thomas Dawson, the son of John Dawson was baptised on 15 October 1786. He married Ann Crossland at Silkstone on 22 January 1816 and they lived at Pot House Farm, West Bretton with Thomas's parents. Their children included Sarah (baptised 14 April 1816), John (baptised 15 August 1819) and Arabella (baptised 6 February 1822) all at West Bretton. John Dawson was recorded in a survey of 1810 as being in possession of 21 acres 3 roods and 5 perches including a farmhouse, barn and stables. Thomas predeceased his father in 1828 aged 40, John died the following year aged 78.

Noah Green married Sarah Dawson at Sandal Magna on 1 October 1846 and David Green married Arabella Dawson, again at Sandal Magna on 9 February 1849.

These two families were now solidly based in Denby Dale and were becoming prosperous. The grocer's shop, established by David was flourishing with Noah in charge and the brothers farming activities would have supplied some of the raw materials for them to sell, perhaps even corn. The Victoria Corn Mill dates to 1835, presumably named after the future monarch. The date may be spurious, in so much as Victoria did not ascend the throne until 1837 but, here was a corn mill right in the centre of the brother's sphere of activity. Family tradition suggests that the mill was built by them, though this is an unsubstantiated claim at present. We have already noted that they were here before the building was erected so it remains a possibility and there is no doubt that they did come

A letterhead showing an idealised view of the Green family premises in the centre of Denby Dale circa 1880. The stable to the left was later demolished in order to build the Prospect public house.

to own it. Unfortunately, White's trade directory of 1838 still only lists David Green as a shopkeeper with no mention of the corn mill.

By 1861, David Green can be found listed in the census returns as a retailer of beer. This is the earliest record for the existence of the *Railway Inn,* perhaps named or re-named at the coming of the railway to Denby Dale in 1850. It was the nearest place of refreshment for those alighting at the station and may go back even further, as a beer house used by the navvies who built the railway and the stonemasons who built the viaduct. There is now no mention of the farm on David's job description but dual occupations, particularly when public houses were involved, were very common and it is likely he was still employed on the land throughout the day whilst Arabella looked after the pub. The *Railway Inn* later became, according to family tradition, part of the corn mill. It most certainly could not have been run from the old Victoria mill building, (again, as suggested by family tradition), because, as we have already noted, this was built in 1835 and the pub was still running up until 1873 alongside the Corn Mill. It is likely that the *Railway Inn* was sited roughly between the Corn Mill and the grocer's shop.

1861 Census Returns – Denby Dale

Name	Relation	Age	Yr. Born	Occupation	Place of Birth
David Green	Head	38	1823	Retailer of Beer	Denby Dale
Arabella Green	Wife	38	1823		Bretton West
Charles E Green	Son	11	1850	Scholar	Denby Dale
Thomas H Green	Son	9	1852	Scholar	Denby Dale
George H Green	Son	7	1854	Scholar	Denby Dale
Ellen Green	Dau.	5	1856		Denby Dale
Agnes A Green	Dau.	10 m	1861		Denby Dale

Above left -David Green, who ran the Railway Inn, (died 1873) and (above right) his wife, Arabella (died 1886). Family tradition remembers that Arabella had decided that the next time David took corn into Huddersfield she would meet him there to have their photographs taken. As can be seen, she turned up in her finery whilst David wore his working clothes.

David and Noah Green's mother, Hannah lived with her son, Noah after the death of her husband, she died between 1851 and 1861. Noah seems to have been successful in business and was able to employ a domestic servant to help his wife with their children and the daily chores.

Name	Relation	Age	Occupation	Place of Birth
Noah Green	Head	46	Grocer & Farmer	Denby Dale
Sarah Green	Wife	45		West Bretton
Sarah J Green	Dau.	13	Scholar	Denby Dale
John E Green	Son	10	Scholar	Denby Dale
Joseph H Green	Son	8	Scholar	Denby Dale
Hannah Green	Dau.	5	Scholar	Denby Dale
Mary Stanley	Servant	18	House Servant	Oughtibridge

Little had changed ten years later, both families had seen their sons and daughters grow up and they still lived almost adjacent to each other. Noah was now aided by three of his children:

1871 Census Returns – Denby Dale

Name	Relation	Age	Yr. Born	Occupation	Place of Birth
Noah Green	Head	56	1815	Grocer & Farmer	Denby
Sarah Green	Wife	55	1816		Bretton
John E Green	Son	20	1851	Grocers Assistant	Denby
Joseph H Green	Son	18	1853	Grocers Assistant	Denby
Hannah Green	Dau.	15	1856	Grocers Assistant	Denby
Mary Hawley	Servant	30	1841	General Servant	Emley

The household of Noah was only separated by the Schofield family from his brother David's household at the pub, and, of course, the two sisters, Sarah and Arabella Dawson were able to spend much of their time together.

1871 Railway Inn – Denby Dale

Name	Relation	Age	Yr. Born	Occupation	Place of Birth
David Green	Head	48	1823	Innkeeper	Denby
Arabella Green	Wife	48	1823		Sandal
Thomas A Green	Son	19	1852	Engine Cleaner	Denby Dale
George H Green	Son	17	1854	Cloth Finisher	Denby
Annie Green	Dau.	10	1861	Scholar	Denby
Emma Green	Dau.	8	1863	Scholar	Denby
Thomas Shaw	Boarder	66	1805		Kirkburton
Joseph Brettoner	Boarder	73	1798	Tailor	High Hoyland

The next household recorded was that at the Post Office, run by Postmistress Mary Wood. The *Railway Inn* had by this time become a boarding house as can be seen from the above census returns.

Noah and David had quietly become the owners of a large area of land in the centre of Denby Dale. We have already noted the corn mill and shop, with frontage, Wood Nook Farm and the dwellings associated with them. They had also acquired some land on the opposite side of the road prior to the building of the houses known as Prospect Terrace and of course they owned the *Railway Inn*.

As with all public houses, the *Railway Inn* was not without its more troublesome occasions, as the *Barnsley Chronicle* reports:

13 January 1872
Putting a Dog on the Fire at Denby – Shocking Cruelty

Thomas Hudson of Scissett, was charged with cruelty to a dog at Denby on the 27th Dec last. The information was laid by Supt. Sykes – Mr Freeman defended. Edward Haigh, the owner of the dog, said that on the day named that he was at the house of David Green, the Railway Inn, Denby Dale, getting a glass of beer. The defendant sat in the same room and gave his dog, about 6 months old, a bit of fat and bread. He then stroked it, got hold of it by the legs and put it into the fire. All its legs were exposed to the heat, and he held it there until its hair and all its legs were burnt. The dog screamed very much. The hair under its belly was burnt off and its feet were swollen. Cross examined: Witness had been in prison once and had come out a short time before. The dog did not sieze the man. He (witness) pushed him away as well as he could. In answer to Insp. Birkill, the witness said defendant wanted him to settle the case for a quart of beer. Frederick Craven, who was also in the house deposed to seeing the defendant put the dog on the fire and hold it there. The dog yelled very much and then ran out of the room. PC Worsley said in consequence of information received, he examined the dog on the 29th ult. He found its legs much swollen and the hair of its belly burnt. When the places were touched the dog yelled out very much. The dog was about 6 months old and would not fly at anyone. Mr Freeman – who defended, said he was instructed that the dog was never put on the fire at all, and as he understood the dog was in Barnsley, he should like it to be seen by the magistrates. He then called Bentley Haigh who deposed to being at the Railway Inn on the day named. He was in front of the fire when the dog flew at the defendant and attempted to bite him, the complainant then kicked the defendant. The defendant never put the dog on the fire. The witness Craven was drunk and the landlord refused to fill him drink. Thomas Hirst said he called at the Railway Inn on the 5th inst. When he saw the complainant and his dog in there. He examined the dog but could not find a single hair burnt. He had been a dog keeper and had had the same breed. By Mr Kaye – He did not know anything about the dog before he called at the Railway Inn, he could not find a single hair burnt. After waiting a short time, the dog was brought into court and examined by the magistrates. At the close of the inspection the chairman said that they had no doubt at all that the defendant had put the dog on the fire. It was a very cruel act and they fined the defendant 20s and costs, amounting in all to £2 2s or two months in default. The defendant said he had no money and would have to go to prison.

An earlier report on 15 October 1870 saw David fined 10s and costs for selling beer after half past eleven at night (see *Ye Olde Townships-Denby Dale*), an offence he had also committed back in 1866.

The death of David Green in 1873 aged only 50 saw the end of the family's tenure at the pub. As he did not make a will administration of the £300 he left was granted to Arabella. It seems likely that the building was now incorporated into the family's corn milling activities. The loss of a public house in Denby Dale did not go unnoticed and local brewers Seth Senior & Sons of Shepley took the opportunity to buy the old stable block associated with the pub and demolish it. They re-developing the site with a new building which became known as the *Prospect Hotel* (by at least 1889 although it was probably soon after 1873), the pub is now known as the *Dalesman*.

After David's death, Arabella left Denby Dale to go and live with her daughter, Ellen who had married John William Elam, a coach-maker, at 32 Birkby Lodge Road, Huddersfield. Prior to her marriage in 1879, Ellen had worked at the *George Hotel* in Huddersfield as a cook. Arabella's daughters, Agnes, Annie and Emma probably left Denby Dale with her. By 1881, Emma can also be found working at the *George Hotel*, as a scullery maid. The hotel was a large one and Emma would have been exposed to people from all walks of life and from far away cities and countries, world's away from the comfortable familiarity of Denby Dale. To illustrate this we can see the guests and staff on the night of the census survey in 1881:

Mary A Botting	Head	37	Petton, Warwick	Manageress/Innkeeper
Emma J Botting	Dau.	12	Brompton, London	Scholar
Joseph S Faulders	Visitor	37	Cardew, Cumberland	Woollen Merchant
Samuel G Bissell	Visitor	24	Australia	Commercial Traveller
John Bailey	Visitor	65	London	Manufacturer
Richard C Harrison	Visitor	38	London	Commercial Traveller
Charles L Freeman	Visitor	56	Kettering, Northampton	Commercial Traveller
John R Campion	Visitor	45	St. Paul's, London	Silk Merchant
George L Stevens	Visitor	35	Chepstow, Gloucester	Woollen Merchant
Lydia A Brownrigg	Serv.	36	Hartshead, Yorkshire	Chambermaid–Inn
Mary E Styne	Serv.	22	Kirkstall, Yorkshire	Housemaid–Dom.
Annie Saul	Serv.	21	Aldwark, Yorkshire	Housemaid–Dom.
Sarah J Turton	Serv.	27	Denby, Yorkshire	Housemaid–Dom.
Margaret Cowan	Serv.	29	Scotland	Cook–Domestic
Eliza Aspinall	Serv.	18	Shepley, Yorkshire	Kitchenmaid–Dom.
Selina Taylor	Serv.	18	Birdwell, Yorkshire	Kitchenmaid–Dom.
Harriet Dowling	Serv.	18	Great Bealings, Suffolk	Still Room Maid–Dom.
EMMA GREEN	**Serv.**	**18**	**Denby Dale, Yorkshire**	**Scullery Maid–Dom.**
Arabella Rennard	Serv.	22	Wakefield, Yorkshire	Barmaid–Inn
Margaret Hagar	Serv.	22	Norwich, Norfolk	Waitress–Inn
Bridget O'Bryan	Serv.	30	Ireland	Laundress–Dom.

Sarah J Garner	Serv.	30	Huddersfield, Yorkshire	Book Keeper (Clerk)
William Bull	Serv.	29	Stamford, Northampton	Waiter–Inn
Walter Fuller	Serv.	22	Chatteris, Cambridge	Plateman–Inn/Dom.
Joseph B Iredale	Serv.	16	Lindley, Yorkshire	Page–Dom.
Samuel Peel	Serv.	26	Grantham, Lincoln	Waiter–Inn
Thomas Creegan	Serv.	24	Sheffield, Yorkshire	Porter–Inn
John D Lardner	Serv.	25	Ireland	Porter–Inn
Harry Preston	Serv.	40	Wakefield, Yorkshire	Boots–Inn

NB – It is interesting to note that of the 20 employees, 17 were unmarried (including Emma), 12 of these being women.

Perhaps Emma struck up a friendship with Sarah Turton of Denby, at least the pair of them could talk about familiar places and people.

Only a year after the death of David, Noah Green passed away, in 1874, he did not make a will and administration of his estate of £2000 was granted to his wife. Sarah remained in Denby Dale with her family and can be found in 1881 running the family shop in tandem with her youngest daughter, Hannah. The census returns record their home as Polygon Terrace, just a short walk up High Street from the shop.

1881 Census Returns – Denby Dale

Name	Relation	Age	Place of Birth	Occupation
Sarah Green	Head	64	Nr. Wakefield	Shopkeeper (Provisions)
Hannah Green	Dau.	25	Denby Dale	Shopkeeper (Provisions)

The year 1874 saw a double tragedy for the family as Noah and Sarah's eldest son, John Edward died at the age of 24. Their eldest daughter, Sarah Jane had died in 1870, aged 22, which left only Joseph Henry, Hannah and Sarah to keep the shop and farm running. That they did and were prosperous can be seen in the 1881 census returns which again show the employment of a domestic servant.

Name	Relation	Age	Born	Occupation	Place of Birth
Joseph Henry Green	Head	28	1853	Grocer & Farmer 14 acres – 1 man 2 boys	Denby
Fanny Green	Wife	28	1853		Denby
Noah Green	Son	0	1881		Denby
Susanne Richardson	servant	20	1861	Domestic Servant	Selby

A pewter teapot, inscribed JHG & FL, which was a wedding present for Joseph Henry Green and Fanny Lockwood in 1880.

The family shop was, of course, still subject to the rules and regulations enforced at the time, one of which Joseph Henry fell foul of in 1885:

1885 Sept 26
Deficient Weights at Denby Dale

Joseph Henry Green, provision dealer, of Denby Dale, was charged with having in his possession, a large scale 1¾ ounce, against the purchaser on the 17th September. Mr Supt. Kane proved that he found the scale in the defendant's shop. Mr J Carrington defended. A fine of 5s and costs was imposed.

Sarah Green died in 1886, the same year as her sister, Arabella, leaving her son, Joseph Henry as the patriarch of the family. Joseph Henry married Fanny Lockwood just prior to 1881, when their first child Noah was born, continuing the by now familiar family name.

Joseph Henry had achieved notoriety in the sporting field in his late twenties as reported in the *Barnsley Chronicle*:

15 July 1876

Denby Dale Athletic Festival

The walking of Green, of Denby Dale, did not commend itself to the unprejudiced observer, it seeming to partake more of a trot than the regular heel and toe. His speed and style of walking, which was not in the least laboured, it was admitted, were good, but the first named requisite was acquired in this instance by unfair pedestrianism, and therefore in that sense not to be admired. He acquitted himself much more satisfactorily at Penistone sports the other week when he took off first prize.

AUGUST, 1890

Sun	-	3	10	17	24	31
Mon	-	4	11	18	25	-
Tues	-	5	12	19	26	-

From J. H. GREEN,
Wholesale & Retail Grocer, Provision & Corn Dealer,
Fruit & Potato Stores, Draper, Clothier, Hatter, Hosier, & General Outfitter,
Boot and Shoe Factor, Ironmonger and House Furnisher,
Sewing Machines, Wringing & Mangling Machines, Fire Proof Safes, Deed Boxes, Knife Cleaners, Brass and Iron Bedsteads, Wire & Wool Mattresses, Fenders and Fire-irons in Brass and Steel, all kinds of Agricultural Implements.
All kinds of Glass, China, and Earthenware.
Foreign and English Cigars, Fancy and Plain Tobaccos, Snuffs, &c.
DENBY DALE.

Wed	-	6	13	20	27	-
Thur	-	7	14	21	28	-
Frdy	1	8	15	22	29	-
Sat	2	9	16	23	30	-

A calendar issued by Greens stores in 1890 lists many of the goods and services they provided besides corn. These included: fruit, potatoes, drapery, clothier, hatter, hosiery, general outfitters, sewing machines, wringing and mangling machines, fire proof safes, deed boxes, knife cleaners, brass and iron bedsteads, wire and wool mattresses, fenders, fire irons, agricultural implements, glass, china, earthenware, foreign and English cigars and plain tobaccos.

He appears on numerous occasions in local newspaper reports and appears to have taken his participation in pedestrianism (a shorter form of an Olympic event such as the 20km walk), very seriously. Indeed, sometimes he got a little carried away.

1891 Census Returns – Denby Dale

Name	Relation	Age	Born	Occupation	Place of Birth
Joseph Henry Green	Head	38	1853	Grocer & Corn Dealer	Denby
Fanny Green	Wife	39	1852		Denby
Noah Green	Son	10	1881	Scholar	Denby
Lucy Green	Dau.	8	1883	Scholar	Denby
Sarah Elizabeth Green	Dau.	5	1886	Scholar	Denby
Annie Lockwood	Niece	17	1874	Mothers Help	Horbury

The now derelict Victoria Corn Mill today, still displaying a sign for Spillers cattle pig and poultry foods.

The view up to Wood Nook with the Prospect (Dalesman) pub on the left and the Victoria Corn Mill on the right.

Joseph Henry died on 21 April 1896 and, as with his forebears, he did not make a will, the administration of his estate of £3758 7s 9d was granted to his wife, Fanny. As their youngest son was still only fifteen years old it would have been Fanny's responsibility to keep the shop and corn mill running until young Noah was old enough to take charge. She also had to care for her younger children though help was more than likely provided by family members. Noah would have quickly grown up, and he would have spent much of his youth watching and learning from his father and within a few years was able to take the burden of the business from his mother. He also married, when he was around twenty years old, to Clara Selina Norton and they began their family by perpetuating the by now familiar family name of Noah with the birth of their first child. Noah and Clara Selina, along with Fanny in the shop, took the business into the twentieth century and were soon to aided in this by their sons, Noah and a second Joseph Henry (born 1907). The twentieth-century trade directories chart their progress:

1912 – Noah Green (grocer).
1922 – Mrs F Green (shopkeeper), Mr J H Green (grocer).
1936 – Joseph Henry Green (corn miller, central stores, telephone Skelmanthorpe 48).

Noah Green 1881–1954, during his school years.

Noah Green and Clara Selina Norton circa 1910.

During this period the family had decided to sell off Wood Nook Farm, which was bought by either Thomas or Walter Norton in 1928/9. Around a decade later it was sold again, this time to Roland Brownhill, it later became the property of Peter Schofield. The old Victoria Corn Mill, though still in use had by now been supplanted by newer buildings. The ground floor had been taken over by the Denby Dale and District Sanitary Laundry Co. run by George Robert Senior by at least 1912. Utilising the well inside the mill the company continued until at least 1928. It was also during this period that Noah's youngest daughter Bessie, married Frank Littlewood. Frank along with Arthur Smithson had been the founder's of another well known Denby Dale business, the joiners – Smithson and Littlewood.

By the 1950s Noah Green was in his 70s and the corn mill and shop was run by his sons, Joseph Henry and Noah aided by Noah's two sons, David and Adrian Green.

A full load of corn, waiting to go out for delivery outside the Victoria Corn Mill during the 1930s.

The bags of corn are piled high on the liveried vehicle, which looks out to the main road and the chemist's shop, circa 1930s.

A family group photograph taken at the wedding of Frank Littlewood and Bessie Green in 1939. Bessie's father Noah, is second right at the back. Her mother, Clara Selina is seated on the last right of the picture.

Bessie Green, behind Croft House, circa 1940s.

It was David Green who was responsible for the foundation of the animal feed side of the business, during the 1960s. He recognised that rather than buying the feed in from other suppliers to sell it on, it would make more sense for the business to manufacture its own. New buildings were erected, machinery installed and *Greenfeeds* was founded, and indeed became the core of the business.

The decision was taken in 2008 to sell off the Denby Dale site. The buildings were emptied in readiness for demolition amidst potential plans for a nursing care home to be built. The animal feed business will continue from its base in Norfolk, though its association with Denby Dale is now over. Amidst the chimneys of the weaving mills and the sirens that signalled dinner-time or end of shift for the workers, the Green family

Noah and Clara Selina Green in later life, circa 1950s.

The Victoria Mill, emptied and awaiting demolition in 2008.

prospered. They arrived in Denby Dale before the first of the mills was built and watched the village and its population expand rapidly. They witnessed the first wooden railway viaduct being built and later its stone replacement. They were still here when the mills began to close in the 1970s and 80s and they are still local today.

The family gravestone of David and Hannah Green, in Cumberworth churchyard.

The family gravestone of Joseph Henry and Fanny Green, in Cumberworth churchyard.

Chapter Four

Elijah Hinchcliffe – Transported Convict

English law has sometimes dealt with its people in a very harsh way, even up until comparatively modern times. I have covered many cases recorded in *the Barnsley Chronicle,* which appeared in the county court sections of the newspaper. I have omitted some of the more serious cases that took place in Denby and its environs, such as rape and serious sexual assault as these have no place in books which exist in large part to celebrate the people of the past and their achievements. In hardly any of the cases my research has brought to light has the sentence been anything other than a short spell in the *house of correction* or a fine and a slap on the wrist.

I then came across an individual who was born in Cumberworth about whom nothing was previously known, and there are still many gaps in his life story which only time and further research may uncover. This individual was forced from the land of his birth because of his crime, suffered many privations during his arduous journey and was forced to carve out a new life for himself against incredibly difficult odds. Elijah Hinchcliffe was transported to Van Diemen's Land. Although this chapter is concerned with only one individual and much of it takes place far from home it is important to remember that Elijah's home was originally Cumberworth. He would have had friends here and been familiar with the sound of the church bell ringing as he spent his early life here.

The concept of transporting criminals to foreign states began in 1615 when the Privy Council authorised it as a condition of a pardon from a death sentence by hanging. Initially they were sent to the American colonies where, on arrival, they were auctioned off to the highest bidders. This was done in order for the shipping contractors to recoup their costs. This continued until the American War of Independence in 1776, by which time an estimated 40,000 convicts had been sent from Britain to America. After losing the war the option of sending British undesirables to America was finished and British prisons became extremely overcrowded. Prison ships or *hulks* moored in the River Thames eased the situation a little but a further solution was desperately required. The authorities now looked towards Australia.

The *'first fleet'* of 586 male and 192 female convicts, together with free settlers and freemen set out on 13 May 1787 and arrived the following January. Transportation to Australia was now established, principally to Botany Bay but this was later extended to include Tasmania.

We must now return to the little we know of Elijah Hinchcliffe's family and early life in Cumberworth.

The Hinchcliffe (or Hinchliffe) surname is common throughout Denby, Cumberworth and the surrounding area. Official records, state that he was originally a native of Cumberworth and the baptism registers record two individuals with this name:

Elijah Hinchcliffe baptised 23 February 1817 to Thomas and Mary Hinchcliffe.
Elijah Hinchcliffe baptised 20 April 1818 to Anne Hinchcliffe (single woman).

Incredible as it may seem, there are only two individuals with this name and they were born so close together, immediately confusing the issue. Before we continue we much decide which child he was.

Thomas Hinchcliffe (a weaver) may have been born in 1781. A marriage can be found for him to Mary Barrow (both from Cumberworth) on 20 September 1802, at Cumberworth, by Banns. They had the following family:

Anne (1803), Martha (1805), Harriet (1807), Giles (1810), Sarah (1812), Phyllis (1814), Elijah (1817), George (1819–1827), William (1822), Ruth (1824), Mary (1826).

Researchers have also discovered that Mary could have been Mary Ingham or perhaps even Martha so there is some confusion over this Elijah's mother's name. Whatever the scenario, the family detailed above had left the Cumberworth area by the time of the 1841 census returns, as their names are absent from the villagers recorded here.

The other baptism notes that this Elijah's mother was Ann Hinchcliffe, noted to be a single woman. This illegitimate Elijah is potentially a more serious candidate for our transported convict. We do not know how deprived of a father figure he was, but it is likely that he grew up against a background of want and adversity.

Elijah's age on arrival in Australia was noted to be 24 which would indicate that he was the first of our two candidates, but ages were sometimes recorded in error, and lies were told, particularly by criminals. Our second candidate would only have been 23 years old on arrival and must therefore become our second choice. As there are no infant burial entries, or indeed, burial entries at all for an Elijah Hinchcliffe at Cumberworth, we can assume that both boys grew to maturity, the records at Cumberworth are silent after this.

The final piece of evidence regarding Elijah's parents comes from Tasmania itself. His prison record states quite clearly that his parents were Thomas and Martha Hinchcliffe. The records also throw up one other salient point, sometime prior to 1841 Elijah had married to a woman we know only as Martha.

In 1841, Elijah can be found living at Dukinfield, on the eastern outskirts, of modern day Manchester, about 23 miles west of Penistone. His reasons for being here are unknown but his stay did not last. As we have noted, he was married at around this time to Martha, though the marriage was not a long one and produced no children. He found work as a general labourer, which was not a well paid occupation. He became associated with a man called Esau Hastings and together they planned a get rich quick scheme. It is possible that the pair had worked together before on burglaries for which no perpetrator had been found, it might also be said that they may have been a pair of hopeless bunglers. Whatever the truth, their plan to rob the property of one Leonard Bryan in Dukinfield went disastrously wrong. Both were apprehended and imprisoned before appearing at Knutsford Quarter Sessions on trial for their crime during the Summer of 1841. Elijah was allocated a number – 449, by which he was known throughout the proceedings. The following gives the damming verdict and judgement of the court:

HINCHCLIFFE, ELIJAH 449
Late of the Township of Dukinfield, in the said county (Lancashire), labourer, hath at this present sessions been indicted and convicted of feloniously breaking and entering the dwelling house of Leonard Bryan and stealing the goods and chattels of the said Leonard Bryan from the said dwelling house. Now it is ordered by this court that the said Elijah Hinchcliffe shall be transported to such parts beyond the sea as Her Majesty, with the advice of the Privy Council shall direct, for the term of ten years to be computed from this time. And it is further ordered by this court that the Master or Keeper of the House of Correction of Nether Knutsford, in and for the said county (Cheshire), to receive into his authority the body of the said Elijah Hinchcliffe and him safely keep and to hard labour in the said House of Correction in the mean time and until he is so transported as ordered.

Elijah's partner in crime, Esau Hastings appears underneath the latter entry in the record, he was tried in the same court at the same time and found as guilty as his colleague, he was given the same sentence and also ordered to do hard labour at the House of Correction.

The authorities made the decision that Elijah (along with Esau) would be sent to Hobart, Tasmania and that they would leave on the convict ship *Barossa*, which was to set sail on 30 August 1841 from Sheerness on the River Medway. The thought of transportation must have been a huge shock to Elijah and he must have harboured secret hopes of escape but the authorities were always a step ahead. It is likely that he was taken from the prison at Knutsford and put on either a special prison coach or a regular coach that travelled between Lancashire and London on a regular basis. If it was the latter then it was not uncommon to see convicts being carried on the roof of the coach, manacled and chained together, poorly clothed and exposed to the elements.

On arrival at Sheerness it is likely that Elijah and Esau were held temporarily on a *prison hulk*, moored at Sheerness. Prison hulks were ships that had reached the end of their sea lives and were converted to floating jails, conditions were harsh in the extreme. It is likely that he was brought ashore as part of a work gang during his brief sojourn here. The food served was barley and oatmeal in the morning and evening and either beef or bread and cheese for dinner. Some of the hulks also contained a chapel and a school in order for those

A prison hulk at Deptford in 1828. (Courtesy of the Taylor Lib.)

so inclined to improve their minds and their morals. The stay here would have been relatively brief before they boarded the *Barossa*, the authorities were wary of the threat of violence or riot on board the prison hulks during the waiting period. The last of the prison hulks was gone by 1857 when the final surviving ship used for the purpose was destroyed by fire.

In most cases, convict ships, such as the *Barossa*, were privately owned merchant ships that were chartered by the British Government to convey prisoners to Australia. The earlier voyages were dogged by serious outbreaks of disease, cruel masters and suffered heavy loss of life. In order to improve this, the English authorities began to review the system in 1801. The ships were despatched twice a year, at the end of May and the beginning of September, to avoid the dangerous winters of the southern hemisphere. Surgeons employed by the early contractors had to obey the master of the ship and on later voyages were replaced by independent Surgeon Superintendents whose sole responsibility was for the well being of the convicts. As time went on, successful procedures were developed and the surgeons were supplied with explicit instructions as to how life on board was to be organised. By then the charterers were also paid a bonus to land the prisoners safe and sound at the end of the voyage.

By the time the exiles, like Elijah, were being transported in the 1840s and onwards, a more enlightened routine was in place, which even included the presence on board of a Religious Instructor to educate the convicts and attend to their spiritual needs. All of this sharply reduced the number of fatalities, indeed, many convicts arrived in Australia in a better state of health than when they left.

The *Barossa* carried 350 convicts, all male, each of whom would have been issued with a suit of clothes, a change of linen, a flock bed, a pillow and a blanket. It is likely that not all the convicts boarded at Sheerness and that the *Barossa* would have called in at other ports in England to pick up more convicts. A contingent of soldiers (say around 30) would also have been on board to keep order. The ship's doctor was Henry W Mahon and its Captain (Master) was John Austin.

Convicts were handed over to the Master of the ship at the beginning of the voyage, upon arrival they would then be transferred into the custody of the Governor of the colony

An example of a convict ship, similar to the Barossa. (Courtesy of the Taylor Lib.)

Convicts being escorted to their ship after awaiting its arrival in Sheerness. (Courtesy of the Taylor Lib.)

by use of indenture. Once on board the convicts were housed below decks and often behind bars, in many cases they were also restrained by chains. Elijah would have been allowed on deck for fresh air and exercise but conditions were very cramped and they slept on hammocks.

A prison below decks, home for Elijah for 136 days. (Courtesy of the Taylor Lib.)

The following detail is taken from a different voyage but illustrates the sort of conditions Elijah might have faced:

> *The food was cooked in a galley shared with the seamen, soldiers and prisoners. The rations included flour, beef, pork, peas, rice, raisins, oatmeal, butter, sugar and vinegar. Each man at sea received lemon juice as an anti-scorbutic. Each was allocated 120 gallons of water and 2 gallons of wine for the voyage. Tottenham and Isabella both put into Rio for fresh water, fruit and vegetables. The Tottenham's sick bay was well supplied with tea, chocolate, sago, scotch barley, ginger, black peppers, allspice, port wine, rice and pearl barley. A barrel of tar, brimstone and vinegar were provided for fumigation. A bathing tub, urinals and spitting pots were available for cleanliness and comfort.*
>
> *In spite of the food and equipment on board being better than many convicts experienced at home, conditions on a long and hazardous voyage were highly unpleasant for men who had lived their lives very far from the sea.*

Held in cages and chained up within them, convicts were held in conditions like these for the 13,000 mile voyage to the other side of the world. (Courtesy of the Taylor Lib.)

The full list of convicts that accompanied Elijah on the trip was:

Addiman, John	Ashburner, Edward	Baker, Thomas	Bates, John
Alcock, Alexander	Ashworth, Joseph	Banks, William (aka William Skipp)	Battlemore, Thomas
Alexander, James	Ashworth, Taylor	Bardsley, Robert	Bean, William
Amey, James	Askey, James	Barnes, John (aka John Hunt and Robert Taylor)	Bentley, Thomas
Amos, William	Askwith, Moses	Barnett, Thomas	Birdsall, John
Anderson, James	Aspin, James	Barraclough, John	Bland, George
Anderton, Robert	Baker, Abraham	Barrett, Henry	Boothman, Richard
Andrews, John	Baker, John (aka John Clarke)	Barrett, Joseph	Bowerman, George
Archer, Thomas (aka Thomas Edwards)	Baker, John	Bartlett, Alfred	Bowman, William

Bradbury, James (aka Thomas Smith)	Clifford, Charles	Eckersley, Joseph	Gore, Thomas
Bradford, William (aka William Green)	Cluinson, Edward (aka Edward Hassell and John Moor)	Edge, Robert	Gorman, John
Bray, William	Collier, Thomas	Edwards, John	Gorrie, Robert
Briggs, Charles	Collinge, Edward	Edwards, Robert	Gould, John
Brimble, Nathaniel	Collins, John	Edwards, Thomas (aka Thomas Archer)	Grant, William
Brindle, Evan	Collis, Joseph	England, George	Grater, Henry
Broomfield, Thomas	Cook, Samuel	English, William	Green, George
Broughton, John	Cooper, John	Evans, John	Green, Richard
Brown, Edward	Copping, William	Evans, Thomas	Griffin, Charles
Brumpton, Samuel	Cotter, James	Everitt, Thomas	Griffin, John
Buck, Job	Cox, Joseph	Fairburn, John	Griffith, Thomas
Burnett, William	Crompton, James	Farn, John	Grove, Edward
Busby, Robert	Davies, Thomas	Featherstone, Charles	Gunn, James
Butler, William	Davis, John	Ferris, Meshack	Hairs, John
Butterworth, Thomas	Davis, Richard Archibald	Finnigan, William	Hall, Henry
Cadman, John	Day, Joseph	Fitzcharles, Alexander	Hampshire, William
Callaghan, Patrick	Deakin, John	Fletcher, Richard	Hargraves, William
Cameron, Peter	Didham, William	Fletcher, William	Harkins, James
Cameron, Roland	Donnison Robert (aka Robert Forster)	Fowler, John	Harrad, John
Campbell, Alexander (aka Archibald Campbell)	Donovan, Thomas	Francis, John	Harrad, John
Carpenter, William	Dry, William	Frost, Joseph	Harrison, Richard
Chambers, Samuel	Duff, Charles	Gale, John	Hart, Daniel
Chopper, James (aka James Grimes)	Dunn, George	Gaskin, William	Hartley, John
Claridge, Benjamin	Dunnett, Thomas	Gaunt, James	Hartley, Richard
Clarke, John (aka John Baker)	Dunsmuir, William	Geddes, Robert (aka Charles Witches)	Haslam, James
Clayton, George	Dunswell, William (aka William Gardner)	Goldsmith, Henry	**Hastings, Esau**
Clayton, George (aka John Thompson)	Dury, Thomas (aka Thomas Durey)	Gomm, Thomas	Hawkins, Joseph
Clegg, James	Dyson, George	Goodluck, George	Hear, John (aka John Kelly)

Heaton, William	Kelly, Archibald	Messam, Henry	Ponchard, Joseph
Hemming, George	Kennedy, Hugh	Milburn, Isaac	Poole, Thomas
Hey, John	Kidd, George	Miles, Thomas	Port, Charles
Hickie, James	Kirton, Joseph	Miller, James	Powell, John
Hills, John	Ladkin, Edward	Milward, William	Pretty, Charles
Hinchcliffe, Elijah	Lagor, John	Mitchell, John	Price, John
Hodgson, Thomas	Laing, James	Mitchell, John	Price, Richard
Holden, Samuel	Lancaster, Abel	Moore, John	Pritchard, Alfred
Holland, Joseph	Lane, John	Morrison, James	Radburn, James
Hollingworth, George	Langthorn, Thomas	Morrison, Thomas	Radford, Edward
Holloway, John	Lavender, Mark	Mulleneux, Henry	Railstone, George
Horobin, Samuel	Law, Thomas	Mumford, William	Rault, Jules
Horrocks, Squire	Lawley, James	Munro, Henry	Rawcliffe, John
Horton, Edward	Leary, John	Murray, John	Read, Richard
Howell, George	Leatherland, Robert	Murray, William	Reckless, Ralph
Hughes, Thomas	Lewis, George	Nadin, William	Redman, John
Hughes, Thomas	Lowe, Joseph	Neale, William	Rees, Richard
Hulme, James	Lowe, Thomas	Newton, William	Rendall, James
Hunt, Thomas	Lymington, Thomas	Norden, Oakley	Richardson, Joseph
Hyams, Henry	Marsh, James	Norden, Robert	Riley, James
Ingham, William	Martin, Samuel	Ogden, George	Roberts, John
Jackson, James	Mason, Samuel	Ogilvie, George	Roberts, William
Jacob, John	McCarthey, James	Orchard, Joseph	Robertson, John
Jacques, Joseph	McCurdie, William	Osborne, Robert	Robinson, John
Jeffrey, John	McDermott, Michael	Owen, David	Ronney, James
Jenkins, George	McDonald, Charles	Palmer, Benjamin	Rooney, James
Johnson, Richard	McDonald, Edward	Parker, John	Roose, James
Johnson, Robert	McDonald, John	Parry, William	Royal, Benjamin
Johnson, William	McDonald, William	Pattison, James	Runciman, John
Johnson, William	McFarlane, John	Pegg, Henry	Salter, Thomas
Jones, William	McGill, Joseph	Phillips, Richard	Sanderson, James
Jordan, David Erasmus	Meldrum, John	Pinder, John	Sandland, Henry
Keegan, James	Mellor, John	Plant, George	Saville, Robert
Keep, Daniel	Meredith, George	Platt, Joseph	Sayers, George

Schofield, John	Smith, William	Thomas, John	Webb, Thomas
Sciavi, Joseph	Southey, Thomas	Thomas, Thomas	White, George
Shardlow, John	Spencer, William	Tilney, William	Whitehead, Thomas
Shaw, Joseph	Stalker, James	Tivey, George	Williams, Henry
Shaw, Thomas	Standring, Robert	Tootall, Joseph	Williams, John
Shaw, Thomas	Stanworth, Henry	Torrif, Alexander	Williams, William
Sheldon, William	Staples, Samuel	Trainor, Mathew	Wilson, Charles
Shepherd, John	Steel, James	Tuck, Joseph	Wilson, John
Shepley, Charles	Steven, Norman	Tuft, William	Winrow, Gregory
Shute, James	Stevens, James William	Tuting, Henry	Winwood, James
Skene, Charles	Stewart, John	Vaun, Richard	Wood, Frederick
Smith, Henry	Sullivan, John	Waller, William	Woods, James
Smith, Henry	Sweeton, Edward	Ward, Thomas	Woods, William
Smith, James	Taylor, Thomas	Warden, Henry	Woolford, Frederick
Smith, Joseph	Taylor, William	Warren, James	Wright, Edward
Smith, Peter	Terry, Thomas	Watson, Thomas	Wright, Thomas
Smith, Thomas	Thacker, Enoch	Webb, Robert	Yerrell, Thomas

The medic on board the *Barossa*, Henry W Mahon, surgeon, kept a log for the male convict ship from 12 August 1841 to 22 January 1842. In it he recorded the medical problems of the convicts including Elijah Hinchcliffe. Elijah was noted to be 23 years old and suffering from 'purigo' between the 9 and 17 of November 1841. He was noted to be cured at the last date. The disease was most likely *prurigo nodularis,* a skin condition in which hard crusty lumps form on the skin that gives off bursts of intense itching. Some of the other complaints recorded were:

Medical Log for the *Barossa* for November 1841, (selected entries)

Thomas Hunt, aged 19, convict; disease or hurt, homorrhoide; dates on sick list, 1–6 Nov. 1841; relieved.

Joseph Eckersly, aged 27, convict; disease or hurt, dyspepsia; dates on sick list, 4–9 Nov. 1841; cured. *Dyspepsia=Gastritis.*

William Jones, aged 26, convict; disease or hurt, sycosis menti; dates on sick list, 5–19 Nov. 1841; cured. *Sycosis menti=Eczema.*

Abraham Baker, aged 19, convict; disease or hurt, scorbutus; dates on sick list, 5–21 Nov. 1841; cured. *Scorbutus=Scurvy.*

Thomas Baker, aged 47, convict; disease or hurt, lichen livid; dates on sick list, 5–30 Nov. 1841; relieved. *Lichen Livid=Dermatitis.*

Samuel Staples, aged 53, convict, disease or hurt, eneurisis; dates on sick list, 5–11 Nov. 1841; relieved. *Eneurisis=Bedwetting, incontinence.*

Robert Strandring, aged 43, convict; disease or hurt, catarrhus; dates on sick list, 6–8 Nov. 1841; cured.

William Lewing, aged 23, soldier; disease or hurt, cynanche tonsil; dates on sick list, 9–11 Nov. 1841; cured.

George Sayers, aged 24, convict; disease or hurt, herpes circin; dates on sick list, 9–18 Nov. 1841; cured.

Thomas Griffiths, aged 45, convict; disease or hurt, erisipelas; dates on sick list, 9–18 Nov. 1841; cured. *Erysipelas=Inflammatory disease, generally in the face marked by a bright redness of the skin.*

Michael McDermott, aged 33, convict; disease or hurt, phlegmon; dates on sick list, 9–11 Nov. 1841; cured. *Phlegmon=Inflamation of Phlegm.*

Elijah Hinchcliffe, aged 23, convict; disease or hurt, purigo; dates on sick list, 9–17 Nov. 1841; cured.

Charles Skine, aged 18, convict; disease or hurt, nyctalopia; dates on sick list, 9–16 Nov. 1841; cured. *Nyctalopia=Night blindness or impaired vision in the dark, probably brought on by being under decks for so long.*

William Bray, aged 20, convict; disease or hurt, opthalmia; dates on sick list, 10 Nov.–4 Dec. 1841; cured. *Opthalmia=Cunjunctivitas.*

George Lewis, aged 19, convict; disease or hurt, diarrhoa; dates on sick list, 13–15 Nov. 1841; cured.

Robert Gorie, aged 28, convict; disease or hurt, rheumatism; dates on sick list, 15–21 Nov. 1841; cured.

John Thompson, aged 28, convict; disease or hurt, diarrhoa; dates on sick list, 19–22 Nov. 1841; cured.

Of the 350 prisoners transported (all male on this crossing) 348 made it to Van Diemon's Land. The crossing took 136 days. Three men died during the voyage, including two convicts, they were: Samuel Bumpton, Isaac Milburn and William Murray. Discrepancies between the number who embarked and disembarked were often due to deaths on board, transfers to other ships en route, or landing at other ports.

In order to try and understand the new land that was to become Elijah's home and the challenges he might face we must now briefly examine the history of this part of Australia.

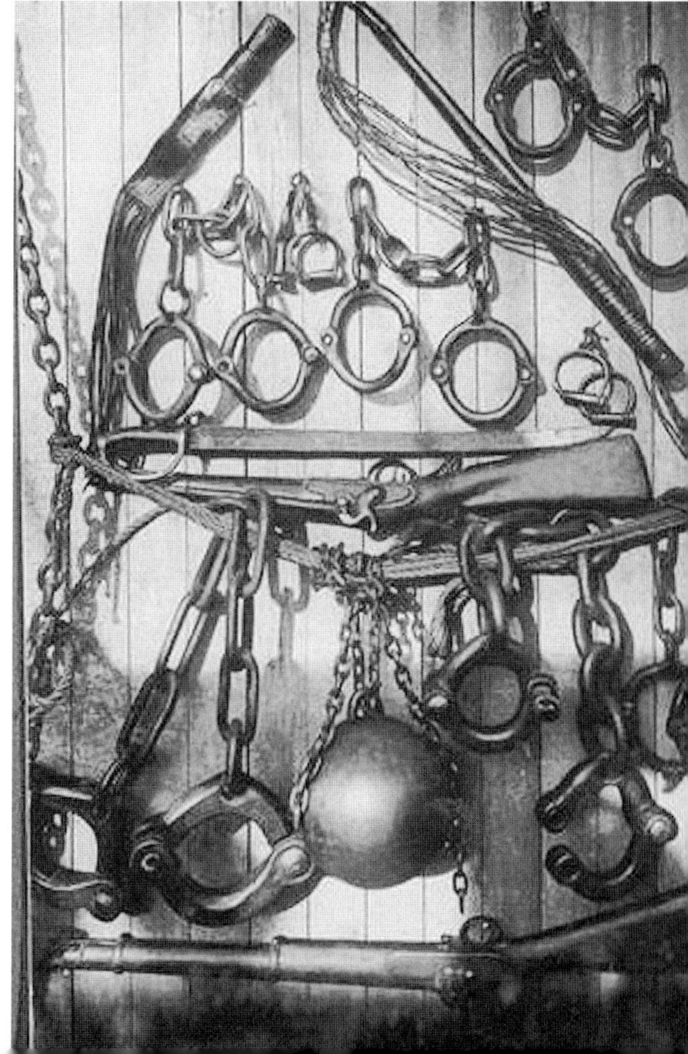

Relics of convict punishment and incarceration. (Courtesy of the Taylor Lib.)

Tasmania

Tasmania was named after Abel Janszoon Tasman, the great Dutch navigator-explorer, who landed in south-eastern Tasmania in early December 1642. He named the island Anthony Van Diemensland, which was later Anglicized to Van Diemen's Land.

Britain's colonisation of Tasmania was partly a ploy to ensure British dominance in international sea power. Both the government in London and its representative in New South Wales, Gov. Philip Gidley King, wanted to secure bases in the south. Accordingly, John Bowen established a camp at Risdon Cove on the Derwent River in September 1803. After the arrival in February 1804 of Lieutenant Governor David Collins (1804–10), following the failure of his colonisation venture at Port Phillip (Victoria), the settlement was relocated to Hobart. In November 1804 William Paterson founded a settlement in northern Tasmania, which soon had Launceston as its hub. This sub-colony was independent of Hobart until 1812.

The survival of the tiny settlements was precarious. Transported convicts always made up much of the European population at that time, and runaway convicts, many of whom became bandits of the rural regions, known as *bushrangers*, challenged formal authority. Scarcity of supplies prompted them to hunt kangaroos, which worsened relations with the Aboriginal population. Collins was passive as lieutenant governor, and his successor, Thomas Davey (1812–17), was certainly no more effective.

Thereafter rudiments of order emerged, first under Lieutenant Governor William Sorell (1817–24) and then under George Arthur (1824–36). Van Diemen's Land gained virtual independence from New South Wales in 1825, allowing fuller scope for Arthur's profound efficiency and determination. Subsequent lieutenant governors were the Arctic explorer-hero John Franklin(1837–43), the man in charge when Elijah Hinchcliffe arrived, Sir John Eardley-Wilmot (1843–46), and Sir William Thomas Denison (1847–54). All found their task difficult.

Tasmania enjoyed much economic prosperity between 1820 and 1840. During that period the European population increased from about 4,350 to more than 57,000. The colony's penal function brought in large sums from the British treasury. Free immigrants and some ex-convicts developed commerce and various resources. Raising sheep for wool advanced quickly from the mid-1820s, and suitable land in the island's eastern sector was soon occupied. Tasmanian entrepreneurs and pastoralists played a dominant role in opening Port Phillip from the mid-1830s. Locals also exploited adjacent seal and whale fisheries, encouraging the growth of shipbuilding and services to support these endeavours. International whalers made use of Hobart's superb harbour; it became a major port for whaling ships. Convict labour assisted in all this and in constructing public works and handsome buildings, in both urban and rural areas.

Indigenous Tasmanians bore the cost of all this economic development. Murderous encounters relating to the Risdon Cove settlement eventually degenerated into the Black War (1804–30), a period of great conflict between the Aboriginal population and European settlers. The hostility became especially intense during the 1820s, as pastoralists extended their dominion. In the Bass Strait seal hunting grounds, Aboriginal women, whose status was often that of semi-slaves, provided domestic and sexual services for the Europeans, and disease ravaged indigenous communities everywhere. Some consciences stirred, and Arthur appointed George Augustus Robinson to placate the surviving Aboriginal population. Consequently, from 1831 virtually all Aboriginal people (about 140 by that time) were relocated to Flinders Island in the Bass Strait in an effort to shield them from hostility on the Tasmanian mainland. Deaths continued, however, and in 1847 the survivors moved back to Tasmania. The last person believed to be of strictly Tasmanian descent, a woman by the name of Truganini, died in 1876.

The experience of convicts was also grim, even if it was rarely so terrible as that of the Aborigines. Altogether, at least 55,000 male and 13,000 female convicts came directly from Britain. Once in Tasmania, most of these offenders served their time in public or private employment, with punishment for misdemeanours. About 10 percent offended more seriously and suffered execution or servitude in the jail stations at Macquarie Harbour, Maria Island, and Port Arthur. After they gained their freedom, some former convicts faced hardship, while others led modest lives and yet others achieved material success.

During its life as a British penal colony, from 1803, 73,500 convicts were transported to the opposite side of the world for crimes ranging from minor misdemeanours to political activities. Life was harsh. Stories of solitary confinement or flogging with the infamous cat o' nine tails are common, the punishment cells, barely large enough to contain a single man, kept in the dark like a wild beast, survive to this day. At nearby Point Puer, boys from 9 to 18 years were housed in a jumble of barracks, workrooms and schoolrooms. The new arrivals were forced into labour gangs to do the hard physical work required to maintain the prison. Of the 38 boys who died there from 1834–1843, 22 were labourers. The boys were given classes in practical trades like joinery, boot-making, carpentry, nail-making and black-smithing. In 1844 alone, 34 brick-makers turned out 155,000 bricks. In the north west corner of the Tasman Peninsula, the ruins of prisoner barracks, solitary cells and a chapel are all that remain of a convict coal mine operated by up to 600 men at its peak. They worked underground in atrocious conditions on eight-hour shifts day and night. Though they toiled during the day under the eye of brutal overseers, they had little supervision at night and contributed to robberies that plagued early travellers. The desperate authorities in the early 1820s devised a method of banishing convicts turned bush-rangers, establishing a hell-hole on a barren island in the middle of the rough, unpredictable Macquarie Harbour, on the west coast. Hobart's docks were the disembarkation point for many chained convicts, who arrived to the noise and bustle of a crowded cluster of warehouses, rowdy taverns and maritime workshops.

These conditions were bad enough, but Elijah would have been made well aware of the consequences of any further serious misdemeanours committed by him.

Port Arthur

For those convicts who re-offended after their arrival at Hobart or for those regarded as the most violent the penal colony of Port Arthur awaited. Port Arthur was named after Van Diemen's Land lieutenant governor George Arthur. The settlement started as a timber station in 1830, but it is best known for being a penal colony.

From 1833, until the 1850s, it was the destination for the hardest of convicted British and Irish criminals, those who were secondary offenders having re-offended after their arrival in Australia. Rebellious personalities from other convict stations were also sent here, a quite undesirable punishment. In addition, Port Arthur had some of the strictest security measures of the British penal system.

The peninsula on which Port Arthur is located is a naturally secure site by being surrounded by water (rumoured by the administration to be shark-infested). The 30m wide isthmus of Eaglehawk Neck that was the only connection to the mainland was fenced and guarded by soldiers and half-starved dogs.

Contact between visiting seamen and prisoners was not allowed. Ships had to check in their sails and oars upon landing to prevent any escapes. However, many attempts were made, and some were successful. Boats were seized and rowed or sailed long distances to freedom.

Port Arthur was marketed as an inescapable prison, much like the later Alcatraz Island in the United States. Some prisoners were not discouraged by this, and tried to escape. One of the most infamous incidents, which was bizarre if nothing else, was the escape attempt of one George 'Billy' Hunt. Hunt disguised himself using a kangaroo hide and tried to flee across the Neck, but the half-starved guards on duty tried to shoot him to supplement their meagre rations. When he noticed them sighting him up, Hunt threw off his disguise and surrendered, receiving 150 lashes.

Despite its badge as a pioneer in the new nicer age of imprisonment, Port Arthur was still as harsh and brutal as other penal settlements. It has been suggested that its use of psychological punishment, compounded with no hope of escape, made it one of the worst. Some tales suggest that prisoners committed murder (an offence punishable by death) just to escape the desolation of life at the camp. The Island of the Dead was the destination for all who died inside the prison camps. Of the 1646 graves recorded to exist there, only 180, those of prison staff and military personnel, are marked. The prison closed in 1877.

Once the *Barossa* reached Hobart on 13 January 1842, after a passage of 136 days, Elijah would have been examined by the Registrar before he and all the other convicts could disembark. The Registrar was required to take an individual description and record the general character and conduct of each prisoner, during the voyage. The men were then classified according to their character and were required to report to the Director on all these points and assist him in naming the term of their probation. The term of the first period of probation was related to the original sentence according to the following scale:

> *7 years or under 10 – 2 years, 10 years or under 14 – 2½ years, 14 years or under 20 – 3 years, 20 years or less than life – 3 years, Life – 4 years.*

Because of the various accents and untruthful information given by the convicts, the details written down by the officials were quite often misleading or unintelligible.

Inspection of convicts upon their arrival in Hobart by the Governor. (Courtesy of the Taylor Lib.)

The following details were recorded by the Registrar about Elijah:

> *Description:*
> *Trade – weaver, height (without shoes) – 5ft 4, Age – 24, complexion – fresh, head – long, hair – light brown, whiskers – none, visage – round, forehead – medium, eyebrows – brown, eyes – dark hazel, nose – long, mouth – long, chin – long, native place – Cumberworth, Yorkshire, remarks – scar on right wrist, cross on left arm, blue mark on right arm.*

The entry for Esau Hastings follows directly after that of Elijah, suggesting that perhaps the two had remained close throughout the voyage, Esau was described thus:

> *Description:*
> *Trade – weaver, height (without shoes) – 5ft 3½, age – 22, complexion – fair, head – oval, hair – dark brown, whiskers – black, visage – long, forehead – medium, eyebrows – black, eyes – black, nose – long, thin, mouth – ?, chin ?, native place – Lancashire, remarks – small scar on forehead.*

Both were required to tell the registrar the nature of their crime, Elijah stated that his offence was:

> *Burglary and stealing clothes and also that he was once fined for drunkeness 5s.*

Esau stated that his offence was:

> *Housebreaking, into Mr Bryants (*Bryan in the Knutsford trial record*) property. I was caught on the premises.*

Further details regarding Esau are recorded. He was the son of John and Rose Hastings, his conduct during the voyage had been good and he was a weaver.

A general view of Hobart around the time that Elijah would have arrived here. (Courtesy of the Taylor Lib.)

Hobart harbour during the mid nineteenth century. (Courtesy of the Taylor Lib.)

Elijah's prison record states that he was a Protestant and could read and write. His gaol report during his time in Knutsford was unknown but he had been orderly during the voyage. The surgeons report regarding any new offences, his conduct and how he was employed simply says 'good'.

After arriving in Hobart, Elijah probably spent some weeks (or months?) in the prisoners' barracks, which were located in Campbell Street, Hobart. These barracks (later Campbell Street Gaol) dated from 1821 and were used to house newly arrived convicts waiting for assignment to settlers, work gangs or penal stations. (The buildings were demolished in 1963.) It was usual for convicts to be put to work in occupations that they were familiar with and as Elijah was recorded as both a labourer and a weaver then he would likely have been placed either on a farm or on a building project.

Soldiers leading a chain gang of prisoners to work.

His early years as a prisoner were not totally without incident. Entries recorded in his prison log recorded that:

20 September 1842 – misconduct at the works – reprimanded.
10 November 1842 – neglect of work and general idleness – 4 days solitary.

Interspersed with the latter, in March and October respectively were the comments good and orderly. Evidently Elijah ignored his warning and so paid the price but there are no further punishments listed, perhaps it was a case of a difficult first year in trying to adjust to his new life. One other item of note from the record tells us that Elijah obtained a ticket of leave on 16 February 1847 although no reason is given for this.

Elijah had obviously come to terms with his new life in Australia. Unless a convict was given an unconditional pardon, which was extremely rare, they were not allowed to return home to England when freed. Elijah was not destined to see any of his family again, including his wife, Martha. After a term of seven years separation from her the marriage was deemed to be legally over and they were both able to re-marry, something that Elijah duly did.

The last place mentioned on his convict record where he was noted to be working was Campbell Town, in the north of Tasmania. Campbell Town records reveal that Elijah, now aged 32 was married on 25 June 1849 to a Caroline Saunders (who was also known as Mayner or Mainer). Caroline was born in Birmingham and she too was (or had been), a convict, which may explain her differing surname. At this point Elijah was noted to be a free man, though in fact he was enjoying his parole, which had been granted on 15 May 1849. He had initially been recommended for a certificate of freedom on 14 March 1848. He had been a convict for over seven years but had achieved an early release, via his parole, which must attest to his good behaviour. He was finally released from his parole and made a free man on 23 July 1852. Only four years after his marriage, Van Diemen's Land ceased to be a penal colony.

Many former convicts made new lives in Australia after being released as with the case of one of Elijah's former inmates on the *Barossa*, Henry Sandland. Sandland, and a James Spark were indicted for breaking and entering a dwelling house on March 18th 1841, at St Martin-in-the-Fields, London and stealing two silver bottles. They were found guilty of theft and were sentenced to transportation to Australia for ten years. Henry was then aged 22 years. A copy of a Secretary of State paper in Whitehall, London states that Henry was in Australia and still alive on December 31st 1842. He died on the 15th October 1869 in the district of Brighton, Tasmania (formerly Van Diemen's Land) at the age of 47 years. But how much evidence has Elijah left for us to follow him?

Elijah and Caroline remained in Campbell Town for just over three years but two months after Elijah was officially made a free man they made the decision to move to Castlemaine, north of Melbourne, Victoria, and caught the ship *Belle Creole*, bound for Melbourne, on the 22 September 1852. We can speculate as to their reasons for doing this with some degree of accuracy. In 1851, Castlemaine was suddenly catapulted into the limelight.

In September, 1851, three shepherds and a bullock driver discovered gold in Specimen Gully, about 5km northeast of present day Castlemaine. Within a month the alluvial bed of Forrest Creek was being worked with 8000 miners on the field by the end of the year and 25,000 by March 1852. Castlemaine was briefly larger than Melbourne, as that city's population moved to Castlemaine to seek its fortune.

Tasmania, home to Elijah for 10 years. (Courtesy of the Taylor Lib.)

Elijah may have been forcibly removed from England but two brothers from Denby Dale left their home shores voluntarily to seek their fortune in Australia. James and Tedbar Wood set sail aboard the *Sultana* in April 1848 and arrived in Victoria in July, where they were joined later by their brother Edwin. Based in Geelong, just to the south west of Melbourne, they too took their opportunities in the gold rush at Castlemaine and were successful. It is possible that they may even have met Elijah and swapped tales from home, though as staunch Methodists they would have sternly disapproved of Elijah criminal background.

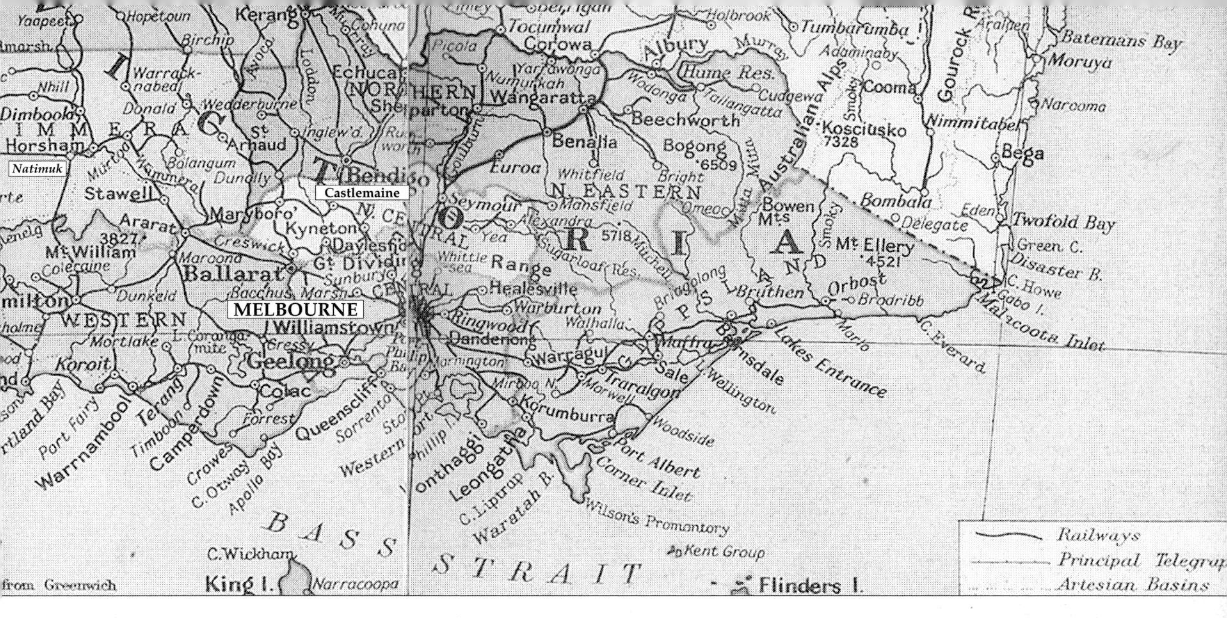

The state of Victoria, showing Melbourne, Castlemaine and Natimuk. (Courtesy of the Taylor Lib.)

Whilst living at Castlemaine, Elijah and Caroline had a son, John Thomas, in 1853, when they listed their religion as Presbyterian. This is the only child currently known to have been born to the couple. John Thomas grew up in Castlemaine and married Elizabeth Ellen O'Grady in the town in 1880. They presented Elijah with seven grandchildren, namely:

John Thomas (born about 1883), Lilly Maud (born about 1884, died aged 5 in 1889), Alice Violet (born about 1885, died aged 4 in 1889), Arthur (born about 1886, died aged 3 in 1889), Lilley Mary (born 1889), Lionel Arthur (born 1890), Leslie Elijah (born 1892) and Hilda May (born 1899).

The three infant deaths in 1889 were an appalling family tragedy and could have been due to the beginning of an influenza epidemic which ravaged the area in 1890–1891. There were, of course, a number of other possible causes, including dysentery and gastro-enteritis which were particularly prevalent in Melbourne at the time.

Of the other children, John Thomas (junior) died in 1941 aged 58 and was buried at Trentham Cemetary in Victoria. Leslie Elijah (named after his grandfather) served with the Anzacs during the First World War and was killed in action in France on 15 November 1916, probably on the British front line. The dreaded letter informing his parents of his death duly arrived and John Thomas requested that his sons *wristlet watch and writing wallet* be returned to the family. Lionel Arthur also fought during the First World War, he survived and married Mary Josine Rooney in Victoria in 1918.

Elijah lived a long life, he spent 57 years in Australia, until his death is recorded at the small country town of Gymbowen, to the west of Natimuk in Western Australia in 1899, aged 82. The only recorded death for a Caroline Hinchcliffe is recorded at Geelong Eastern Cemetary in 1876 and it seems likely that she predeceased Elijah by 23 years.

Elijah almost made it to the twentieth century, and what a tale he would have been able to tell to his grandchildren. Caught stealing, trial, hard labour, prison hulks, the voyage on the *Barossa*, solitary confinement, marriage, gold rush, the list goes on. What a fascinating Grandfather this Cumberworth born man, must have been.

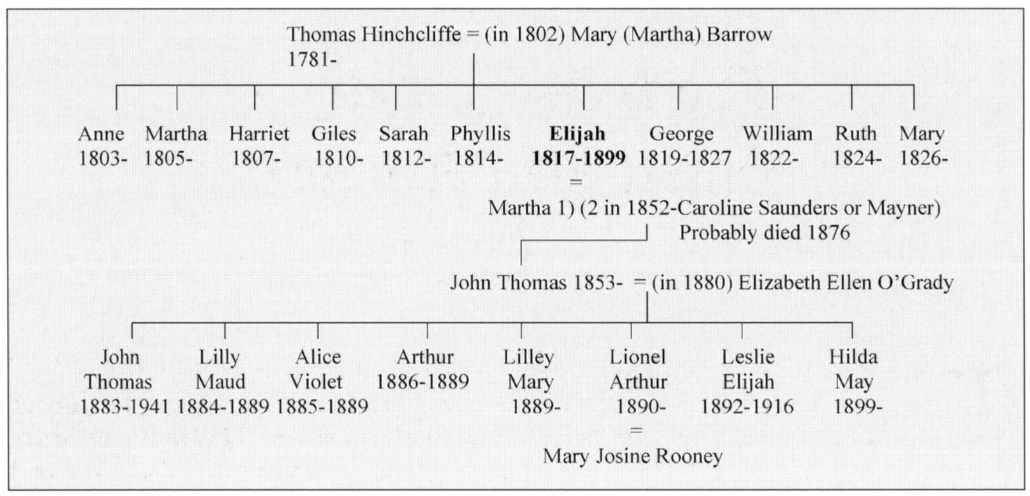
Thomas Hinchcliffe = (in 1802) Mary (Martha) Barrow
1781-
Anne 1803-
Martha 1805-
Harriet 1807-
Giles 1810-
Sarah 1812-
Phyllis 1814-
Elijah 1817-1899
George 1819-1827
William 1822-
Ruth 1824-
Mary 1826-
=
Martha 1) (2 in 1852-Caroline Saunders or Mayner)
Probably died 1876
John Thomas 1853- = (in 1880) Elizabeth Ellen O'Grady
John Thomas 1883-1941
Lilly Maud 1884-1889
Alice Violet 1885-1889
Arthur 1886-1889
Lilley Mary 1889-
Lionel Arthur 1890-
Leslie Elijah 1892-1916
Hilda May 1899-
=
Mary Josine Rooney

Chapter Five

The Kelso Family – Music Hall Artiste's

Three members of a family with the surname George, who originated in Westminster, London were to make their stage name KELSO popular throughout the North of England and further afield during the late nineteenth and early twentieth centuries. They toured with the fairgrounds and entertained at the towns and village feasts and then, once the season was over, they returned to base, which for William (Billy) Kelso, the oldest of three brothers, was eventually Denby Dale.

The name of Kelso has survived amongst the memories of many of the older residents in Denby Dale and district, usually accompanied by a smile or even a knowing laugh. Very few know anything more than the family name or perhaps the title of a play that the family performed, one in particular, *Maria Marten or Murder in the Red Barn*, which we shall return to later.

The fact that the family were travellers, from at least Easter to September, gave them the distinction of being considered to be *gypsy's*. The magnificent old touring caravan which once parked up in Norman Croft being further proof of this. The old prejudices that followed travellers around would have surfaced and suspicions been aroused as to the activities of these people as the more sedentary local families adjusted to their presence.

William Nicholas Henry George, who we will now refer to as William (Billy), was born on 10 July 1865 at 35 Castle Lane, Westminster to William Nicholas Frederick and Sophia George (formerly Blake). William N F George was noted to be a 'time keeper, traveller', which meant that he had found temporary work as the man responsible for ensuring the workers arrived and left on time at a business somewhere close by. I say temporary as the word *traveller* indicates that the lodgings they occupied were not a permanent address. The informant on William N H George's birth certificate was an E George, obviously a close relation so it may be that William and Sophia were lodging with a family member at the time of the birth of young William.

Sophia George, n'ee Blake, pictured before her death in 1886.

In Memoriam of
SOPHIA BLAKE,
THE BELOVED WIFE OF WILLIAM GEORGE,
WHO DIED AUGUST 10th 1886,
Aged 44 Years;
And was Interred at Salford Cemetery, Near Manchester,
August 13th.

A long time I was with pain opprest,
Which wore my strength away,
And made me wish for endless rest,
That never will decay.

"WE ALL DO FADE AS A LEAF."

Funeral card, commemorating Sophia George.

The smog-burdened streets of a London twenty years or so before the emergence of Jack the Ripper, coupled with poor sanitation and disease in the densely crowded city probably hastened the family's departure. By 1868, the couple had moved to Chatham in Kent where their second son, Henry was born. Sometime between 1868 and 1877, the family made their way north where the third son, Thomas was born, in Bradford. The family were still itinerant and by 1881 were living at 31 Hollingwood Street, Salford in Lancashire. We can finally catch up with them in the census returns for that year:

William George	38	London	Traveller (Commercial)
Sophia George	36	Lambeth	
William N George	17	London	Labourer in Mill (Cotton)
Henry George	13	Chatham	Scholar
Thomas George	4	Bradford	
Frederick George	2 months	Salford	

As we can see, William (Billy) George had taken up employment in the well-known Lancashire industry of cotton weaving but he had different dreams and aspirations to this! Between 1881 and 1885 he had changed his life and his career.

He married a woman we know only as Rebecca Ada at Bishop Auckland on 5 January 1885 and just under nine months later the couple had a child, William on 1 October 1885 at Manse Place, Airdrie, unfortunately, William (who became known as Willie) was dumb from birth. William (Billy) was still moving around the British Isles. On the birth certificate of Willie, William (Billy) George was recorded as being a *variety artist*. This more than adequately explains his constant changes of address, but exactly what did he mean when he described himself as such and where did he get the motivation from?

William (Billy) married twice, a subject we shall return to later, but of importance here was the profession of his father noted on his second wedding certificate. William N F George was noted to be a music hall artiste. Finally we begin to understand the reason for the constantly changing towns recorded in the baptisms of his and Sophia's children, they followed the feasts and fairs around Britain and their children were born in caravans on the show grounds where they worked. William (Billy) was simply following in the footsteps of his parents.

Feasts and fairs were a popular form of mass entertainment during the nineteenth century. During the earlier years these might take the form of booths and side-shows featuring fortune tellers, Punch and Judy, waxwork imitations, freak shows, jugglers, illusionists, peep shows and fire-eaters. Refreshments would have included hot peas, gingerbread and nuts. There may have been the odd fairground ride, such as a swing boat or a merry-go-round which relied on horsepower, but these were less common. The boxing booth, shooting galleries, roll-a-penny and later on, slot machines accompanied some or all of the above, depending upon the size of the fair of feast. The advent of steam power saw a revolution in feast and fairground entertainment, beginning around the 1860s, and rides powered by steam engines saw ever more dynamic and exciting attractions created. From the 1890s steam powered musical organs added to the noise of the occasion, providing music for the rides and some of the side shows. It was during this period that the bioscope or cinematograph shows were introduced, these early films had no soundtrack but were accompanied by sound effects to give them more impact. The *Barnsley Chronicle* recalls the Scissett Feast of 1872:

> *13 July 1872*
> *Scissett Feast*
> *The annual feast at Scissett was held on Monday and Tuesday, on both of which days the village presented a very animated appearance. There was a good deal of attraction. The road near to the house of Mr J Schofield, the Crown Inn, was crowded with stalls and c. A field in the rear of the house was also well stocked with steam merry-go-rounds, pea booths and shooting galleries, which did a 'roaring trade' on both days.*

Added to all this was the travelling theatre. Up until the mid nineteenth century religious critics of the time regarded such entertainment as morally harmful and the authorities had used this excuse as a cover in order to be able to suppress potential political propaganda. Therefore, theatre shows were only permitted by the issue of a licence by the Lord Chamberlain's Office. From the mid nineteenth century constraints began to be eased and the travelling theatre became a feature of feast and fairground sites. This *rag and stick* theatre as it was affectionately known, grew in popularity and the spicy melodramas portrayed were always well attended. Occasionally these theatres were so popular that they stayed long after the annual feast had moved on, even into the close of season period when the company usually returned home.

Like his father, William (Billy) became involved with the travelling theatre, though he was by no means limited to melodramas. More often than not he described himself as a comedian and this versatility would have lent his acting and his ability to communicate with the audience further quality. He did not, however, perform under his own name, the William part of it was simply shortened to Will or Billy but his stage name now became *Kelso*.

He was joined in the family act by his brothers, Henry and Thomas, the act being named, the Kelso Brothers, the company being the *Kelso Empire Portable Theatre.*

Portable theatres were large tarpaulin tents, rectangular with a stage, gallery, seating, along with heating and lighting. They could be assembled and dismantled easily. The performers involved would have had to find lodgings locally each time the theatre moved on, but William (Billy) Kelso and his family would have stayed in the comfort of his own luxurious caravan. Throughout the summer season they would have followed the village feasts and fairs but in winter they would have erected the theatre more permanently and endeavoured to obtain a licence to perform in the town or village for as long as possible.

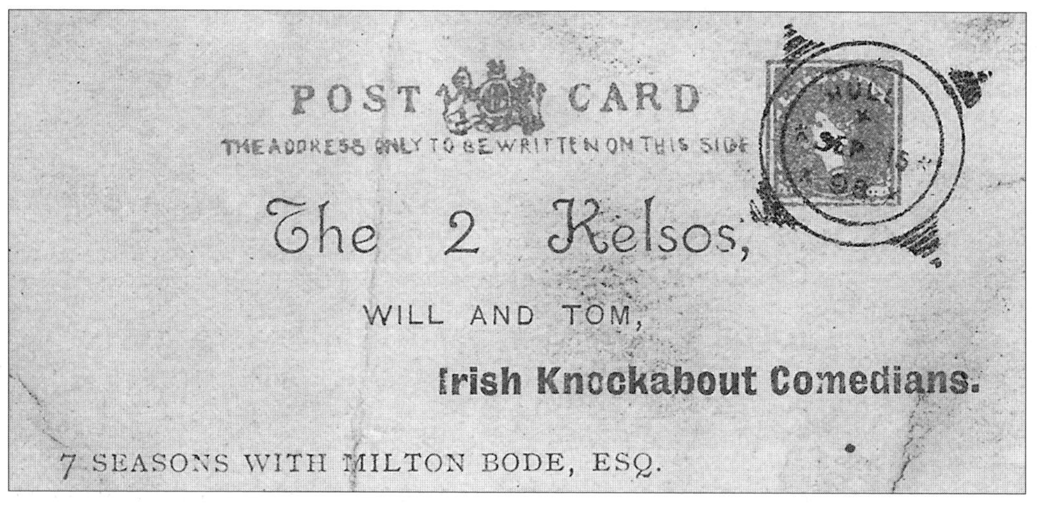

Postcard advertising the 2 Kelsos and their association with Milton Bode, dated 15 September 1898.

As people had little leisure time or disposable income the theatre had to come to them and although the performers did not become wealthy or famous they brightened the lives of Britain's lower class work force. If a show was proving particularly popular it could prove tempting to perform right up to the termination of the licence. It was not unknown for the manager to have to apply urgently for a new one in order to have enough time to take down the stage and tent.

William (Billy) and Rebecca Ada, whom he had almost certainly met through his travels with the portable theatre had two more children besides Willie, they were Frank and Harry. On 16 September 1896, they had set up the theatre in the market place at Batley, other applications for licenses included the places: Penistone, Thurlstone, Farsley, Lowmoor, Skelmanthorpe, Chapeltown, Hemsworth, Slaithwaite, Hightown, Liversedge, Ossett, Clayton West and Cleckheaton. We can also find Billy working with his brother, Tom, in 1898 from a postcard which advertised their act. *The Two Kelso's – Will and Tom – Irish Knockabout Comedians*, the postcard is dated 15 September and is stamped with the Hull post-mark.

William Billy Kelso, circa late nineteenth century.

The postcard also advertises the fact that the pair had spent seven seasons with Milton Bode although it does not say where. This was obviously something that the brothers were extremely proud of and was of use in gaining further employment. Another business card, this time for Billy Kelso alone exists and it is possible that it dates to the following year, 1899. On the card Billy calls himself a comedian and stage manager and the legend now reads *8 seasons with Milton Bode.* If this is correct then Billy Kelso at least, probably along with Tom, spent a season each year, on stage as a comedian, working at a theatre, owned by Milton Bode, from 1891 when he was 26 years old to 1899 when he was 34.

Theatre mogul and impresario Milton Bode, born in 1860 in Birmingham, reputedly ran away from school and joined a travelling circus. He had become an actor by 1886 and managed his first stage production, of *The Count of Monte Cristo* in 1887. He later became the owner of numerous theatres and achieved notoriety for his productions of plays and pantomimes. He employed some of the most famous comedians and actors of the day, including Dan Leno in 1898 and Charles Chaplin in 1903. In 1900 he leased the Theatre Royal at Huddersfield with Edward Compton but sold it on in 1918 to Alfred Wareing. Milton Bode died of heart failure in 1938.

From the latter we can be sure that the theatre in question was not Huddersfield, but it could have been at Bristol, Carlisle, Wolverhampton, Bath, Reading, Cheltenham, Birmingham or Glasgow.

Shortly before 1905, Rebecca Ada died, but it wasn't long before William (Billy) re-married, to music hall artiste, Minnie Hayes.

Minnie Hayes was born in 1873, the daughter of Richard Salt (a mechanic) and was a widow when she married Billy on 10 March 1905, when they both recorded themselves as music hall artistes. At the time they were living at the same address, 50 Ashton Terrace, Teall Street, Wakefield. Minnie performed under a stage name and although she now became Minnie George, her publicity photographs all bear the name Minnie Parker. The couple began a family with the birth of twins, Albert and Minnie, who were born 6 August 1906 at the feast ground in Shelf. The information on their birth certificates was provided on 14 September by Minnie though by now the family had moved on to the feast ground at Wyke near Bradford. Minnie was a fine singer and actress in her own right and the frequently updated publicity photographs of her in costume attest to her versatility. Living out of a caravan with her family would not have been an easy existence and being pregnant and giving birth during a life on the road must have been uncomfortable at times to say the least. It is also likely that she would have had the skills to make and mend costumes and was probably a trustworthy cashier. As the young family grew up they would have been employed in selling tickets and refreshments as a sideline. By around 1910, Billy Kelso had formed and marketed a double act with his son, Frank. Named *Keith and Kelso,* for reasons unknown, there are numerous publicity photographs still in

Minnie Parker, circa late nineteenth century.

Publicity photographs of Minnie Parker in various costumes, all circa 1900–1910.

Publicity shots of Minnie Parker in various costumes, all circa 1900–1910.

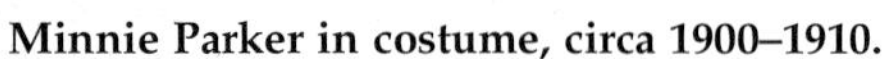

Minnie Parker in costume, circa 1900–1910.

As this photograph states, Mrs W Kelso, a portrait of Minnie, for once not in costume, circa 1910.

Frank Kelso (centre), with his step brothers, Albert and Alfred, circa 1916.

The autograph of Minnie Parker.

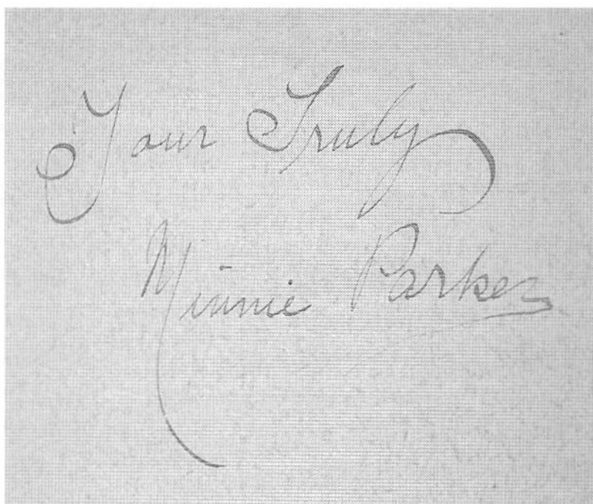

Publicity stills of *Keith and Kelso* performing, aka William (Billy) and Frank Kelso, circa 1910.

Keith and Kelso, **publicity still, circa 1910.**

William (Billy) Kelso seated, with his son, Frank, the postcard is marked *Keith and Kelso*, circa 1910.

existence of the pair in costume and wearing heavy makeup. Thankfully one of the pictures bearing their names is identical to one marked Keith and Kelso.

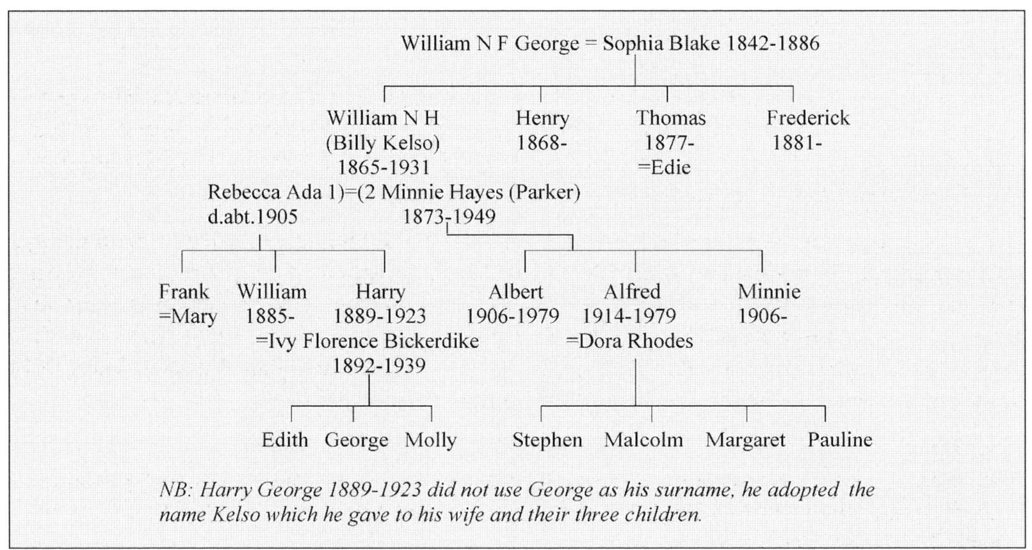

The Kelso brothers did not perform alone and regularly advertised in *The Stage* newspaper for other artistes to join them. *The Stage* was a nationally available monthly paper which covered all the disciplines in the entertainment industry but was primarily involved with the theatre. It was founded in 1880 at 3d for 12 pages but became weekly in 1881. The paper continues today as the bible for anyone working in television, films, theatre and suchlike. Actors in portable theatre companies would regularly be paid out of a share of the takings but the following adverts make no mistake about the potential earnings for suitable candidates.

17 January 1901
Wanted, company of dramatic and variety artistes, also pianist, for Portable Theatre. To open shortly. Address, H Kelso, Bijou Theatre, West Melton, near Rotherham.

24 January 1901
Wanted for portable (Melton Mowbray) to open February 11th, few good responsible people. New management. Harry Kelso, Bijou Theatre, West Melton near Rotherham.

It would seem that the brothers had gone their separate ways by this time. These two advertisements are the last we hear of Henry Kelso. It is possible that he died during his early 30's though it may be that he simply lost touch with his family.

28 August 1902
Wanted, for Portable Variety Theatre, a young, useful lady. Must do turn. Lowest terms, etc. W Kelso, Varieties Feast Ground, Cleckheaton.

23 July 1903
Wanted for portable varieties, a smart young violinist. Must read at sight. Open Friday, July 24th. Will Kelso, Varieties, Feast Ground, Dewsbury.

24 September 1903
Wanted, ladies and gents in all lines; pianist, violinist, scenic artist. Must open at once. Money sure. Write, T Kelso, theatre, Meltham.

24 September 1903
Wanted, for first class portable theatre, gent for lead, gent for juveniles, and responsible couple, capable of turns preferred to study and gag. Must open Monday next. No fares to people unknown. This is not a Ghost Show. Old friends write. Lowest terms, etc., to the original William Kelso's Empire Theatre, Honley.

The latter appears to be even more evidence that the brothers had gone their separate ways by this time. Billy Kelso is calling his theatre the *original* in a similar manner to some modern day pop bands that have split due to personal and performing differences and have restarted with new musicians. We do not know how long the three Kelso brothers performed together on a regular basis, but it would appear that Tom Kelso had certainly been running his own shows prior to 1903, and Henry prior to 1901.

17 September 1903
Wanted, leading lady and gent, lady and gent for juveniles, gent for heavies and producer. Useful people and pianist write. All must have wardrobe and be attentive to business. Write or wire, Tom Kelso, the Founder of the Original Theatre, Meltham.

On 22 October 1903, Tom placed an advertisement in *The Stage*, stating that, due to ill health he was trying to sell his portable theatre, *everything new, playing to good business.* He was based in Skelmanthorpe at this time. A week later he placed another advert in order to sell *a*

A postcard advertising Tom Kelsos latest production, dating to around 1903.

duck canvas tilt, length 66ft. over all 41ft., nearly knew, cheap for cash. Tom was at this time only 26 years old and whatever his illness was, it was not life threatening. The fact that the portable theatre was almost brand new suggests something happened suddenly in Tom's life which caused him to abandon his immediate plans. It is unknown as to whether there was any acrimony between the brothers, but the fact that both were advertising themselves as the *Original Theatre* is highly suggestive.

The adverts in *The Stage* continued but were now placed by William (Billy) Kelso alone:

1st June 1905
Wanted, for portable variety theatre, a young useful couple for dramatic and variety business; also a young violinist, to read at sight, also an honest girl as servant and a smart lad to look after organ and lamps. Lowest summer terms. Long engagement. W Kelso, Birstall, near Leeds.

8 October 1908
Wanted, for Will Kelso's New Portable, a young leading man, with turn and wardrobe. Will Kelso, Theatre, Catcliffe, Rotherham.

18 August 1910
Wanted, a young responsible gent, with turn. A good shop to good steady man, people been with me before wire. Will Kelso, Portable Theatre, Delph, near Oldham.

Some of the performers who worked with the Kelsos over the years. Clockwise from the top left, Norman de Vere, W H Irving *'The Yorkshire Lad'*, Gertrude Elliott and Jessie Brentwood.

Little Hatch, a take-off of the world famous Little Titch, who also worked with the Kelsos.

The adverts regularly request previous performers to apply and the George family photographic archive is littered with signed postcards of some of these people, including Little Hatch (a take-off of the world famous Little Tich), Jessie Brentwood, Rici Millar, Gertude Elliott and Norman de Vere.

The beginning of the First World War saw feasts and fairs closed down between 1916 and 1919 by order of the government. Showmen's engines and horses were sequestered for active service and many actors joined up to fight. In addition to this, feasts were felt to be inappropriate, given the circumstances of the war and the huge slaughter involved. Somehow William (Billy), now 51, and too old to fight, and Minnie continued to entertain a populace, many of whom were overburdened with emotion and grief. There may have been no feasts or fairs but the Portable Theatre continued.

In 1916, the Kelso Empire Portable Theatre travelled to South Kirkby, Birdwell, Askern, Great Houghton, Cudworth, Shafton and Thurnscoe. They also stayed at Kirkburton, in Dean Field but the district council had a problem with the sanitation of the site and the Kelsos made out an application to move to Honley Paladium. All these locations are within a relatively small and localised area. The lives and characters of the people being entertained would have been generally similar. It would seem that the Kelsos were slowing down somewhat and not travelling so far afield.

In 1917, they performed in April at Scissett Feast, this was followed with stays at Slaithwaite, Marsden, Holmfirth, Kirkburton, Clayton West and Denby Dale. On 3 July 1917, they made an application to move to Denby Dale and this would appear to be when the family finally settled down at Robinson's Croft, later, Norman Croft, opposite the *Prospect*

The stylish caravan that William (Billy) and Minnie Kelso and their family called home during the early twentieth century.

Hotel, just off Wakefield Road. This caused some controversy in the village, not regarding the site, but about the very presence of a Portable Theatre and its owners being in the village for the long term! William (Billy) and Minnie rented the croft and lived in their caravan on the land. There were also two cottages and one house (all now demolished) on the site. The Robinson family lived in the house and Amanda Robinson and the Waddington family occupied the two cottages. This is how the croft was once known as Robinson's Croft, rather than the more familiar Norman Croft of later years. William (Billy), now 52 years old, had finally hung up his coat at a permanent location, though the Kelso's still toured throughout the summer and performed locally in Winter.

Inside the ornate touring caravan.

Roninsons Croft, later Norman Croft, in the shadow of the viaduct, where the Kelsos finally settled in 1917. Note the cottages that have long since been demolished, the barn, now also demolished and the two caravans in the yard. Circa 1917.

Wakefield Road, Denby Dale. The entrance to Norman Croft is just before the gas lamp in the centre of the photograph. Circa 1930s.

The Croft, just behind the Kelso family home.

On 17 October 1917, William (Billy) Kelso was reported to the Chief Constable for putting on shows of an immoral nature. He had set up the theatre at the Scissett feast ground, behind the *Crown Inn*. A plain-clothes officer was despatched to attend the show and report back his findings. The officer was satisfied that the show itself was of a good and wholesome nature but it was also noted that two of the female performers employed by William (Billy) were supplementing their income by taking local men into a nearby dye-house and accepting money for their favours. The two women were fired immediately upon discovery. There had been opposition and prejudice directed towards the company of travelling theatres since their conception, particularly towards the actresses. On occasion, the church would rouse itself and hold an open air service outside the theatre in order to aid the sinners inside. The fact that portable theatres, unlike the permanent ones, did not pay any rates, may also have been a problem.

The advertisements placed in *The Stage* from 29 March until June 1917 were all made whilst the family were based at Scissett. On 27 September 1917 they were asking for performers to join them at Denby Dale:

> *Wanted, Lady for male parts. Wardrobe found and smart chambermaid used to six pieces weekly. Open Monday. Lowest etc. Will Kelso, Portable Theatre, Denby Dale.*

So far, we have followed the Kelsos from feast ground to winter pitch, we have noted some of the family partnerships and we have seen how they advertised for performers to act or sing in their shows. We also know that William (Billy) provided the laughs expected of a comedian, which would have warmed up the audience for the main event. The one thing we have not touched upon is the nature or titles of the melodramas they performed. Oral tradition remembers that they put on a performance of *The Man in the Iron Mask*. It is also interesting to note that Willie, the son of William (Billy), dumb from birth, also worked on stage, in a play which had a part specifically written for a dumb person, unfortunately the name of the part and play are long forgotten.

One particular melodrama associated with William (Billy) and Minnie Kelso, and still remembered by the older inhabitants of the district was based on a real life tragedy. To try and understand the type of play that the Kelsos would perform and the scope and content, not to say, popularity, we must examine the original tale in some detail, then we might imagine the play being performed at Norman Croft, Denby Dale, on a cold winter's night.

Maria Marten or *Murder in the Red Barn*

Maria Marten, the 26-year-old daughter of mole catcher, Thomas Marten of Polstead, Suffolk, had begun an adulterous relationship in 1826 with William Corder (born 1803), the son of John Corder, a yeoman farmer. Maria already had a son by Peter Mathews. William Corder was short but muscular but was known to be a liar and a cheat. He and Maria conceived a child (which was destined to die as an infant) and upon the insistence of Maria's parents the couple agreed to marry. On 18 May 1827 Corder had arranged that Maria would meet him at the building on the family farm known as the *Red Barn* from which they would travel to Ipswich by horse and gig to be married. At Corder's request, Maria went dressed as a man to avoid any unwanted notice.

Several months passed and the Marten family had heard nothing from Maria and could not understand how she could leave her young son for so long. Corder was still in touch with the family though his explanations regarding his 'wife' were always vague and improbable but he kept up the pretence of the marriage by stating that she was well and happy. Eventually, Thomas Marten was prevailed upon by his wife to make a search in the *Red Barn*, and along with a friend he began his investigation, prodding the floor with his mole spud. Upon finding a patch of soft earth he dug out around 18 inches and discovered a body stuffed into a sack. Maria's decomposing corpse was recognised by her sister, Ann, from a broken tooth, her hair, clothing and belongings.

The later surgeon's report stated that murder had been caused by a sharp instrument being plunged through the orbit of the eye into the brain.

Shortly after the discovery, William Corder was tracked down in London, where he had married (to a woman he had known for only three weeks, whom he had met through an advertising agency) and begun a new life running a boarding house for females with his wife. He was taken to Polstead for the inquest and sent to Bury St. Edmonds to stand trial. On being caught, Corder was found to be in possession of a passport from the French Ambassador and seems to have been about to leave the country, he was also found to have two pistols, powder and shot, bought, apparently, on the day of the murder. The trial took place on 7 and 8 August 1828 though before this his wife had believed that her husband was being put on trial for bigamy. He protested his innocence to the murder but was duly found guilty and was sentenced to death by hanging, his body to be anatomised. Just prior to the sentence being carried out, Corder confessed, he said that he and Maria had quarrelled about the burial of their child and other matters. A scuffle broke out between them and he took his pistol from his jacket pocket and fired, Maria fell dead. He denied that he had stabbed her, though many at the time thought this to be only a partial confession. He appears to have killed her in order to keep secret an unknown previous offence.

Corder was executed on 11 August at the County Gaol in Bury St Edmonds in front of thousands of spectators as by now the story had become national. His body was cut open and laid out on show whereupon thousands of people filed past to view it before final dissection. The surgeon in charge later had an account of the trial bound in leather made from Corder's skin.

After the trial doubts were raised about Corder's guilt, in particular Maria's stepmother fell under suspicion as she was only a year older than Maria and it was suggested that she and Corder had been having an affair.

The story had provoked numerous articles in newspapers and songs. Plays had begun to be performed whilst Corder was awaiting trial and along with tales of highwayman and suchlike, the story was popular for *penny gaffs*, cheap plays, performed in the back rooms of public houses. The excitement surrounding the affair led to many dramatic embellishments being added to the tale. The *Red Barn* itself was torn to pieces by eager souvenir hunters and what was left standing eventually burnt down in 1842, even Maria's gravestone was chipped away to nothing. As an interesting aside, the *Red Barn*, or site of it, is currently the home of Baroness Rendell of Babergh, better known as crime writer Ruth Rendell.

Interest in the case did not fade away and the story became the most performed play of the nineteenth century.

William (Billy) Kelso would have played William Corder as an older man and a cold blooded monster and Minnie Parker the innocent he preyed upon, her reputation and children by other fathers washed over. It was said within the Kelso family that Billy murdered his wife more than two hundred times.

A sentimental ballad composed soon after Corder's execution is likely to have been included in the performance of the play and sung by William (Billy).

Murder of Maria Marten

or

Confession and Execution of William Corder:
The Murderer of Maria Marten

(originally published by Catnach Press Ballads, 1828)

Come all you thoughtless young men, a warning take by me,
And think upon my unhappy fate to be hanged upon a tree;
My name is William Corder, to you I do declare,
I courted Maria Marten, most beautiful and fair.
I promised I would marry her upon a certain day,
Instead of that I was resolved to take her life away.
I went into her father's house the 18th day of May,
Saying, 'My dear Maria, we will fix the wedding day.
If you will meet me at the Red Barn, as sure as I have life,
I will take you to Ipswich town, and there make you my wife.'
I then went home and fetched my gun, my pickkaxe and my spade,

I went into the Red Barn, and there I dug her grave.
With heart so light, she thought no harm to meet me she did go,
I murdered her all in the Barn and laid her body low;
After the horrid deed was done, she lay weltering in her gore,
Her bleeding, mangled body I buried under the Red Barn floor.
Now all things being silent, her spirit could not rest,
She appeared unto her mother, who suckled her at her breast;
For many a long month or more, her mind being sore oppress'd,
Neither night nor day she could not take any rest.
Her mother's mind, being so disturbed, she dreamt three nights o'er,
Her daughter she lay murdered beneath the Red Barn floor;
She sent the father to the barn when he the ground did thrust,
And there he found his daughter mingling with the dust.
My trial is hard, I could not stand, most woeful was the sight,
When her jaw-bone was brought to prove which pierced my heart quite;
Her aged father standing by, likewise his loving wife,
And in her grief her hair she tore, she scarcely could keep life.
Adieu, adieu, my loving friends, my glass is almost run,
On Monday next will be my last, when I am to be hang'd;
So you young men who do pass by, with pity look on me,
For murdering Maria Marten I was hanged upon the tree.

Mickie Kelso, circa 1920.

The latter is but one example of what must have been a much larger repertoire performed by the Kelsos, but it is, perhaps, as near as we can get to the flavour of one of their shows.

William (Billy), Minnie and Tom were not the only Kelso's in the business as shown by the survival of a photograph of Mickie Kelso who signed herself as the niece of William (Billy). Mickie was most likely the daughter of Tom, or possibly Henry. Mickie also advertised in *The Stage* magazine:

> *12 August 1920 – Wanted, to open Monday 27th, good joint couple for change nightly stock. Turn preferred. Well up in farces and used to gagging. Mickie Kelso, Seham House, Mexborough.*

The licence applications by William (Billy), for performances continue until 1925, for instance, in 1918 the Kelsos were at Dean Field in Denby, in

1922 they were at Kirkburton, in 1923 at Emley show ground and later, New Mill show ground. But, times were changing and the British public were now embracing a new, more exotic form of mass entertainment. The bioscopes and cinematographs had now been superseded by motion pictures, and television was around the corner which would gradually become available to the masses. The final application for a licence to perform was made in 1925 and included Denby Dale, Skelmanthorpe, Scissett and New Mill. The listing of Skelmanthorpe is interesting as the village had its own theatre from 1913/14. The Palace was home to variety/novelty acts, and plays up until 1934 when it was replaced by the Savoy Picture House. The Kelsos were in direct competition with a permanent establishment and one has to assume some gnashing of teeth.

Some travelling shows lingered on but their heyday was long past and for the Kelso family it was time to call it a day. William (Billy) was, by now, 60 years old, his wife, Minnie was 52.

William (Billy) Kelso died on 4 March 1931 at Storthes Hall Mental Hospital aged 65. His death certificate noted that he lived at Norman Croft, Denby Dale and was a retired comedian. Minnie received a letter from her brother in law, Tom Kelso, which was dated a day later:

37 Brighton Terrace, Brixton, London, SW9 March 5th 1931.

Dear Minnie,

Your mine to hand. It is with the deepest regret and sorry, that we hear of the passing away of our brother and your husband, William. You have our united and sincere sympathy in your sad bereavement, God Rest his Soul.

We are more than sorry that we cannot come to Denby Dale, owing to the fact that we have just lost almost all our money through taking shows on tour. We sincerely hope that you will bear up under these most trying circumstances. We would be pleased to hear from you later on.

Your affectionate Brother and Sister

Tom and Edie Kelso

Evidently Tom had returned to London believing that the pickings here would be much richer and was sadly disappointed. It is possible that he travelled here soon after selling his portable theatre in 1903, leaving the field clear for his elder brother in the north whilst he touted for work in the more affluent south.

William (Billy) was predeceased in 1923 by his son, Harry, who was born Harry George but adopted his families stage name for the rest of his life. His wife, Ivy Florence, and their three children all inherited the surname of Kelso. Harry had opened a shop on Church Street in Honley

Harry Kelso, youngest son of William (Billy) Kelso's three sons by his first wife, circa 1920. Harry stands outside his shop on Church Street in Honley.

selling tobacco, sweets and suchlike; and the name on the signboard above the shop was H Kelso.

Minnie George (Parker) outlived her husband by eighteen years. Her travelling days were over and after his death she left Norman Croft and moved to a property on Norman Road and it is likely that the ornate old touring caravan was disposed of at this time. For pleasure she would frequent the *Prospect Hotel* across the road and no doubt, on occasion, she would have been pressed into a song. One of the last photographs of her, shows her outside the *Prospect Hotel* wearing a top hat and tails, very much the ringmaster. The event may have been the celebrations held in the village to mark the end of World War Two and if so, it is fitting that Minnie took a part in them. Minnie died on Boxing Day 1949 aged 76. The informant on the death certificate was her son, Alfred George who was noted to be living with his family at Wood Nook at the time. He moved from here in 1951 but did not go far, only the short distance to Dearnside Road.

The last picture of Minnie Parker, outside the Prospect Hotel. Dressed in top hat and tails, she looks the perfect ringmaster, circa 1945.

A studio portrait of Albert George, circa 1925.

Albert George at the wheel of his car, circa 1940s.

Frank and Albert George had by this time set up another business known as the Kelso Brothers, but this one had nothing to do with variety and performing. We have already noted that Frank was one half of the double act, Keith and Kelso and it is known that his brothers Harry and Willie were also involved with the portable theatre. William (Billy's) elder children by Minnie Parker may have had some small involvement but Albert and Minnie were only 19 when their parents retired. We know that Alfred sold refreshments such as peanuts and fishcakes at the shows but as he would only have been a teenager when the decision was taken to stop performing he never got the chance to get involved and eventually found employment at Kenyon's weaving mill.

Albert, by 1931, had found work at T B & H Firth, a Denby Dale haulage contractor but disillusioned with this he and his elder half brother, Frank began a food dealers business run from a warehouse at the site of the family home in Norman Croft. First registered on 17 July 1936, the bulk of the business involved delivering orders by way of two, liveried, company lorries. Of course they also sold goods to any customers who visited the Croft. During the dark years of the Second World War, just like any other retailer of groceries,

Kelso Brothers license to sell food from their mobile premises, 24 October 1939, less than two months after Britain had declared war on Germany.

Licence No. 337

FOOD CONTROL

LICENCE TO TRADE IN FOODSTUFFS BY RETAIL.

The Food Control Committee for the district of

KIRKBURTON

hereby license

Kelso Bros

as a Retail Dealer in

Fruit (Fresh Tinned) Vegetables (Fresh Tinned) Chocolate Cream (Canned) Potatoes Rabbits Fish (Fresh Tinned)

in respect of the business carried on at

Mobile Premises - Delivery Vans

Signed on behalf of the Food Control Committee

Signature [signature]

Date 24 OCT 1939

10/39—[7731] 32461/4074 200m 10/39 4039 G & S 704

License by the Ministry of Food to Frank and Albert Kelso, February 1942. Note the lines through the various items listed which were scarce or subject to rationing.

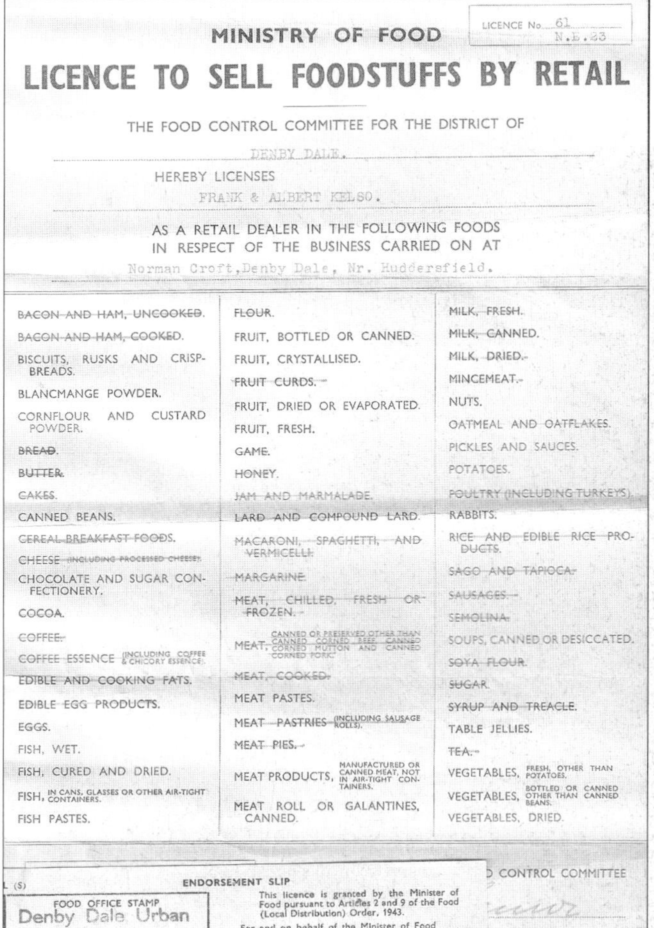

LICENCE No. 61 N.E.23

MINISTRY OF FOOD

LICENCE TO SELL FOODSTUFFS BY RETAIL

THE FOOD CONTROL COMMITTEE FOR THE DISTRICT OF

DENBY DALE.

HEREBY LICENSES

FRANK & ALBERT KELSO.

AS A RETAIL DEALER IN THE FOLLOWING FOODS IN RESPECT OF THE BUSINESS CARRIED ON AT

Norman Croft, Denby Dale, Nr. Huddersfield.

~~BACON AND HAM, UNCOOKED.~~	~~FLOUR.~~	MILK, ~~FRESH.~~
~~BACON AND HAM, COOKED.~~	FRUIT, BOTTLED OR CANNED.	MILK, ~~CANNED.~~
BISCUITS, RUSKS AND CRISP-BREADS.	FRUIT, CRYSTALLISED.	MILK, ~~DRIED.~~
BLANCMANGE POWDER.	~~FRUIT CURDS.~~	~~MINCEMEAT.~~
CORNFLOUR AND CUSTARD POWDER.	FRUIT, DRIED OR EVAPORATED.	NUTS.
~~BREAD.~~	FRUIT, FRESH.	~~OATMEAL AND OATFLAKES.~~
~~BUTTER.~~	GAME.	PICKLES AND SAUCES.
~~CAKES.~~	HONEY.	POTATOES.
CANNED BEANS.	~~JAM AND MARMALADE.~~	~~POULTRY (INCLUDING TURKEYS).~~
~~CEREAL BREAKFAST FOODS.~~	~~LARD AND COMPOUND LARD.~~	RABBITS.
~~CHEESE (INCLUDING PROCESSED CHEESE).~~	~~MACARONI, SPAGHETTI, AND VERMICELLI.~~	~~RICE AND EDIBLE RICE PRODUCTS.~~
CHOCOLATE AND SUGAR CONFECTIONERY.	~~MARGARINE.~~	~~SAGO AND TAPIOCA.~~
COCOA.	~~MEAT, CHILLED, FRESH OR FROZEN.~~	~~SAUSAGES.~~
~~COFFEE.~~	~~MEAT, CANNED OR PRESERVED OTHER THAN CANNED CORNED BEEF, CANNED CORNED MUTTON AND CANNED CORNED PORK.~~	~~SEMOLINA.~~
~~COFFEE ESSENCE (INCLUDING COFFEE & CHICORY ESSENCE).~~	~~MEAT, COOKED.~~	SOUPS, CANNED OR DESICCATED.
~~EDIBLE AND COOKING FATS.~~	MEAT PASTES.	~~SOYA FLOUR.~~
EDIBLE EGG PRODUCTS.	MEAT ~~PASTRIES (INCLUDING SAUSAGE ROLLS).~~	~~SUGAR.~~
EGGS.	~~MEAT PIES.~~	SYRUP AND TREACLE.
FISH, WET.	MEAT PRODUCTS, MANUFACTURED OR CANNED MEAT, NOT IN AIR-TIGHT CONTAINERS.	TABLE JELLIES.
FISH, CURED AND DRIED.	MEAT ROLL OR GALANTINES, CANNED.	~~TEA.~~
FISH, IN CANS, GLASSES OR OTHER AIR-TIGHT CONTAINERS.		VEGETABLES, FRESH, OTHER THAN POTATOES.
FISH PASTES.		VEGETABLES, BOTTLED OR CANNED OTHER THAN CANNED BEANS.
		VEGETABLES, DRIED.

...D CONTROL COMMITTEE

L (S)

ENDORSEMENT SLIP

FOOD OFFICE STAMP

Denby Dale Urban District Food

This licence is granted by the Minister of Food pursuant to Articles 2 and 9 of the Food (Local Distribution) Order, 1943.

For and on behalf of the Minister of Food, [signature]

Frank and Albert's two liveried mobile sales wagons parked up in Norman Croft. The Prospect Hotel and Victoria Corn Mill can be seen in the background, circa 1950s.

Kelso brothers warehouse, now demolished, in Norman Croft, circa 1950s.

No. 6 PLATOON
"B" COMPANY
70th WEST R.DING (STAINCROSS) BN.
HOME GUARD

TO ALL RECRUITS :—

COMMENCING SUNDAY AUGUST 23RD 1942, YOU WILL ATTEND PARADES AS FOLLOWS :—

SUNDAYS — AT 9.0 A.M. PROSPECT HOTEL, DENBY DALE.

TUESDAYS - AT 7.15 P.M.
THURSDAYS - AT 7.15 P.M. } PARADE GROUND, NORMAN ROAD, DENBY DALE.

RECRUITS WILL ASSEMBLE FIVE MINUTES BEFORE THE ACTUAL TIME OF PARADE.

ALL THOSE IN POSSESSION OF UNIFORM WILL WEAR IT. IF UNABLE TO REPORT AT 7.15 P.M – DO SO AS SOON AS POSSIBLE.

ANY MAN ABSENT FROM ANY PARADE MUST HAND IN THE FOLLOWING DAY AN EXPLANATION OF HIS ABSENCE, IN WRITING TO PLATOON HEADQUARTERS. IF WORK IS THE CAUSE, A CERTIFICATE SIGNED BY YOUR EMPLOYER MUST BE SUBMITTED.

UNLESS LEAVE OF ABSENCE HAS BEEN GRANTED, THE ONLY REASONABLE EXPLANATIONS OF ABSENCE ARE –

(1) EMPLOYMENT
(2) ILLNESS.

BOTH SUPPORTED BY THE REQUIRED CONFIRMATION.

THE FOLLOWING ARE NOT REASONABLE EXCUSES – "GARDENING" — "PICTURES" — "FORGETFULLNESS".

18 AUG 1942

J. A. Loveday. Lieut
O.C. 6 PLATOON

DENBY DALE.

A letter sent out to number 6 Platoon, B Company, 70th West Riding Division, Home Guard, based at Denby Dale, informing them of the parade grounds at the Prospect Hotel and Norman Croft.

they experienced the effects of rationing and became limited as to the goods they could supply. Norman Croft had another use during the Second World War, as a parade ground for the Denby Dale Home Guard.

The family grocery business thrived until Frank and Albert decided to retire, around 1960–1965. In July 1959, planning permission was granted to Albert George for a bungalow in Norman Croft, and he lived here up until his death in 1979. The property is still owned by the present day generation of the family, though as I write Norman Croft is being built upon, new houses occupy the site of the old grocery warehouse.

Throughout their working lives the Kelsos dealt with almost continual change and had learned to become versatile and adaptable within their private and public lives. They brought a joy to the Denby and district area in an era before consumerism, mass media and cynicism. Their like has now gone, but their fascinating story has lived on in the oral recollections of the older inhabitants of the area reflecting the impact they once made upon the district.

The gravestone of William and Minnie George in Cumberworth churchyard.

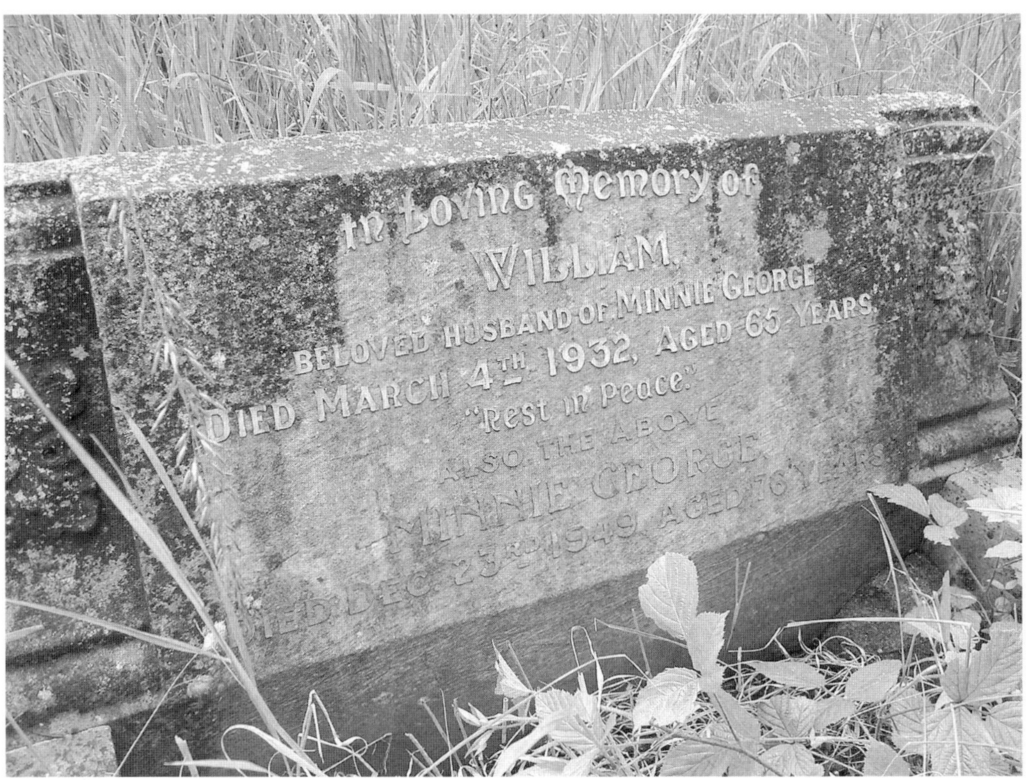

Chapter Six

Deeds & Misdeeds

Including Excerpts from the Barnsley Chronicle

1411

Prior of the Convent of Pontefract O'Clun as appropriators of the parish church of Silkstone with dependant chapel of Cumberworth. John Helwys (Helways), John Robynson, John Stevenson and Richard Nic(h)ols, laymen of Cumberworth.

1500/1

William Burdet of Denby, created an acolyte at York on 6 March 1500/1.
(An acolyte was a person in minor holy orders, next below the rank of a sub-deacon. William is currently unknown but could have been the brother of Richard Burdet, Lord of Denby who died in 1546).

1565

Mathew Wentworth, Henry Jessop and Alice his wife and Charles Turton, three messuages with lands in Cumberworth and Shepley in the parish of Kirkburton.

1587 September 30

Confirmation of a bargain and sale. Thomas Bosvill of New Hall, esq., to William Mosley and Joan, late wife of William Scozzar. Manor of Canonhall, with all lands. For 30 years, at 10 marks per year.

1587 October 28

Defeasance of bonds. William Hewett, citizen and clothworker of London, and Thomas Hewett, his son, to Jarvis Bossevile of Newhall, Yorks., esq., and Thomas Bossevile, gent., his son and heir. Confirming a bargain and sale of 28 Sep 1587, by which the Bosseviles sold to the Hewetts the following:- capital messuage of Cannon Hall, parish Caltheron, Yorks., capital messuage of Rawe Roode, par. Caltheron, in the occupation of Charles Walker; capital messuage of Jowett Howse, par. Caltheron, in the occupation of Thomas Oxley; capital messuage of Brodeyates, being an inn in the same parish, in the occupation of Charles Wainwright: water mill, in the occupation of John Mitchell, and one parcel of ground called Millfields, 12 acres.

1624 October 9

Exemplification of a final concord. Thomas Pasley of Cawthorne, Yorks, yeoman to Thomas Oxley of Skellmanthorpe, Yorks, yeoman. 1 close of meadow or pasture called South Carr, butting on the lands of Thomas Barneby, east, north and south, and on the lane leading from Silkstone to Bargh, on the west; a close of pasture or arable called Long Middle Carr, and 2 closes of meadow, pasture, or arable, called the Boscroftinges now divided into 4, one of which lies to the east of the water which runs to Bargh; close of pasture or arable called the Bight. All of these contain, together, 27 acres, and were parcels of a messuage in Barnby, once the inheritance of William Champney of Frickley, and now in the tenure of James Beamont. For £200 and 50/–.

1629 February 3

Mortgage by demise for 7 years. John Brooke of Gigleswicke, Yorks, clerk, and Elizabeth, his wife, to Thomas Oxley of Skelmanthorpe, Yorks, yeoman, and Edith Oxley, daughter of Thomas. Moity of a capital messuage with appurtenances in Barneby, now in the occupation of Thomas Pasley: and a moity of all rents from these, lately the inheritance of William Champney. For £200, paid to William Brooke, father of John Brooke, with the consent of John and Elizabeth Brooke.

1632 December 1

Deed of partition. Edmund Ogden of Bullhouse, Yorks., gent., and Mary his wife; Richard Ogden of South Elmshall, Yorks., gent., and Mary, his wife, and William Riche of Bullhouse, Yorks., gent., and Isabell, his wife, all of the first part, and Thomas Pasley of Barnby, Yorks., yeoman and Thomas Litlewood, jun., of Burthwaite, Yorks., yeoman, of the second part.2 messuages in Cawthorne, now occupied by Alexander Fanley and William Mitchell, and called Brookhouses. For £460.

1639

Cumberworth was noted for having a disorderly alehouse. Ralph Mellor and Abrahan Hepworth of Cumberworth contemptuously and obstinately have taken upon themselves to keep ale house in Cumberworth without a licence contrary to the statute. Ordered that the churchwardens shall levy and distrain on their goods the sum of 20s for the use of the poor. This method of using fines to reduce the poor rates was a popular custom of legal procedure of the period.

1640 July 23

John Firth of Cumberworth was summoned to court along with Anthony Jenkinson of Shafton to be sworn in as High Constables for the Wapentake of Staincross in place of Richard Cudworth and George Cowper, who had completed 3 years in office.

1641 September 1

Erecting a house without planning permission was as difficult then as it is now. Each house had to have a minimum of 4 acres of land attached to it for farming purposes otherwise it was illegal and an order could be made for it to be demolished. On the above date Robert Hepworth of Cumberworth had provided a house for Edward and Sarah Brooke without the necessary 4 acres, according to the statute to the heavy expense and grievance of the inhabitants of the parish of Silkstone in which parish Cumberworth was then situated.

1662 August
Petition of the churchwarden and inhabitants of Denby for the removal of Pheobe Slack, August 1662.

1668 January
Petition of 10 inhabitants for a security against the abusive behaviour of William Robinson of Denby, January 1668.

1668 October 18–19
Lease and release. Edith Oxley of Skelmanthorp, Yorks, spinster, younger daughter of Thomas Oxley, late of the same place, dec'd, confirms that, on the marriage of William Brooke, her nephew, and the son and heir of Elizabeth Brooke, of Skelmanthorpe, widow, sister of Edith Oxley, and Anne Richardson, second daughter of Richard Richardson of Northbirch, Yorks, gent, she settled the following.

Capital messuage with appurtenances, in Barnbie, lately in the tenure of Thomas Pasley, and now in the tenure of Robert Fawley, together with all buildings and lands belonging, to be to the use of Edith Oxley for life, then to the use of William Brooke, and his heirs.

1672 April 16
Petition for the removal of Walter Poole and wife Dorothy from Cawthorne to Denby 16 April 1672.

1674 October
Petition of the churchwardens and overseers of Penistone that Thomas Haigh of Denby accepts Mary Mitchell, a poor apprentice, October 1674. With note of order that Haigh takes on the apprentice.

1679 June
Order to the Constable of Denby for the removal of the child of William Howes to Ragnall, Nottingham, June 1679.

1694 March 2
Will and probate of John Sotwel of Cathill, par. Silkstone, Yorks.

(i) annunity of £20 to wife Elizabeth, to be payable out of his messuage at Cathill and a close called the Great Royds in Thurlston. (ii) to wife Elizabeth, various furnishings in the parlour and chamber over the parlour, and she is to have the use of these rooms for life. (iii) to eldest son, John, £20, in lieu of his child's portion. (iv) to eldest daughter, Mary Dawson, one shilling. (v) to Richard Sotwell, his son, £100. (vi) to William Sotwell, his son, £150. (vii) to Edward Sotwell, his son, messuages and lands at Cathill and Thurlston. Will dated 3 Jan 1694. Probate 2 Mar 1694.

1721 September 30
Will of William Couldwell of Kexbrough, par. Darton, Yorks., yeoman.

(1) to nephew Thomas Wroe, £10, to be paid 12 months after the death of his wife. (2) to nephew Charles Wroe, £10 as above. (3) to niece, Elizabeth Wroe, £10 as above. (4) to

niece Mary Wroe, £10 as above. (5) to wife, Anne Couldwell, all profits of his real estate in Kexborough, for life. (6) to newphew Richard Couldwell of Cumberworth, his real estate in Kexborough. (7) to wife Anne, all is personal estate. Will dated 30 Sep 1721. Probate granted 25 Jul 1722.

1739

Final Concord. John Marshall of Lower Denby als Nether Denby, par. Peniston, Yorks., tanner, to Walter Spencer Stanhope of Cannon Hall, Cawthorne, Yorks., esq. Messuage at Raw Green, Cawthorne, now in the tenure of John Longley, with all appurtenances. For £52 10s.

1747 June 5–6

Deed to lead the uses of a fine (by lease and release). Jonathan Parkin of Bretton, par. Silkstone, Yorks., miller, to John Field of Rawroyd, par. Cawthorne, Yorks., yeoman. 2 messuages in Skelmanthorpe and several closes of land called the Croft, the two Over and Nether Lidgitt Roods. For 10/–.

1751 April 15

Copy of the will of William Shooter of Cumberworth Half, par. Emley, Yorks., yeoman.

(i) to son George, £10. (ii) to son William, £10, at aged 21. (iii) to daughter Sarah, £10. (iv) to daughter Tabitha, £10. (v) to daughter Elizabeth, £10, at aged 21. (vi) his close of land called Longleys, in the township of Cumberworth, par. High Hoyland, and messuage at Clayton, par. High Hoyland, called Smith House, with the barn and two closes belonging, are charged with the payment of the above legacies. (vii) remainder of the estates to be to the use of his above mentioned children, plus his daughter Martha Shore, his sons Joshua and Joseph Shooter.

1752 May 1

Declaration of the uses of a fine. John Shooter of Clayton, par. High Hoyland, Yorks., Cordwainer, eldest son and heir of William Shooter, late of the parish of Emley, of the first part: Joseph Shooter of Hardwick, par. Wragby, Yorks., Cordwainer and Joshua Shooter of Marshall Mill, Clayton, carpenter, sons and executors of William Shooter, of the second part, and Edward Armitage of Smithy Ridge, West Bretton, Yorks., yeoman, of the third part. Parties agree to levy a fine in a close of land, arable, meadow or pasture, called Langleys, situated in Cumberworth Half, par. High Hoyland, and in a messuage called Smith House, in Clayton, par. High Hoyland, and a barn and 2 crofts or closes belonging.To be held to the use of Joseph Shooter and Joshua Shooter.

1752 September 1

Abstract of a final concord. Plaintiffs: Edward Armitage and William Allen. Deforciants: John Shooter and Richard Moxon and Mary his wife 2 messuages, 2 gardens, 1 orchard, 3 acres land, 3 acres meadow, 3 acres pasture, common of pasture and common of turbary in Clayton, Cumberworth Half als Skelmanthorpe, Hoyland Swans.

1754 March 16

Will of Joseph Armfield of Cawthorne, Yorks., yeoman.

(1) to sister Grace Armfield, widow, of his late brother Thomas Armfield dec'd., 6 dwelling houses and all appurtenances, in Cawthorne, for life.

(2) to Sarah Fish, daughter of John and Martha Fish, the messuage or dwelling house, with garden and stable, now in the possession of Isaac Sugden.

(3) to John Fish, brother of Sarah, a house, mistall and garden, in the possession of Jonas Beaumont.

(4) to Martha Fish, mother of John and Sarah, a dwelling house in which Faith Allison now lives, and a garden belonging, for life, and, thereafter, to her son John.

(5) to Ann Fish, daughter of Martha, the dwelling house in which he now lives, with outhouses, garden, and all household goods.

(6) to Martha Fish, daughter of John and Martha, the house in which James Barber now lives, with the gardens adjoining.

(7) to William Fish, son of John and Martha, the dwelling house in which widow Winter now lives and the gardens belonging.

1763 October 21–22

Lease and release. Joseph Shooter late of West Hardwick, par. Wragby but now of Purston Jacklyn, par. Featherstone, Yorks., cordwainer and Hannah his wife, to Daniel Dyson of Skelmanthorpe, par. Emley, Yorks., carpenter. Messuage called Smith House, in Clayton, par. High Hoyland, and 1 barn and 2 crofts or closes of land belonging. For £39 19s. 3d. The property to be subject to the recited mortgage to Jonathan West.

1787 May 23

Will of John Ellis of Toppitt, par. High Hoyland, Yorks., husbandman. Messuage, and close of land in Clayton, par. High Hoyland, to wife Elizabeth, for life. on her death, the above property to younger daughter Isabell, wife of Timothy Lockwood. All his tenant right and interest in a cottage lying on Toppitt wastes, to his wife Elizabeth for life, and, thereafter to his eldest daughter Sarah, wife of Joseph Hampshire. Will dated 23 May 1787.

1788 June 2–3

Mortgage.

John Ellis of Toppit, par. High Hoyland, Yorks., husbandman, to Joseph Hodgson of Upper Heaton, par. Kirkheaton, Yorks., gent. Messuage called Smith House, in Clayton, par. High Hoyland, and one barn and 2 crofts or closes of land belonging. To recover £80 principal plus interest.

1792 June 26–27

Mortgage in fee (by lease and release).

William Fish of Gunthwaite, parish of Peniston, Yorks., farmer and Margaret his wife, of the first part: John Lisle of Cawthorne, Yorks., schoolmaster, of the second part: John Batley of Cawthorne, Yorks., gardener, of the third part. Reciting a bond of 30 Apr 1789 by which Fish owes Batley £56 13/6d., and that Fish wishes to borrow a further £18 16/6d. from Batley, making a total of £75. The following premises are thus pledged as mortgage: Messuage, dwelling house or tenement with the garden and foldstead belonging, in Cawthorne, and now in the tenure of Benjamin Lockwood: close or parcel of ground called the Croft alias Micklethwait Croft situated in Cawthorne, containing 3 roods. To secure payment of £75 principal plus interest. The parties further agree to levy a fine in the above lands.

1796 December 20–21

Lease and release, with discharge of mortgage.

William Fish of Gunthwaite, par. Cawthorne, Yorks., farmer and Margaret, his wife, to Thomas West of Cawthorne, Yorks., esq. Reciting mortgage discharge and conveyance of 20 and 21 Dec 1796, and that, although it was not entered in the conveyance, it was understood by the parties that the premises be pledged by way of mortgage, with redemption on payment of £20 plus interest. By this deed, Fish sells the equity of redemption and releases the mortgaged lands to West.

For £11 10/–.

1798 December 5

Lease for a year.. John Hodgson of Halifax, Yorks., eldest brother and heir at law of Joseph Hodgson, late of Upper Heaton, par. Kirkheaton, Yorks., gent., dec'd., and Edward Hodgson of Ledgers Mill, par. Mirfield, Yorks., miner, another brother, both being administrators of the goods of Joseph Hodgson, and Timothy Lockwood of Toppit, par. High Hoyland, farmer, and Isabell his wife, of the one part, to Sarah Hampshire of Emley, Yorks., widow. Messuage called Smith House, in Clayton, par. High Hoyland, with a barn and 2 crofts or closes of land belonging. For 1 year, at a peppercorn rent.

1800 December 16

Will and probate of Sarah Hampshire of Emley, Yorks., (i) to brothers in law Timothy Lockwood and John Hampshire, all the reversionary interest in a freehold messuage and close of land belonging, with all appurtenances, in Clayton, par. High Hoyland; in all the cottage standing on the waste at Toppit within the manor of Denby cum Clayton: all other personal estate, on trust to pay the rents and receive the profits of these properties until her youngest child reaches 21; the money to be used for the maintenance of all her children. Will dated 16 Dec 1800. Probate 4 Mar 1807.

1819 October 15–16

Lease and release. John Hampshire of Kendall, Westmoreland, manufacturer, eldest son and heir at law of Sarah Hampshire, dec'd., of the first part: Timothy Lockwood of Toppitt, township of Clayton West, par. High Hoyland, Yorks., farmer, and Isabell his wife, of the second part: Timothy Lockwood as surviving trustee for sale of lands under the will of Sarah Hampshire, of the third part: John Bedford of Gilcar, par. Emley, yeoman, of the fourth part, and Benjamin Haigh of Nether Denby, par. Penistone, Yorks., gent., of the fifth part. Reciting mortgage of 2 and 3 Jun 1788: that default was made: will of John Ellis of 23 May 1787: lease and release of 5 and 6 Dec 1798: will of Sarah Hampshire, 16 Dec 1800: that her youngest child is now 21 years old, and that there is still due on mortgage £102. Lands as recited in above deeds. For £300 (viz. £102 paid to Lockwood by Bedford, and £198 paid to Lockwood and his wife, by Bedford. The parties further agree to levy a fine in the above, to Benjamin Haigh.

1828 December 14

This night, Mr William Norton, of Clayton West, near Huddersfield, who had been declared a bankrupt, made his escape from the house of Mr John Lancaster, sheriff's officer of Huddersfield. Mr Norton had been apprehended, and was afterwards confined in a room four stories high, which was considered perfectly secure, but it was discovered that he had contrived to descend into the street by means of a rope, one end of which was fastened to his bedstead and the other stretched across the street and tied to the rails of the Methodist chapel. It is supposed that he had obtained a quantity of small twine (which was found in the room after his escape) and that he had during the night let down one end of it into the street and drawn up the rope, by means of which he effected his escape. A reward of £20 was offered for his apprehension.

(William was the brother of the manufacturers Joseph Norton (1800–1874) and George Norton (1806–1865) of Nortonthorpe Mills, Scissett.

William bounced back from his adversity and can be found, along with other members of his family, creating and designing new ideas for applications in the weaving industry. The patents for these are still held at the British Library:

Norton Patents held at the British Library

Inventors and Inventions – Patent Leeds Central Library.
Looms for Weaving Piled Fabrics.
Description: Improvements in weaving piled fabrics, relating to the manufacturing of double cloth from two destined foundation warps and a separate pile warp. Description 2: William Norton, Kirkburton The full patent is comprised of 4 pages of text and 17 diagrams. Patent/Application Number: 2775 Location: Kirkburton Publication Date: 8/12/1855 Application Date: Creator: William Norton.

Inventors and Inventions Type: Patent Leeds Central Library.
Looms for Weaving. Norton & Collier's Specification.
Description: An improvement in looms for the weaving of figured and twilled fabrics. Description 2: Joseph Norton, High Bridge Mill, Clayton West, High Hoyland, 10 pages text, 2 diagrams Patent/ Application Number: 8412 Location: High Bridge Mill, Clayton West, High Hoyland, Skelmanthorpe, Publication Date: 4/3/1840 Application Date: Creator: Joseph Norton Contributor: George Collier

Inventors and Inventions Type: Patent Leeds Central Library.
Power Looms.
Description: Improvements in power looms, whereby varieties of patterns and changes of fabric may be woven in the same piece without the aid of a jacquard or engine, with the weaver having the means of altering and varying the pattern as required. Description 2: Walter Norton, Clayton, West Huddersfield The full patent consists of 3 pages of text; there is no diagram. Patent/Application Number: 378 Location: Clayton, West Huddersfield. Application Date: 12/2/1864 Creator: Walter Norton.

Inventors and Inventions Type: Patent Leeds Central Library.
Tipping pile fabrics.
Description: Improvements in tipping pile fabrics and in apparatus to be used for such purpose Description 2: Benjamin Norton, Nortonthorpe Mills, Full patent – 7 pages and 3 diagrams Patent/

Application Number: 3915 Location: Nortonthorpe Mills near Huddersfield Publication Date: 1/6/1869 Application Date: 22/12/1868 Creator: Benjamin Norton.

Inventors and Inventions Type: Patent Leeds Central Library.
Weaving Cut Pile Fabrics.
Description: Improvements in weaving cut pile fabrics, which are particularly applicable in the production of piled checks or plaids, or when weaving other fabrics. Description 2: Walter Norton, Clayton, West Huddersfield. The full patent is comprised of 4 pages of text and 1 diagram. Patent/Application Number: 222 Location: Clayton, West Huddersfield Publication Date: 26/1/1864 Application Date: Creator: Walter Norton.

Inventors and Inventions Type: Patent Leeds Central Library.
Weaving Velvets, &c, Norton & Hellawell's Specification (provisional).
Description: 'Improvements in weaving velvets and other piled fabrics, and in apparatus employed therein,' According to this invention I form each wire or rod of two thin steel blades fixed or held together at their ends only. Description 2: Thomas Norton, Cattlehurst Mills, Huddersfield, & Henry Hellawell, Kitchenroyds, Denby Dale, Full patent 2 pages text Patent/Application Number: 381 Location: Cattlehurst Mills, Huddersfield, & Kitchenroyds, Denby Dale, Publication Date: 29/1/1874 Application Date: Creator: Thomas Norton Contributor: Henry Hellawell.

Barnsley Chronicle Extracts

NB: Date of the paper first – then the article.

1872

6 January 1872

Gambling at Cumberworth

Wilson Kilner, Wilson Pell, Alfred Stephenson, John Lister Woodhouse, Joe Noble, Joseph Addey, Joseph Senior, Fred Booth, Job Morley and Henry Jackson, all young men, were charged with playing at pitch and toss at Cumberworth on the 16th Dec. last. Mr Freeman appeared for the defendants. PC Worsley said about a quarter past four in the afternoon of the above day, which was a Saturday, he saw the defendants gambling with money at the low end of Cumberworth. He watched them for a considerable time, and at last, Jackson and Pell observed him, and gave the signal, when they all went away. In answer to Mr Freeman, witness denied telling a butcher named Senior at Cumberworth the same evening that he was unable to identify one of the parties. A witness named Noah Senior spoke to witnessing a number of men playing for some time, and to speaking to Pell, Morley and Jackson. The butcher, Senior, already named, was called by Mr Freeman and stated that the policeman had told him on the same evening that he was unable to identify any of the parties. Mr Cooke said the magistrates had no power to impose a penalty. If the offence were proved the parties must go to prison without the option of a fine, but they were unwilling to send a number of respectable looking young men like them to the House of Correction and after the evidence of the last witness they should give them the benefit of any doubt which there might be and let them off. They however, ought to know, and to let their companions know at the same time, that where a charge was fully proved the offenders must go to prison. The defendants were then discharged.

6 January 1872

Farewell of a Clergyman at Skelmanthorpe

On Sunday last, the Reverend C W Houlbrook, curate of Skelmanthorpe preached his farewell sermon to a very attentive congregation, who were deeply affected during the delivery of the sermon. In the vestry before the service the surpliced choir presented to the Reverend gentleman among themselves in recognition of his faithful ministrations and indefatigable labours in the Sunday school and his raising the choir to such a state of efficiency. On the Sunday previous, the reverend gentleman presented each member of the choir with a handsome prayer book as a parting gift.

20 January 1872

Fatal Accident to a Denby Dale Colliery Proprietor

On Monday an inquest was opened before Thomas Taylor Esq. at the house of John Lockwood, the White Hart Inn, Denby Dale touching the death of Mr Thomas Schofield, colliery proprietor and brick maker who came to an untimely end by an accident at the Denby Dale railway station on the previous Friday. The evidence went to show that the deceased, who owned two collieries, one at Cumberworth and the other at Denby Dale, was at the Lancashire and Yorkshire Railway Station on the afternoon of the previous Friday. Several of his own wagons were in the sidings and were being filled with coal. Whilst he was at the station he got on the brake of one of the wagons as he had often done before, the brake was at a certain point. As the wagon was in motion he jumped off but the wagon caught his coat and dragged him on until it pressed his body through a space of 6 or 8 inches. The Station Master, Mr Robinson, on seeing the danger ran to the assistance of the deceased and whilst on the road he called out 'mind your legs Thomas'. It would appear that the deceased heard the warning as he drew his legs up, but could not get free from the wagon, which as stated, dragged him on until it pressed him through the small space named. He was removed to his home as quickly as possible, where he died at a quarter to four in the afternoon, in the 45th year of his age. The jury after hearing the evidence, returned a verdict of 'accidentally killed'. The deceased had been twice married, but only leaves one daughter, who is also married, together with a widow to lament his loss. He was

The White Hart, Denby Dale, circa 1950.

a native of Denby Dale but it was not until about 15 years ago that he can be said to have permanently resided there. The cause of death is believed to have been a rupture of the bladder. Mr Schofield, had for many years officiated as a local preacher in connection with the Wesleyan Methodist body. His remains were interred on Wednesday at Cumberworth Parish Church and, notwithstanding the miserable weather, there was a large concourse of people. His funeral was attended by upwards of 100 of the circuit leaders and local preachers belonging to the body which for so long he had been faithfully devoted and by whom he will be missed. In politics he was a conservative and took an active part in connection with all movement of a political character in the Scissett district. He was generally and deservedly respected by all classes of society. He was brother to Mr Schofield, boot and shoe dealer, Market Hill, Barnsley.

27 January 1872

Stealing a Smock at High Flatts

John Taylor and Thomas King, two youths who said they were on tramp, pleaded guilty to stealing a smock, value 2s 6d on the 19th inst. at the property of Samuel Horne at High Flatts. Martha Horne, wife of the prosecutor, said she washed the smock and put it out to dry on some grass about 11 o'clock on the 19th inst. about half past two o'clock she missed it and gave information to the police. The smock produced by PC Settle was the same. It was her own make and was worth 5s 6d. Edwin Dearnley, a boy, spoke to seeing the prisoner, Taylor, leave the prosecutors yard about half past twelve o'clock. He had something white under his coat. He joined the prisoner King and they both went on the road towards Huddersfield. Joshua Hoyle, a plasterer, said that he was at the Huddersfield Model Lodging House on the 21st inst. when he bought the smock, produced by the prisoner, King and gave him 7½ d for it. The smock was wet at the time and he dried it before the fire. PC Settle, one of the West Riding constabulary stationed at New Mill near Huddersfield deposed to apprehending the prisoners in Huddersfield, and on charging them with the robbery they both denied it and said they had come from Halifax. Committed for one month each.

3 February 1872

Assault at Skelmanthorpe

William Lawton, weaver of Skelmanthorpe, was charged with assaulting a youth named George Edward Hinchliffe, in the employ of Messrs. Norton Brothers, manufacturers of Nortonthorpe. The complainant said he had to go to Skelmanthorpe for some medicine as well as to get a £10 and a £5 note changed. He went to Mr Senior's shop and got the notes changed. When he was returning to the works he was met by the defendant who said he would go and help him to spend the money. He refused, when the defendant knocked his hat off. Witness called out for Mr Senior, whose son came to his assistance. The defendant was not sober. Mr Senior deposed to hearing complainant crying out. Witness ran to his assistance and asked defendant what he was doing with the lad. The defendant did not speak at first, but afterwards he replied 'You go to hell'. Witness got hold of the defendant and took him off the complainant, when he fell on him and struck and kicked him. The defendant, who said he was so drunk that he knew nothing about the case, was committed to the Wakefield house of correction for one month with hard labour.

3 February 1872

Drunk and Refusing to Quit at Clayton West

George Barraclough was charged with being drunk and refusing to quit the house of John Shaw at Clayton West on the 27th ult. The landlord said that the defendant went to his house drunk and began to be quarrelsome. He (complainant) ordered him out, but he refused to leave. Several previous convictions were put in by the police and the defendant was fined £1 and costs, in all £1 14s or one month in default.

3 February 1872

Refusing to Quit the George Inn, Denby

Jonathan Heppinstall or Norton, was charged with being drunk and quarrelsome in the house of Nancy Taylor, the George Inn, Denby on the 17th ult. Mrs Taylor deposed to the defendant going into her house and calling for a glass of beer. A butcher, named, Thomas Morley, who lived at Denby Dale, was in the house and the defendant wanted to quarrel with him. She asked him to go out, but he refused several times and used abusive language. PC Simpson deposed to hearing a row in the complainants house and on going in found the defendant using some very filthy language. He refused to go out when he ordered him and witness dare not eject him because there were a lot of his friends in the house. Hadfield Holmes gave corroborative evidence, and said the defendant pulled 5s out of his pocket and wanted to fight him.

He refused, and as the landlady asked him (witness) to assist her: he did so. The defendant denied ever commencing a disturbance but on the other hand, said Morley insulted him and asked him whether he was representing the county or the borough, called him a bastard, asked whether his name was Heppinstall or Norton and said he could not heir his fathers property. He wished the bench to understand that Morley was a single man and the landlady, being a widow, he took the chair at that house. (Laughter). Wm. Whittaker and Enoch Taylor, son of the complainant were called to prove that Morley commenced the disturbance, and that the defendant had left the house as soon as he had drunk his glass of beer off. Mr Kaye said there was the same disposition on the part of the bench to put an end to drunkenness at Denby as there ever was.

Fined 20s and costs, in all £1 17s, or one month in default. The money was paid.

17 February 1872

A 'Ghost' at Denby Dale

We are informed, upon the authority of a veracious Denby Dale correspondent that during the past week a considerable amount of pertubation has been created among the natives of that secluded locality by the nocturnal freaks of a 'ghost', which draped in the orthodox ghostly costume – a white sheet – and carrying a couple of ominous looking tapers, has marched in stately silence along the secluded bye-ways of the neighbourhood. The visit, it was alleged, boded no good, the lights were regarded as omens of dire portent; but what the sequel would be was impossible to divine. At last one native, more courageous than the rest, thought he would sound the ghost upon the subject, and at the same time try and find out whether it possessed the ghostly quality of being ' as the air, invulnerable'. A smart, and, so far as the ghost was concerned, sharp and unexpected tap on the top of the head settled the latter point. As to the former, it was not deemed necessary to pursue the inquiry further, for a sharp pull at the skirt of the drapery, laid bare the burly form of a Denby Dale day labourer, who had probably adopted this ruse as a preliminary to a series of hen roost expeditions. It is needless to say that the 'ghost' beat a speedy and somewhat undignified retreat, and that it is not likely to resume its nocturnal wanderings for some time to come.

24 February 1872

Assault at Denby

Hadfield Holmes was charged with assaulting Jonathan Norton of Gunthwaite at Denby Dale, on the 14th inst. Mr Barrett appeared for the complainant and Mr Freeman for the defence. Complainant had been a witness against the defendant in the court two or three weeks ago, and the present assault seemed to have originated in the ill feeling created by those proceedings. Defendant had sworn at complainant, struck him over the nose, and threatened to 'cut his head right off'.

Fined 20s and costs in all £1 19s.

24 February 1872

Assault at Skelmanthorpe

Richard Senior charged John Gleming with assaulting him on the 18th inst. at Skelmanthorpe. Complainant deposed to being at Skelmanthorpe on the day named, when the defendant met him, struck him several times, and tore his coat, which cost 4s repairing. Emma Woodhead, a young woman, spoke up to the complainant and defendant who were scuffling. She saw the defendant strike complainant in the face and then run away. For the defence a girl named Ellen Dyson was called, and spoke to hearing complainant challenge defendant to fight and seeing him strike him. She got hold of his coat to prevent them fighting. The bench fined the defendant 1s and costs amounting in all to 20s 6d.

24 February 1872

A Denby Police Officer Sued for Damages for Assault

Burton V Simpson

This was a plaint brought to recover £10 for damages for an assault. The plaintiff was James Burton, farmer, of Clayton Hall, who sued Joseph Simpson, a police officer stationed at Denby. Mr Burton of Wakefield appeared for the plaintiff; and Mr Barrett, of the same place for the defendant. Mr Burton briefly stated the case, which arose out of an affray on the 7th December, last year at Ingbirchworth. Mr Burton called the following witnesses. The plaintiff said he was at Penistone on 7th December last and was returning home in Mr Wood's cart. Plaintiff was riding and Mr Wood was leading the pony up the hill. Two persons were walking by the side of the cart. When they got a little nearer the top of the hill, the defendant, Simpson came and asked who they were. Wood said he knew them all. He said to him (plaintiff) 'Who are you?', Wood said 'It is Burton, of Clayton Hall'. The defendant said 'that will not do for me' and then got on the wheel of the cart and said he would handcuff me. He pulled the handcuffs out. When the other persons had got about 150 yards from where he was, he managed to get away from the grasp of the defendant and went to the Wagoners Inn at Dunkirk. The defendant came into the house and said, 'you are my escaped prisoner'. Witness gave his name and the landlord said he knew him. Mr Brooke, who was in the room said he would be bound for him. He was a farmer and had about 200 acres of land. Mr Peace, a manufacturer of Denby Dale, was there, and the defendant asked him to assist him. Plaintiff got the handcuffs on his wrists and was pushed into a corner. Defendant than said 'Now you – I will give you something'. His Honour: Do you mean to say you had not struck him?. Plaintiff: I did not. I struggled to get free. The defendant pulled his staff out and struck me on the head and knocked a tooth out. Defendant then sent for a Doctor, as he was afraid I should bleed to death. The defendant tried to get them off, and tried to break them as he had not his key. The defendant summoned him and several others before the magistrates for cruelty and assaulting him in the execution of his duty. The plaintiff here produced the summons, which was issued by the magistrates and gave evidence as to the expenses incurred in the charge. Cross examined:- He had been at Penistone and was returning to Ingbirchworth about 4 o'clock in the afternoon. About 300 or 400 hundred yards from where the affray took place the horse slipped. At the time they passed some horses on the road. Witness, Wood, Firth and another man were with the cart. Wood was out of the cart but was not beating the horse. The neighbours did not come out and say, 'go into him, go into him'. The brass hoop did not come off the whip and we never offered a man sixpence to put it on. Witness and the other persons were sober. The pony did not run against the wall to get out of the way. His Honour: You need not go into the cruelty. I shall not inquire into that. Mr Barratt said he put the questions in order to test the credibility of the plaintiff and his witnesses. His Honour: the cruelty has nothing to do with it. If it be proved that the police officer did what they say he did it was illegal. Mr Barratt contended that if the men were guilty of cruelty the officer had a right to take him into custody. His Honour: do you mean to say that he would be justified in taking him into custody when he knew him, and when a farmer, farming 200 acres of land said he would be bound for him?. Mr Barratt said he did and there was an express section for it. He handed the section to His Honour. Cross examination continued – When he was in the public house he never kicked the defendant nor got hold of his throat. He struggled because defendant wanted to handcuff him. When he ran away and overtook the three persons on the road they never said he was to be off as fast as he could. He delivered milk in Clayton on the second day after the assault and was only attended by the doctor for a few days. He had a bit of a 'switcher' on the night in question. It was not an 'ash plant'. He never made use of it over the police officer. He was not aware that the police officer had bled when in the public house. He had no beer or brandy at the public house which he left a short time after the defendant had gone. William Wood deposed to being with the plaintiff in the cart when the horse fell. He got out and got hold of the pony's head. He did give him a 'tickling up with the small end of the whip', to make him start. The plaintiff was in the cart. When they got about a hundred yards away the defendant came and got hold of the ponies head and said Who is it? He replied 'You know me'. Defendant asked who it was that was in the cart. He witness replied 'Its Burton of Clayton Hall'. The defendant then got hold of the plaintiff and dragged him out of the cart. He and the others in the cart went on, and when they got to the Wagoners Inn at Dunkirk, the officer came in and said to the plaintiff 'You are my escaped prisoner'. Plaintiff said he had given his name twice but the defendant said that would not do, as he (defendant) would have to apprehend him. They had a scuffle for about half an hour when the defendant pulled out his truncheon and struck plaintiff about the head and on the muscles of his arm, until he had no use of it. Defendant put the plaintiff in a corner, and whilst he was bleeding, put the handcuffs on. The paintiff bled very much, and all the company complained, and said he would bleed to death. He (witness) saddled his horse and went to Skelmanthorpe for a doctor. After the defendant had got the plaintiff in the corner he struck him, saying he would 'give him it then'. The plaintiff, defendant and Mr Peace were scuffling together for a long time. He could not tell which of the persons threw each other. Thomas Haigh gave similar evidence. Mr Barratt said the summons was not taken out by the police at all. It was taken out by Mr Smith, an agent of the Royal Society for the Prevention of Cruelty to Animals. He contended that, according to the Act, notice ought to have been given by the plaintiff of his intention to sue, as it was provided that he could pay the money into court, if he thought proper. His Honour: Do you mean to say that if a police officer, in taking a man into custody half kills him, he could claim the protection of that Act? Mr Barratt said he thought so. His Honour: Then I decide against you. The defendant was then called and said that he was stationed at Ingbirchworth, and was on duty near that village about 4 o'clock on the 7th December. He heard a sound as if proceeding from heavy strokes and some person swearing. He went to the place and found four persons near a cart. The plaintiff was in the cart, beating the horse with the thick end of a stick most unmercifully. Wood had hold of the horse and laid the whip, which he was using, over it. He said to the plaintiff 'What are you doing with this horse? And took hold of Burton's stick and took it from him. He knew Brook and Tyas, but Burton was a perfect stranger to him. Defendant asked him what was his name and the plaintiff said 'You go to hell'. He asked who was in the cart, but he never said 'that will not do for me'. He first got to know the plaintiff's name at the public house. He got hold of the horse's head and said he should stick to it until he got his name. He knew the names of the others. When he got hold of it, Wood and Brook also got hold of the horse's head and dragged him away. The plaintiff leaned over the cart and seized him by the collar, and put his knuckles into his throat. He got the plaintiffs stick, but Wood and Tyas took it from him. His Honour, ordered Tyas to stand up. Both stated that they never took a stick from the defendant, but Tyas said he could not say what kind of a stick it was. The defendant continued: Plaintiff got out of the cart, and, with the assistance of Wood, took away his (witness) stick. The plaintiff struck him the face several times and he was also kicked. Wood dashed Brook against him, and he fell on the ground. He told Mr Smith about the cruelty, and he (Smith) laid the information. Then they got away, and he afterwards went to the Wagoners Inn at Dunkirk. He said to the plaintiff 'I intend to re-apprehend you for assaulting me and for cruelty to this horse'. He said he would not go. He did not ask his name there. Wood told him his name, but he did not believe him, and said he should re-apprehend him. Mr Haigh, at the request of His Honour was called and said: The plaintiff said 'My name is James Burton of Clayton Hall'. Witness continued: No person ever said he lived at Clayton Hall, and was a farmer and would be bound for him. Wood got the handcuffs from him, and he and Brook pushed defendant about and put him out of doors. Wood and Burton struck him several times. He pulled his truncheon out and was about to strike plaintiff on the arm. The truncheon caught him in the eye, and he struck after he got the handcuffs on. The plaintiff became frantic, and tried to throw the tables over. The defendant was cross-examined at some length, but nothing material was elicited. Mr Boothroyd, of Denby, gave corroborative evidence. William Haigh, weaver of Ingbirchworth, also gave evidence to the same effect. Wm. Holmes, joiner of Ingbirchworth, said he heard a noise. On going to the door he saw a man beating a horse which was standing. The horse fell. Fenton Walshaw spoke to being on the road and seeing Wood strike the horse with the thick end of his whip stock. The horse fell down, and Wood struck it before it got up. Mrs Haigh, of Ingbirchworth, gave similar evidence as to the ill treatment of the horse. Police constable Worsley deposed to going to the Wagoners Inn, and giving

PC Simpson his key to unlock the handcuffs. Simpson was bleeding very much and seemed to be in an exhausted state. His Honour in summing up, said the plaintiff had called no person as witness who was not interested in the case, and who had to do with the transaction. The plaintiff had to choose to rest his case on their evidence and he and his witnesses had been flatly contradicted. The most important point was whether the plaintiff was struck after he had got the handcuffs on or before. If it had been satisfactorily proved that he was struck after, he would have been entitled to a verdict beyond all doubt. There were witnesses which ought to have been called, who were not. The case was a doubtful one, and he should non-suit the plaintiff. If there was a word of truth in what the witness said about the cruelty, the persons charged ought to have been convicted. There was wilful perjury on one side or the other.

2 March 1872

Assaulting a Hawker at Ingbirchworth

James Atkinson was charged with assaulting Edward Haigh, a hawker, at the Fountain Inn, Ingbirchworth. The parties had been arranging the basis of an 'amicable arrangement' but the magistrates declined to allow the case to be settled out of court. Defendant had purchased a skirt from complainant, on condition that the latter spent the money, 4s 3d., for the good of the company. The money was tabled and the skirt handed over, but complainant declined to spend the money for the good of the company. Defendant upon that, committed the assault with which he was now charged. Fined 10s and costs, in all £1 9s 6d.

16 March 1872

Drunk at Skelmanthorpe

Edward North was charged with being drunk at Skelmanthorpe on the 2nd inst. The defendant was found by the police officer stationed in the district in front of the Commercial Inn, creating a disturbance and refusing to leave. Fined 5s and costs, in all, 17s 6d or 14 days in default.

Huddersfield Road, in the centre of Ingbirchworth , circa 1905. (Courtesy of Old Barnsley)

23 March 1872

Scissett – Death of Mr Herbert Camm Dickinson

We regret to state that Mr H C Dickinson, died at his residence, Mill Bank, High Flatts, on the evening of Friday last. He had been in failing health for some time and his death was not unexpected. Mr Dickinson was President of the Scissett Conservative Association since its formation in 1865 and was also the Chairman of the Conservative committee for the Scissett district in the elections of 1865 and 1868. His high character and extensive property gave him great influence and his death will be seriously felt by the Conservative party in the Scissett and Penistone polling districts. His great business ability and public spirit, together with the esteem in which he was held by all classes and parties will cause his death to be regarded as a public loss, and has cast a gloom over the districts.

8 June 1872

Shameful Assault at Cumberworth

Edward Kilty pleaded guilty to assaulting a young woman named Ann Tyas, a factory worker, at Cumberworth on the 22nd ult. Complainant said she was returning from her work at the factory, at 6 o'clock on the day named, along with another young woman named Eliza Green. As they were going along, defendant began to kick Green's can about. She interfered, and said if the can were hers then the defendant should not do so. Defendant set upon her, and kicked her several times over the legs, which made her very stiff, and she could scarcely work for three days afterwards. In answer to the Bench, Sgt. Batty said the defendant was one of a gang who had assaulted Alan Buckley, but the case had been made up. Police constable Burns spoke to meeting the defendant the same evening at Scissett, when he put his hands out and wanted to know if he wished to take him. The Officer replied that he did not, if he would go home quietly. The defendant said he could not take him, and threatened that if ever he meddled with him he would kick him to death. He was very drunk. Defendant said there had been some sports in a field that day. A hole was dug and filled with water, into which they pushed each other. The liquors were given to them, and they were made drunk by the landlord. Supt. Sykes said the police had very little authority at Skelmanthorpe, and sometimes lynch law was almost in force. The bench said the assault was a brutal and unprovoked one. The defendant would be committed for two months, and at the end of that period he would be required to find securities to keep the peace for six months – himself in £5 and two sureties of £5 each – towards Thomas Burns and all other Her Majesty's subjects or be imprisoned until he found them.

8 June 1872

Denby Dale Wesleyan Band of Hope

The first anniversary of this society was held on Saturday in the Wesleyan Chapel, Denby Dale. A public tea was provided, of which a goodly number partook. After tea, there was a public meeting in the chapel, the President of the Band, the Rev. W H Major occupying the chair. The speakers were the Rev. J Scott, Independent, Clayton West; Mr Thomas Dinsdale, Home Missionary, Clayton West; Messrs. Blacker and Hawkin, Barugh; Mr Ellis, Denby Dale; Mr Melling, Penistone; and Mr Owen Scatchard, Heckmondwike. The usual votes of thanks being given, the meeting was brought to a close by singing the doxology and prayer.

Denby Dale brass band, circa 1912.

15 June 1872

A Skelmanthorpe Case in the Court of Chancery

In the Court of Chancery on Wednesday, before Vice-Chairman Mallins, the case of Dowse v Beanland was heard. The plaintiff in this case was John Dowse, medical practitioner of Skelmanthorpe, in the County of York. The bill was filed for the purpose of obtaining an injunction to restrain the defendant from practising as a Surgeon within 10 miles of Skelmanthorpe. For many years the plaintiff had practised as a medical man at Skelmanthorpe having succeeded his father in the business. In November 1868, having occasion for an assistant, he engaged the defendant, Beanland. Upon the arrangement being made an agreement in writing was entered into to by which the defendant agreed to become the plaintiffs assistant; and it was further agreed when he ceased to act in such capacity not to practise as a surgeon or apothecary, or to enter into the service of any person, as assistant surgeon within 10 miles of Skelmanthorpe. The defendant continued to serve plaintiff until the 25th April last, when disagreements having arisen, he left. Since then he had resided at Shelley Woodhouse, within 1 mile of Skelmanthorpe and was practising as a surgeon. The court, therefore, was moved, for an injunction to restrain the defendant from so doing. R Cotton QC and Mr Beaumont were for the plaintiff; Mr N Higgins QC and Grosvenor Woods for the defendant. The Vice – Chancellor in giving judgement, after adverting to the facts of the case, said that the defendant, in utter disregard of the agreement into which he had entered, had commenced practice within 1 mile of Skelmanthorpe. His defence, first of all, was that he was an infant. It turned out that in order to obtain employment he had stated himself to be 24 when under age. He further alleged that the agreement was not read over to him. The gentleman who witnessed it, contradicted this, and his Honour was of the opinion that the defendant fully knew what he was about, and his defence entirely failed. His attempt to show that the plaintiff was not a properly qualified surgeon was discreditable. The order would therefore be that the defendant be restrained from practising as a medical man within ten miles of Skelmanthorpe.

20 July 1872

A Clayton West Shoemaker Robbed at Barnsley

Yesterday at the Barnsley Town Hall, before the Mayor, J Tyas and Mr F H Taylor, Mary Pacey, a prostitute and Thomas Rooke, were charged with stealing a watch, the property of George Henry Beever, a shoemaker, of Clayton West at Barnsley on Monday last. The prosecutor said he went into the Three Cranes dram shop at half past eight o'clock on Monday night. He saw the prisoner, Pacey, there, and she asked him to sit down beside her. He did so, and paid for two pennyworth of wine for her. He had occasion to go into the back yard, when the prisoner, Pacey, followed him and got hold of his coat on both sides. She put her hand into the left hand side pocket and also into his right, saying she wanted his money. He gave her three half-pence and told her to go away. The prisoner, Rooke, was standing by, and Pacey, at once seized his watch and got it. At the time she got the watch she called out 'Tom'. The prisoner, Rooke, then went up to him and throttled him and held him whilst Pacey got away. Several witnesses gave corroborative evidence, and the apprehensions having being proved, the prisoners were committed to the sessions for trial.

10 August 1872

Laying the Corner Stone of Denby Dale District Undenominational Schools

(due to the length of the original article this report has been heavily abridged)

Hitherto, the children of the village have had to walk to Denby church school, distant, as we have already said, about a mile and a half.

Some months ago, the Rev. Job Johnson, Vicar of Denby, called a meeting of the inhabitants for the purpose of considering and deciding upon a proposal to establish an infant school at Denby Dale for children up to 5 or 6 years of age. The proposal did not meet with general favour, and that for two reasons. In the first place, Mr Johnson wished it to be a church school, whilst there was a strong feeling that it ought to be an Undenominational one; in the second place, an infant school was not deemed sufficient to supply the wants of the population. Admitting that there was ample accommodation in Denby school to which it was proposed by Mr Johnson, to transfer the children after they had reached the age of 5 or 6 years, the distance was too great, especially taking in to account the bleak and exposed character of the road during winter. No decision could be come to on that occasion and a second meeting was held by adjournment in the Primitive Methodist chapel. Meanwhile a third movement had been inaugurated by the Wesleyan's with a view to the establishment of a Wesleyan school. The adjourned meeting was attended by all parties, including Mr Johnson. The Wesleyan's had among their own members obtained promises of liberal subscriptions amounting to, we believe, £300; and Mr Walter Norton stated that if the Wesleyan's could raise £300 for a denominational school, he would undertake to raise a similar amount for an Undenominational one. Meanwhile the Wesleyan's decided upon going in with the Undenominational party and so soon was that announcement made, it was felt by nearly all that the Undenominational movement was virtually an accomplished fact. A good deal of unpleasantness between Mr Johnson and the promoters of the new movement was the result, but our object being here to simply record facts, not to give opinions, into that we do not enter.

A grant of £372 10s was made towards the cost of the building. It was at first feared that there would be some difficulties with respect to the site, but these, on being faced, happily vanished. Mr Silverwood of Shelley, one of the land owners of the district, on being applied to, at once agreed to sell the trustees a most eligible plot of land situated on the left hand side of the road leading to Clayton West, for little more than the nominal price of 1s per yard. Not only that, but he also contributed a handsome subscription to the building fund, together with an extra strip of land free of any charge whatever.

The plans for the new building were prepared by Mr Edward Hughes, architect of Huddersfield, who we may state in passing, was a pupil of the distinguished, Sir Gilbert Scott. Accommodation is to be provided for 200 children, namely, 120 boys and girls and 80 infants. The leading contractors for the work are as under:

Mason work – Messrs Henry Mellor and Son, Denby Dale. Joiner do., Mr Cockcroft, Huddersfield, plumbing and glazing, Mr John Taylor, Thurlstone, and slating a Bentley firm. The total cost will be about £1500. Building operations are now being pushed forward with vigour, and given favourable weather it is anticipated that the premises will be completed by Christmas.

There is a numerous body of trustees and the following gentlemen constitute the building committee: Messrs. Walter Norton (Chairman), Henry H Peace, John Brierley (Secretary), Zaccheus Hinchliffe and Joseph Whittaker.,

Saturdays ceremony was as fixed for 5 o'clock in the afternoon. The day was dull with occasional though by no means heavy rain, and as a consequence the turn out of 'Dalers' was neither quite so gay or quite so numerous as it would doubtless have been under more brilliant weather auspices. But there were other circumstances, which imparted a holiday character to the day. The members belonging to the Independent Order of Oddfellows MU, have, for a series of years, been in the habit of holding their annual banquet on the first Saturday in August at the house of Mr John Lockwood, the White Hart Inn, the Denby Dale band turned out in full uniform to grace the banquet; and the consequence was that long before five o'clock, the residents and loungers in the neighbourhood of the White Hart, of whom there were not a few, had quite a lively time of it. The local 'Forresters' also held a court, and we believe, dined at Cumberworth, and subsequently joined in the procession from the White Hart to the site of the new buildings. The procession, which was formed about half past four, marched in the following order:–

Denby Dale Band, Trustees and Managers of Schools, Architect, Builders, Joiners etc., Odd Fellows, Skelmanthorpe Band, Foresters, Friends of the Cause.

A substantial wooden platform had been erected on the site of the building, on which was placed a table bearing two elegant bouquets of flowers, with chairs for the gentlemen who were to take a leading part in the proceedings, while forms were provided for the ladies, most of whom, however, preferred a standing view of the ceremony. It was nearly half past five when proceedings commenced, at which hour the following, among others were on and near the platform, viz: Mr Walter Norton, who presided as chairman of the building committee, Mr Henry H Peace, of Denby Dale, who had agreed to perform the ceremony, Wright Mellor Esq., Mayor of Huddersfield, John Kaye Esq., JP Clayton West, Joseph Norton Esq, JP, Nortonthorpe, J Firth Bottomley Esq, barrister, London, the Revs.

W H Major, Denby Dale and C Hatherley, Skelmanthorpe, Messrs. R Norton, A Peace, Jos. Armitage, Z Hinchliffe, J Brierley, J Brownhill, Thos. Mellor, E Hughes (Architect), Tedbar Wood, W Savage, Jas. Peace, John Kenyon, Job Peace, Thos. Ellis, Mrs Walter Norton, Mrs H H Peace, Mrs Hy. Silverwood, Miss Kaye, Mrs A Peace, &c., &c.

17 August 1872

Assaulting a Landlord

Joseph Gawthorpe, a beer-house keeper at Cumberworth, charged a rough looking young man named William Lawton with assaulting him on the 6th inst. Mr Parker appeared for the prosecution. Complainant stated the defendant and some others went into his house in an intoxicated state, and because he refused to fill defendant any beer he became very abusive and kicked complainant on the legs so severely that he could not walk for four days afterwards. The bench fined the defendant 10s and costs.

17 August 1872

Clayton West – Manchester Unity of Oddfellows.

The Robert Burns Lodge, No. 243 of this Order, held its anniversary on Saturday last, at the house of Mr Joshua Riley, Commercial Inn, when the younger members sat down to an excellent repast, served up in first class style by the host. The above lodge consists of 240 members, but only 150 reside in the neighbourhood, and 80 are under 30 years of age. The lodge is worth £2280 0s 6d. The gain since January last has been £160.

31 August 1872

Assault at Cumberworth

Seth Senior was charged with an assault on George Fearnley at Cumberworth. Defendant had first punched a female and then knocked defendant down. Defendant denied the charge. Fined 2s 6d and costs, with the alternative of one months imprisonment in default.

31 August 1872

Licensed Houses in the Petty Sessional Division of Staincross

Townships	Population in 1871	No of Public Houses	Beerhouse – to sell on premises	Beerhouse to sell off premises	No. of wine licenses to sell off premises	By 1871 census – the number of inhabitant to every license
Clayton West	1531	4	3			219
Cumberworth	2485	10	2		1	191
Denby	1637	6	1			234
Gunthwaite	83					
High Hoyland	239	1				239
Ingbirchworth	303	2	1			101
Penistone	1557	11	2			119

Cumberworth included inns at Skelmanthorpe. Denby included inns at Denby Dale.

7 September 1872

Denouncing a Magistrate and Slandering the Bench

George Mallinson, described as a weaver, from Denby Dale, was charged with obstruction. The charge was proved by PC Esslement, who said he was in Queen Street on Saturday night, when the defendant came and asked him to lock up a thief. He enquired who the 'thief' was, and defendant replied 'John Kaye, Esq. of Clayton West'. He went on to say that Mr Kaye had robbed him of a bank-book and cheque for £100,000! Witness told him to go about his business, and left, but he was called back when he enquired what he was there for if he would not lock up a rogue and a thief. He then went on to say that all Barnsley Magistrates were liars and rogues, and witness was at last obliged to lock him up. Defendant now repeated his allegations to the magistrates in general and Mr Kaye in particular and enquired what the police were for if they were not to lock up rogues and vagabonds. He also alleged that Mr Norton and come and challenged him on the street. A man named John Fretwell, from Denby, here came forward and said he had never known the defendant do anything wrong. He was remanded for inquiries to be made as to his mental condition.

Two days later ...

George Mallinson, who was remanded on Monday on the charge of obstructing the highway, in order to test his sanity was again brought up. In answer to the bench, the prisoner still made a rambling statement and said that Edward Faulkner had sent a present to Mr Kaye for him. Mr Newman asked what the present consisted of, and how much it was. The prisoner – 'It was a £100,000 cheque! – laughter. He was ordered to be handed over to his father, who promised to take care of him.

7 September 1872

Assault at Skelmanthorpe

Caleb Lawton was charged with assaulting James Nussey at Skelmanthorpe on the 8th of June. The complainant said he was on the road in a cart when the defendant stopped the horse, pulled him out and having got him down kicked him over his legs and body, and injured him so that he had been confined to his house for several weeks. He never gave the defendant any provocation for what he did to him. The doctors bill amounted to £2 1s 6d, which the defendant said he could not pay. The bench committed the defendant for one month to the Wakefield House of Correction without the option of a fine.

7 September 1872

Application for Beer Licenses off the Premises

William Rowley, Kitchen Royd, Cumberworth to sell off the premises. In this case Supt. Sykes said the rating was insufficient, and Mr Norton, the owner of the property, objected to the license being granted. Refused.

21 September 1872

Official List of Yorkshire Collieries & their Owners 1869–70

Included were:

California at Shelley owned by Mathews & Co.

Duke Wood at Clayton West owned by Norton Bros. & Co.

Box Ings, owned by Seth Senior & Son.
Cumberworth, owned by J Sheard.
Kirk Style, Cumberworth, owned by Henry Ellis & Co.
Toppit, Clayton West owned by J Hargreave & Co.
Denby Dale, owned by Thomas Haigh.

5 October 1872

Charge of Furious Driving at Denby

Isaac Barraclough and William Wood, were charged under the Highway Act with furious driving at Denby Dale on the 12th ult. Mr Parker defended. John Moxon of Denby said about 10 o'clock at night on the 13th ult. he had been to the well for some water and was returning home when he heard a conveyance coming along the road at a rapid rate. He got on the footpath and it passed instantly. After it had gone a short distance he heard the trap upset. He ran to the place and found the two defendants under the cart. He assisted to get them out, when it was found that they were seriously injured. PC Worsley gave corroborative evidence. The defence was the pony was only two years old and it ran away and upset the cart as stated involving in addition serious injuries to the defendants. The bench said they were willing to accept the defence and would give the defendants the benefit of the doubt. Case dismissed.

26 October 1872

A Skelmanthorpe Man Committed for Stealing Ducks at Cawthorne

At the Barnsley Town Hall yesterday, George Woodhead, a weaver, residing at Skelmanthorpe, was charged with stealing two very fine ducks, value 7s, the property of Mr C Wemyss, Cawthorne, land agent to the Cannon Hall estate. PC Stewart who is stationed at Cawthorne said, on the morning of Thursday last, about 2 o'clock, he apprehended the prisoner in Cannon Hall Park, Cawthorne, on suspicion of having stolen two ducks, which he had in his possession and which were quite warm. The ducks appeared to have been recently killed. In answer to his question as to where he had got them, the prisoner said he got them in trade. He afterwards said he had bought off Benjamin Wragg of Over Moss near Huddersfield, for 5s. He then locked him up at Barnsley, and afterwards charged him with stealing the ducks from Mr Wemyss's premises in answer to which he said 'I did not steal them'. Mr Wemyss deposed to seeing ten ducks, his property, on some water near his house at noon, on the 23rd inst. He was called up early on the morning of the 24th inst. by the police officer, and on examining the ducks he found two to be missing. Those produced were the two he had missed. The prisoner was sentenced to two months imprisonment.

9 November 1872

Cattle Straying on the Highway

John Horne, a farmer, residing at Denby, was charged by the Denby Board of Health with allowing cattle to stray on the highway. The charge was laid under the Highway Act by Benjamin Kendray, the surveyor of the highways for the district. The case was clearly proved and the Bench fined the defendant 21s and costs.

30 November 1872

Damage to an Oak Tree at Denby

Samuel Hanwell, a boy, was charged with damaging an oak tree in a field occupied by Mr Peace at Denby, on the 19th inst. The lad, it appeared, was caught in an oak tree breaking off the boughs, and, as he had been caught before, a summons was taken out against him. The case, was however, not pressed, and the lad was discharged with a reprimand.

30 November 1872

New Branch Line at Clayton West

On Wednesday, Mr John Kaye JP, of Clayton West, cut the first sod of a proposed branch line of railway from Clayton West to Shepley in the presence of a large number of people. The new line will commence at the Ox-Ings, in Shepley, joining the main line from Huddersfield to Shepley there – and run to Skelmanthorpe, where the first station will be erected, on one side of the road from that place to Emley, and it will then run forward to Clayton west, which will be the terminus. A station will be erected there, on Scott Hill. The line will be nearly straight and the gradient will be 1 in 70 to 80; and it will be three miles and a half in length. No engineering difficulties of any moment will be presented, but a tunnel, which will pass through a bed of rock and shale, will have to be constructed at Shelley Woodhouse, and will be between 500 and 600 yards long.

The ceremony having concluded, the procession headed by a brass band, re-formed and returned to the New School where luncheon was served. Mr J Norton JP, of Nortonthorpe presided.

7 December 1872

Extraordinary Charge of Assault from Skelmanthorpe

Hiram Lodge, Henry Gawthorpe and Herbert Senior, three youths were charged with assaulting William Bedford of Scissett, at Skelmanthorpe on the 27th ult. Complainant said

Railway wreckage at Clayton West after coal trucks had broken loose at Skelmanthorpe in 1913.

that he had been to the cutting of the first sod of the new railway on the day in question and was returning home, about three o'clock when the three defendants, one after the other, kept 'poising' at him. He had had no liqueur, having been at the place only about an hour and he had given the defendants no provocation whatsoever. First one defendant kicked at him, then the second and then the third. How they were for drink he could not say: they might have had some ale in the field. In cross-examination by the defendants, complainant admitted coming out of the 'Dog and Gun' but he had only one glass there, and he never wanted any of them to fight. Lodge, in answer to the Bench said, 'We never did kick him'. Gawthorpe said, 'He was so drunk that he could not stand; and Senior said he asked, 'Does anyone want to fight?' They made answer 'No'. Complainant in answer to the query as to whether he had any witnesses said 'There is James Lee, but he won't come forward for fear that they should kill him!' Mr Cooke thought it must be a rough country over there. There were means, however, for compelling a witness to attend and for protecting him at the same time. Defendant said there was also William Wharam. The case was adjourned for the production of both these parties.

The three defendants were each fined 2s 6d and costs, in all 12s 6d each.

7 December 1872

Serious Assault at Denby – The Kicking Practice

Henry Jackson was charged with assaulting Robert Chipchase at Denby on the 24th ult. The complainant said he arrived at the Denby Dale station by the half past nine train in the evening from Penistone. As he was leaving the station in the company of a railway porter, defendant ran against him and knocked his hat off. He asked him why he had done so, when he treated the affair as a joke. When he got down to the bottom of the hill, defendant knocked his hat off again and then went into the Railway Tavern. Witness went into the house and remained there until ten o'clock, when the landlord turned the company out. The defendant and eight or ten others got round him and defendant began to kick and strike him. Another person also struck and kicked him. One struck him under the jaw and another kicked him on the nose, giving him two black eyes with which he could barely see for a week. The defendant alleged that he never was there, and called a young man named James Smith, who declared that the defendant never touched the complainant. He however admitted that he went near to him but never touched him. The Chairman intimated that he did not believe the witness. Mr Milner said that when he saw the complainant a week ago, he seemed to have been very badly used. Several previous convictions having been put in against the defendant, who it was also stated, had been before the Huddersfield Bench. The Chairman said they had decided not to allow the defendant the chance of paying a fine this time. They committed him for one month to Wakefield House of Correction as he was a great nuisance to Denby Dale.

28 December 1872

Sudden Death of a Married Woman at Denby Dale

On Tuesday last an inquest was held at the house of Aaron Hanwell, the Star Inn, Denby, before Thomas Taylor Esq., coroner, touching the death of Esther Biltcliffe, wife of John Biltcliffe, aged 30 years, who died suddenly on the morning of the 21st inst. The deceased was taken ill and her husband went to Skelmanthorpe to get medical aid but could not get any. A verdict of 'died in childbirth' was returned.

1885

14 January 1885

Skelmanthorpe Local Board

The monthly meeting was held in the board room on Wednesday evening. Present: Messrs. Benjamin Norton (Chairman), Henry Senior, Samuel Field, George Lodge, William Ewart, Robert Wadsworth, George Brook and Edwin Field.

17 January 1885

Butchers and Gentle Driving – An Illustration at Clayton West

William Wood, butcher, was charged with furious driving on the 31st ult. at Clayton West. PC Robinson, said that on the night named defendant, who had charge of a light cart and horse, was driving through Clayton west at a furious rate. He was driving towards Scissett. Another witness gave corroborative evidence and said defendant was driving at the rate of 14 or 16 miles per hour. For the defence, James Hirst, who was with the defendant in the trap said, Wood, who was driving, was sober, having only had two three-penny worth's of whisky. He was not driving at more than 7 or 8 miles per hour. It appeared defendant had been up 16 times before, and in the list of offences there were several for furious driving. He was fined 20s and costs. Defendant said he was only driving at the rate of 6 miles per hour; in fact he could not have driven in a more careful way if his Worship had been with him. Mr T Norton said he had taken no part in the case, but he could not give defendant a good character. He was a most reckless driver, and he wondered he had not killed himself before now.

17 January 1885

Shocking Shooting Fatality at Huddersfield – A Skelmanthorpe Woman Shot

A shocking occurrence took place early on Tuesday morning at Lockwood, Huddersfield, by which a Mrs Blackburn, a widow, about 45 years of age was shot dead by Mr Thomas Walter Holmes, of 14 Bentley Street, Lockwood, a clerk in the employ of the Huddersfield Banking Company, into whose employ she entered as housekeeper on Thursday last. Mr Holmes is a widower, with three sons, all living at home with him.

About 4 o'clock on Tuesday morning he was roused by an unusual noise, and he got up and dressed himself. He took a light in one hand and a loaded six chambered revolver in the other, and went down his bedroom stairs leading to the lobby opposite the front door of the house. While he was going downstairs the revolver accidentally went off. The noise of the discharge awoke Mr Holmes's sons, who were sleeping in the rooms above, and on their asking what was the matter, their father told them. The eldest lad, James, went down with a light, behind his father. They found the door of the back room closed, and on opening it and getting into the room they saw that their was a light in the kitchen below. Mr Holmes went to the top of the stairs leading to the kitchen and called out 'Who's there?' No reply came, but he says he saw someone moving about at the bottom of the stairs, and he fired his revolver down the stairway. He and his son then went down into the kitchen, and there found the housekeeper, Mrs Blackburn, lying on the floor, bleeding from a wound near the right eye. It was of course, evident, to Mr Holmes, that he had shot her, and he sent his son for Mr Hall, surgeon, and his assistant, Mr Greenhow, attended speedily and found that the poor woman was dead. Police Sergeant Bottomley was informed of the occurrence, and went to the house, and Mr Holmes stated the above circumstances to him and handed him the revolver, four chambers of which were still loaded. The Sergeant did not apprehend him, but subsequently the police took Mr Holmes into custody, and removed him to the police station. A spent bullet was found in the passage at the foot of the bedroom stairs and that was the bullet first discharged, when, as Mr Holmes says, the revolver went off accidentally. It is now believed that Mrs Blackburn got up early to commence the washing. A somewhat curious circumstance is that Mr Holmes' 1st housekeeper, who had been ill, died a few days ago, and was buried on Wednesday. The fatality has caused great excitement in the town and much sympathy is expressed on all sides. Mrs Blackburn, who was 45 years of age, belonged to the neighbourhood of Skelmanthorpe. Mr Holmes was formerly a clerk in the Gurney's Bank, London, which stopped some years ago, and he had been in the service of the Huddersfield Banking Company for about 14 years and was regarded as a very excellent servant. The news created much astonishment among his confreres at the bank. Mr Holmes is a Baptist, and no later than Sunday last conducted the service at Rehoboth Baptist Chapel, Lockwood. It was stated that before his wife died she was for a long time a confirmed invalid, and this increased rather than lessened his tendency to extreme nervousness. Holmes was charged at Huddersfield on Wednesday with the manslaughter of Mrs Blackburn. The Chief Constable stated the facts and asked for a remand until Friday, pending the coroners inquest. Mr S Learoyd, who appeared for the accused, said that no one was more bowed down by sorrow for the sad occurrence than Mr Holmes. It would be shown that when the case was gone into it was purely a case of misadventure. The prisoner did not fire at anyone, but had a settled conviction in his own mind that burglars were in the house, and he fired to frighten them away. The magistrates granted bail; but expressed a hope that the prisoners friends would take great care of him and prevent him from doing any harm to himself.

11 February 1885
The result of the latter case:
The case showed how dangerous it was for persons who were timid carrying firearms. The jury returned a verdict of not guilty, and the prisoner was discharged from the manslaughter charge.

24 January 1885
Calling a policeman 'A Blockhead' at Cumberworth
On Wednesday at the county police court at Huddersfield, Charles Dearnley, labourer, Cumberworth, was charged with having used obscene language at Cumberworth at 3:20 p.m. on the 11th inst. Mr Walter Armitage defended. Police Constable Ashworth produced on a sheet of paper the obscene words which he alleged the defendant made use of towards him. Mr Armitage: Did not defendant mistake you for a person he knew named Lockwood (pronounced Lockud)? – No Sir, he did not – And did you not mistake what he said and say that you would teach him to call you a blockhead? No Sir. The defence was that no bad language was used, and that the policeman had brought the case to gratify personal spite. Defendant was fined 5s and 8s costs.

Fundraising at Cumberworth during the First World War.

7 February 1885

By Norton Brothers and Co. Ltd

In the high court of justice Chancery Division, the other day, before Mr Justice Kay, a petition by Messrs Norton Brothers & Company, of Nortonthorpe Mills, Scissett was heard. It was a petition for the reduction of its capital, not by writing off lost capital, but to be allowed to pay back to each shareholder £1 per share out of its accumulated profits. The company had been a most prosperous one, and the shareholders had been paid large dividends. The company was incorporated in 1874 with a nominal capital of £300,000, divided into 30,000 shares of £10 each and £8 had been called up. The directors considered that it would be desirable not to part with the whole of its accumulated profits in the form of dividends and bonuses, so it was resolved at a meeting of the shareholders to return £1 a share which would be equal to £22,500. It was not proposed to reduce the liability of the shareholders, although there was an affidavit by the chairman that the company had no debts and there were no creditors as far as he was aware. It was now proposed to reduce the capital of the company to £270,000 divided into 30,000 shares of £7 each. The company carried on business at Huddersfield. The consent of the court was asked to dispense with the words 'and reduced'. Mr Graham Hastings, QC and Mr Grosvenor Woods appeared in support of the petition. His Lordship made the order asked for in the petition.

7 February 1885

Charge of Game Trespass against an Ingbirchworth Farmer

Ira Mitchell, farmer of Annat Royd, Ingbirchworth, was charged with trespassing in search of game on land over which Mr Tinker of Epworth, has the right of shooting. Jonas Batty, a

John Henry Horns, grocer and drapers store on Wellthorne Lane, Ingbirchworth. The store can be found in the trade directories of 1912 and 1922. (Courtesy of Old Barnsley)

keeper, said that on the 14th Jan. he was on duty on the farm of Mrs. Fanny Gill, Spicer's Farm, which adjoined the defendants farm. He saw the defendant come across with his dog and gun upon Mrs Gill's land. When defendant saw him, he turned and ran back on to his own land. Witness spoke to him across the fence and defendant said 'I was only going to see where that hare had gone'. Witness asked him what made him go back and he made no reply. Mrs Gill's son proved that the shooting was let. Replying to defendant he said it was a fact that defendant and he often trespassed on each others farms. Fined 5s and costs.

7 February 1885

Another Game Trespass at Ingbirchworth

Arthur Jackson, labourer, was similarly charged. Batty, the keeper, said that he had found the defendant on the same day as he had found the defendant in the previous case with two dogs coursing a hare over land on which Mr Tinker had the right of shooting. He also heard the defendant cry 'Look out' to some persons on the road. Defendant pleaded guilty but denied that he ever had a dog in his life or that he was in search of game on the day in question. The young man, Gill said that he saw the defendant in the field on the date named. Fined 10s and costs, 22s 7d.

18 February 1885

The Education Act at Denby

John Moore and Thomas Laundon, both of Denby, were charged with neglecting to comply with the provisions of the education act. Mr Edwin Wilcock, compelling officer to the Penistone Union School Attendance Committee proved the case. The boy Laundon had not made one attendance out of 40, he was 13 years of age and had not passed the necessary standards, he had only passed the second Standard. In this case an attendance order was made. Moore had attended 46 out of 136 attendances.

21 February 1885

A Melancholy Affair at Clayton West

On Sunday morning last a very sad discovery was made at Clayton West. It seems that a widower named George Shaw, 53 years of age, a weaver, who lived at Hill Top, Clayton West, had been drinking during the week ended Saturday last. On Saturday he came home and got into bed in his clothes and about half past 8 o'clock he was seen by his son, Walter. Nothing more seems to have been seen of him until about 9 o'clock on Sunday morning, when William Shaw went into the house and found the deceased hanging by the neck by a hank of cotton, which was fastened to the handrail of the stairs. Life was extinct. At the inquest, which was held at the 'Shoulder of Mutton Inn', on Tuesday, a verdict of 'suicide whilst of unsound mind' was returned.

7 March 1885

A Careless Carter at Scissett

William Sunderland, a carter, employed by a firm of spirit merchants, and for whom, Mr Rideal appeared was charged by PC Mansfield with leaving his horse and spring cart unattended on a public road in Scissett village, on the 24th ult. The officer spoke to watching the horse and cart from 20 minutes to seven o'clock until 7 opposite the Crown Hotel, and defendant failing to turn up, witness went inside and found him in the bar with a glass of spirits in his hand. The offence was not denied, a fine of 5s and costs 15s 6d being imposed.

21 March 1885

Drunk at Skelmanthorpe

Joshua Fretwell, labourer, pleaded guilty to being drunk on the 7th inst. at Skelmanthorpe, where he was found by two police officers, lying in the middle of the road, cursing and swearing. Fined 5s and costs, 14s 6d.

25 April 1885

Denby Dale v Hoylandswaine

Denby Dale batted first: Hinchliffe 7, F Lockwood 10, Kenyon 8, A Lockwood not out 14, Peace 0, Wood 13, did not bat – Mellor, Whiteley, Lister, Broomhill. Total 52.

Hoylandswaine – 29 all out.

9 May 1885

Attacking a Salvationist at Denby Dale

A young man named Samuel Rawnsley living at Denby Dale, was charged with being drunk on the 5th inst. at that place. John Crossland, a stout looking man, on being sworn, said he belonged to the Army and had given up drinking 'and all masks of games'. He was on his way to the barracks when defendant went to him and asked him to lend him sixpence. He refused to lend him one and defendant then kicked him. Defendant was drunk. Wallace Morley, on being sworn to speak the truth, remarked, 'I belong to Jesus, and I will'. Witness then said he found defendant drunk. PC McDonald said he saw defendant who was drunk. A fine of 10s and costs, or one month in default was imposed.

16 May 1885

Sudden Death in a Chapel at Skelmanthorpe

On Sunday evening last, a woman named Hannah Haigh, of Queen Street, Skelmanthorpe, fancy goods weaver, 63 years of age, died suddenly in the Primitive Methodist Chapel, Skelmanthorpe. It seemed that the deceased had been suffering from heart disease for some time, and had been attended by Dr. Greenhalgh of Skelmanthorpe. On Sunday evening she went to Chapel where the anniversary services were being celebrated and after the service had gone on some time, she was observed to be seized with a fit. She was removed by Zepho Booth and Joseph Kaye, but died almost immediately. Dr. Greenhalgh certified that heart disease was the cause of death.

23 May 1885

Suicide at Ingbirchworth

On Thursday morning, James Haigh, innkeeper of the Travellers Rest, Ingbirchworth, near Penistone, committed suicide by cutting his throat with a razor. The deceased, who has for some time been subject to epileptic fits, had just shaved himself, when it is supposed he was seized with a fit, which caused him to commit the rash act. He has, however, been in a low and desponding state of mind for some time and has been an out patient of the Huddersfield Infirmary.

30 May 1885

Cricket – Denby Dale v Wombwell

Denby Dale batted first: Mellor 1, Brownhill 1, Lockwood 12, J Peace 11, A Peace 1, Wood 2, Hinchcliffe 0, Dewhirst 0, Holmes 3, Lister 32, Senior 2, McDonald 6, extras 15 – total 86. Wombwell made 77 all out in reply.

Denby Dale cricket team, probably in 1887. Back row includes: O Haigh, S Kenyon, C Kilner, Fred Lockwood and Tom Gaunt. Front Row, left to right: James Brownhill, H Mellor, ?, James Henry Dewhirst, J Haywood, Oliver Lockwood, James Peace (the owner of Inkerman Mill), Harry Lockwood and Jim Turton.

Sam Shepley (stood left), Headmaster of Denby Dale school 1903–1934 and an unknown colleague with the school cricket team, circa 1920s.

Denby Dale cricket team, first eleven, Thomas Albert Hinchliffe stands with hand on hip in the centre of the photograph, circa mid 1880s.

27 June 1885

Assault at Denby

Isaac Peel and David Turton of Denby, were charged with assaulting Lazarus Schofield, a workman employed by Messrs. Norton Bros. on the 21st inst. at Denby. Mr J Carrington prosecuted. Complainant said he was returning from a meeting at the Salvation Army Barracks to his home on Sunday evening last. When he got opposite the White Hart public house he met the defendants who were drunk. He was then wearing a blue ribbon, as a temperance badge. Turton seized him by the throat, and asked what he was wearing the badge for. Peel said 'Does thou not know what he is wearing it for, he is nothing but a b——— blacksheep'. About fourteen weeks ago trade was very slack and witness went to work at a farthing a wire less money. Since then he had been seriously abused. Fined 2s 6d each and costs, 13s 6d.

25 July 1885

Skelmanthorpe – A Forgiving Complainant

Shaw Crossland of Skelmanthorpe, was charged with breaking panes of glass, value 8s, the property of Edward Hinchcliffe, weaver of Skelmanthorpe, on Saturday night. Complainant said the defendant lived next door but one to him, and on Saturday night he came and broke the windows. He was sorry and complainant did not want to press the case. To pay damage and costs 17s 6d.

25 July 1885

A Property Dispute at Ingbirchworth – Haigh versus Roebuck

This was an action brought to recover a sum of £5 14s for rent. Mr Clegg appeared for the plaintiff and Mr Rideal defended. Defendant was the tenant of a house at Ingbirchworth belonging to the plaintiff, for which, Mr Holmes, innkeeper of Ingbirchworth, was agent. Notice was given to the defendant on Nov. 1st, 1884, to quit on the 1st of May. Defendant sold the whole of his goods and left on the 6th of June, but paid no rent. The defence was that the owner had agreed to allow the defendant a week in which to sell his goods and forgave him the rent owing. Mr Wilby, auctioneer, of Penistone was called, and said plaintiff agreed to forgive defendant the rent owing, if he would give up possession on 6th June. Verdict for the plaintiff for £2 17s, half the plaint and hearing fees and no other costs.

22 August 1885

Assault at Skelmanthorpe

At Wakefield west Riding Court, on Monday, John Senior, blacksmith, Skelmanthorpe, was charged with assaulting an elderly man named Joseph Lodge, a weaver, at he same place, on Sunday, the 2nd inst. The two men and several others went to Flockton feast. On returning home at night the defendant began 'capering' on the road with another man and knocked against the complainant and when he remonstrated the defendant assaulted him. The defendant was ordered to pay £2.

22 August 1885

Vagrancy at Denby

John Ray, a tramp, was charged with begging at High Flatts on Monday last. PC Mansfield proved that he found defendant begging at the place named; he had about a shilling in his possession. Sent gaol for 14 days.

22 August 1885

Neglecting to Send Children to School at Skelmanthorpe

For neglecting to send their children to school, the Skelmanthorpe School Board prosecuted the following persons, the cases being proved by Allen Jackson, the compelling officer:- Benjamin Micklethwaite of Scissett, James Firth Jun., Mercy Addy, Richard Jackson of Skelmanthorpe. A fine of 5s was imposed in each case.

5 September 1885

Damaging Growing Grass at Denby

Frederick Longden, a young man, was charged with treading down growing grass in a field at Denby, on the 28th ult. Aaron Wood, the occupier of the land, proved the case. Defendant was ordered to pay the damages and costs.

12 September 1885

Educational Grants in Barnsley & District for Elementary schools in 1884

Clayton West – Kayes Undenominational £129 17s 6d
Denby – National £102 8s 6d
Denby Dale – Undenominational ££153 4s 0d
Skelmanthorpe Board £175 12s 6d
Skelmanthorpe National £135 16s 4d

19 September 1885

Aggravated Assault on a Wife at Scissett

Charles Blackburn, a young man, was charged with an aggravated assault on Mary Jane Blackburn, his wife, aged 21 years, at Scissett on the 6th inst. Mr John Carrington prosecuted. Complainant said they were married on the 1st November 1884, at Denby church, and had a baby six months old. About half past ten o'clock her husband returned home drunk, but went out again. On returning a second time, his mother got him to bed. Witness had gone to bed and defendant began to strike her and also used his feet. He got hold of her to throw her downstairs. At the time she had her baby in her arms. She then went downstairs and was sitting in a chair in front of the fire when her husband came down, opened the door, and pushed her out of the house. She had to take her baby and go and sleep at the house of her Aunt. Defendant in answer to the charge, said all the trouble arose from the interference of the complainant's parents. She often was away from home and neglected his house. He expressed his regret for the assault, and promised not to offend again in such a manner. The Bench cautioned him, and bound him over to keep the peace for six months. He was also ordered to pay the costs.

19 September 1885

Charge of Stealing Cucumbers

Joseph Dyson and Henry Ellis were charged with stealing twenty cucumbers, the property of John Bedford of Scissett on the 5th inst. Mr John Carrington defended. Prosecutor said he saw his greenhouse safe on the night of the 5th inst. next morning he found it broken open. Several days after, he saw the defendants at a public house at Scissett. Dyson said 'Hast thou got thy cucumbers back?' Me and Ellis fetched them, and we will fetch thy pigs next; or we will make them as thou cannot fetch them' There was no confirmatory evidence, and the Bench dismissed the case, both defendants denying the charge.

A Cawthorne Methodist Chapel outing, posing for a photograph at Broad Oak Farm, Gunthwaite, circa 1900.

The eighteen local ladies who made and baked the 1928 Denby Dale Pie. They were led by Mrs Jonas Kenyon and included Mrs Crossland, Mrs Firth, Mrs Barraclough, Mrs Cunningham, Mrs Littlewood, Mrs Stanger, Mrs Mosley, Mrs Lockwood, Mrs Senior. Mrs Wood, Mrs Cooper. On the back row, number 5 is Mrs Fenton Kilner Smith, front row, number 2 is Mrs Henry Horn, number 7 is Mrs Albert Kilner, number 8 is Mrs John Auckland. The latter women were from Lower Cumberworth.

The new Wesleyan Reform chapel, on Barnsley Road, during construction in 1908.

A days outing from the Wesleyan Reform chapel on Barnsley Road, around 1930.

Waiting for a train at Denby Dale station during the 1940s.

Members of the Wesleyan Reform Chapel, Denby Dale, outside the home of Mrs A Crossland at Upper Denby, circa 1916. In the doorway, Miss N Travis, Mrs J N Peace, Willie Hirst, J A Riggott. Back row: R A Morris, J W Heath, G Boothroyd, H Morris,. Centre row: Mrs S Woodhead, Mrs F Broadhead, Mrs H Heath, Mrs A Crossland, Mrs S A Green, Mrs W Haigh. Front row: Mrs Gibson, Mrs B Senior, Mrs A Bedford, Mrs J Hirst, Mrs J E Hirst.

A gathering of an unknown Friendly Society in Denby Dale. If any readers can supply further information about this photograph, please write to me via the publishers.

A gathering of an unknown Friendly Society in Denby Dale. If any readers can supply further information about this photograph, please write to me via the publishers.

19 December 1885

Game Trespass near Gunthwaite

Thomas Fretwell and John Fretwell, brothers, pleaded guilty to trespassing in pursuit of game on land near Gunthwaite, belonging to Mr W S Stanhope of Cannon Hall. Mr C J Tyas prosecuted. A game watcher named Gertrick, said he saw the defendants on the 18th ult. in a field near Gunthwaite. They had a dog with them, which set up some partridges. Thomas Fretwell, who had been in trouble before, was fined 20s, and the other defendant 10s and costs. The fines and costs amounted to £2 16s or one month in default.

Bibliography & Selected Sources

Archbishop Sharps Manuscript Volume 3, Circa 1690's
Barnsley Archives & Local Studies
Barnsley Chronicle Archives 1872 & 1885*
Bisset. A B – *York Clergy Ordinations 1662–1699*, Borthwick Institute 1998
Bisset A B – *York Clergy Ordinations 1700–1749*, Borthwick Institute 2000
Borthwick Institute, York
Crockford's Clerical Directories, 1910, 1936, 1940, 1950
Cross. C – *York Clergy Ordinations 1500–1509*, Borthwick Institute 2001
Cross. C – *York Clergy Ordinations 1510–1519*, Borthwick Institute 2002
Cross. C – *York Clergy Ordinations 1520–1559*, Borthwick Institute 2002
Cross. C – *York Clergy Ordinations 1561–1642*, Borthwick Institute 2000
Dale. B – *Yorkshire Puritanism & Early Nonconformity* 1909
Elliott. B – *The Making of Barnsley*, Wharncliffe, 2004
Foster. R F – *W B Yeats – A Life*, Oxford University Press, 2005
George family, private archives
Green family, private archives
Heath. C – *Denby & District*, Wharncliffe, 2001
Heath. C – *Denby & District II*, Wharncliffe 2004
Heath. C – *Denby & District III*, Wharncliffe 2006
Heath. C – *Ye Olde Townships – Denby Dale, Scissett, Ingbirchworth & District*, Wharncliffe 2007
Hunter. J – *South Yorkshire V1*, 1831
Hunter. J – *South Yorkshire V2*, 1833
Jackson, B – Cawthorne 1790–1990, Cawthorne Victoria Jubilee Museum, 1991
Johnson family, private archives
Knutsford Quarter Sessions, Cheshire Archives, Chester
Lawton. F – *Historical Notes of Skelmanthorpe & District*, 1895
Pratt. C T – *History of Cawthorne*, 1882
Slinn. S – *York Clergy Ordinations 1800–1849*, Borthwick Institute 2001
Stirling. A M W – *Annals of a Yorkshire House*, Lane (London) 1911
Surtees Society, *Four Yorkshire Diaries – John Hobson* 1875
Usher. D – *York Clergy Ordinations 1750–1799*, Borthwick Institute 2002

* *The years that have been researched and published in previous volumes include – 1869, 1870, 1876, 1884, 1888 and 1896.*

Index